PURITY AND IDENTITY IN Ancient Judaism

OLAMOT SERIES IN HUMANITIES AND SOCIAL SCIENCES
Irit Dekel, Jason Mokhtarian, and Noam Zadoff, editors

PURITY AND IDENTITY IN Ancient Judaism

FROM THE TEMPLE TO THE MISHNAH

Yair Furstenberg

translated by Sara Tova Brody

OLAMOT SERIES IN THE
HUMANITIES AND SOCIAL SCIENCES
In association with
INDIANA UNIVERSITY PRESS

This book is a publication of

Indiana University Press
Office of Scholarly Publishing
Herman B Wells Library 350
1320 East 10th Street
Bloomington, Indiana 47405 USA

iupress.org

Originally published in Hebrew

© 2016 by The Hebrew University Magnes Press

© 2023 by Olamot Center, Indiana University

All rights reserved
No part of this book may be reproduced or utilized in any form or by any means, electronic or mechanical, including photocopying and recording, or by any information storage and retrieval system, without permission in writing from the publisher. The paper used in this publication meets the minimum requirements of the American National Standard for Information Sciences—Permanence of Paper for Printed Library Materials, ANSI Z39.48-1992.

Manufactured in the United States of America
First Printing 2023

Cataloging information is available from the Library of Congress.

ISBN 978-0-253-06771-5 (hdbk.)
ISBN 978-0-253-06772-2 (pbk.)
ISBN 978-0-253-06773-9 (web PDF)

Cover illustration: Ostracon (Yadin and Naveh, Masada 452). Photo by Yael Yolovitch. Courtesy of the Israel Antiquities Authority.

CONTENTS

Preface vii

Note on Translations and Editions xvii

Abbreviations xix

Introduction: From Pharisees to Rabbis   1

Part I
The Varieties of Purity

1. Biblical Foundations, New Conceptions   19
2. Exclusive Paths to Purity from Qumran to Jesus   41

Part II
Communal Identities

3. The Purity of the Pharisees   63
4. Outsider Impurity and the Forms of Judean Sectarianism   84
5. Inclusion and Marginalization   111

Part III
Tradition and Invention

6. Changing Social Contexts: Purity after 70 CE   143
7. The End of Purity   165

Epilogue: The Rabbinic Movement within Shifting Religious Cultures   183

Notes 189

Bibliography 233

Subject Index 251

Source Index 255

PREFACE

For the last two centuries of the Second Temple period, Palestinian Jews contested the meaning of their Judaism. From the Hasmonean period circa 140–37 BCE to the destruction of the Second Temple in 70 CE, Jews fervently debated questions concerning the proper observance of the Torah, the role of the Temple and priests, the nature of Jewish identity, and the imminence of the messianic era. This transformative period in Jewish history also saw the emergence among many groups of a new commitment to an intensified observance of Jewish law. This devotion penetrated all aspects of daily behavior and surpassed the general obligation to the biblical covenant with the God of Israel. The diverse forms of observance of even minute details of law came to reflect competing ideologies, ranging from priestly conservatism and sectarian separatism, through the Pharisees' more accessible forms of piety, to the universalist approach of Hellenistic Jews and the preference of moral over ritual law among the Jesus movement. The discourse of law was a major arena for ideological expression within the diversity of Second Temple Judaism, and the field of purity played an exceptional role within this discourse.

The numerous disputes over the meaning and nature of purity within Second Temple Judaism fused legal, ethical, and ideological considerations, and disagreements over legal details frequently provided a platform for ideological clashes. Purity supplied the Jews of the Second Temple period with a practical and ideological vocabulary for an array of distinct approaches and a rich grammar for formulating competing worldviews.

The power of purity discourse in ancient Judaism lay in the wide range of its usages, encompassing everything from bodily experiences to moral status.

The Hebrew Bible considers various unpleasant, disturbing, or even contagious pathological conditions or creatures as sources of impurity. These include swarming things, corpses of animals or people, and various skin eruptions or genital discharges. The Israelites were careful to stay away from these impure substances and cleansed themselves immediately after coming in contact with them. There were negative consequences to any exposure that one might have with such impurities. Importantly, the Torah warns impure Israelites not to desecrate the holy realm; they may neither enter the Temple nor eat holy foodstuff. Presumably, in the biblical worldview, these decaying occurrences undermine the living power of holiness, and the divine realm must be strictly separated from the contaminating forces of corruption. Considering the threat of decay, which clashed with the perfect divine order, it is not surprising that impure things were not only disgusting and physically unpleasant but could also arouse moral uneasiness. Therefore, the Hebrew Bible believes that moral corruptness is an impurity as well and that sinners spread contamination through the land. And while the priestly laws of the Torah provide ways to remove bodily impurity, through washing, sprinkling, or sacrifice, sinners who defile the land through their abominable actions are banished from God's presence.

Due to the power of purity discourse to set both ritual hierarchies and moral values, it served the different sects during the latter part of the Second Temple period to define their own qualities as well as the image of Judaism. In this period, the concern for ritual purity extended far beyond its limited biblical roots, and alongside some common practices, each group promoted a unique form of purity observance and ideology. Ultimately, the contrast between pure and impure became an identity marker that distinguished Jews from gentiles, priests and sectarians from other Judeans, and (according to the Gospel of Matthew) those preparing for the Kingdom of the Heaven from the nonbelieving Pharisees. Thus, the questions of who are the pure, from whom and what they should separate, and what sets of beliefs and practices are material to this status permeated intersectarian discourse, thereby defining both religious ideologies and group identities within the Second Temple period.

Of all fields of law, purity observance was the most charged among Jews of the period. It directly impacted social differences and served as the most transparent indicator of each group's worldview. The intersectarian debates over purity included the means for securing the purity of the Temple and Jerusalem and who was allowed to access these holy places as well as the nature of the distinction between Jews and gentiles and the possibility of conversion. Furthermore, are sinners in general considered impure, and with whom may they maintain social relations? A major arena of the discourse of purity pertained to daily eating practices. Thus, the difference between washing hands before the meal, as the Pharisees demanded, and immersing in a ritual pool advocated by the Essenes, reflected differing conceptions of purity. At the same time, others such as John the Baptist and his followers believed that the looming messianic era entailed new forms of purification that would transform the human state and emancipate it from the hold of impure powers. As the teachings of Jesus illuminate, for Jews of the period these distinctions carried clear ideological and ethical ramifications, encapsulating the worldview of each group.

This book thus argues that the language of purity provided a powerful tool for organizing legal, social, and ideological boundaries, and its study is therefore pertinent for understanding the forces that shaped the varieties of Second Temple Judaism and its later offshoots.

Following the historian of the Second Temple period Flavius Josephus, it is customary to refer to three major groups who advocated their ideological alternatives to Judean society: the Sadducees, Essenes, and Pharisees. The Sadducees belonged to the priestly elite. They held conservative views concerning the exclusive authority of the Torah and maintained the biblical notion of a collective reward and punishment in this life, rejecting any form of afterlife. There are no texts that may be securely attributed to the Sadducees, but we may surmise from other references to their legal positions, that also with respect to the issue of purity they upheld the concerns of the Priestly Code in the Pentateuch for the purity of the holy realm, including the Temple, the priests, and their consecrated foods. The second group, the Essenes, who scholars generally associate with the members of the group whose writings were found in the caves at Qumran, were organized in separate communities and maintained a strict regimen based on a stringent interpretation of the Torah, as we learn from their legal writings preserved in Qumran. Evidently, the Qumran sectarians believed Jerusalem and the Temple to have been polluted both ritually, since the authorities adopted the lenient policy of purity, such as that promoted by the Pharisees, and morally, through the corruption of the Temple priests. They were therefore compelled to distance themselves from the impure multitude and live in the desert. The writings of the Qumran sectarians also reveal their dualistic tendency, which divided humanity into the pure sons of light and impure sons of darkness, as well as a strong eschatological awareness in expectation of the annihilation of the government of the spirits of impurity. Paradoxically, despite the marginality of this sectarian network of communities, we probably know more about them through their legal, liturgical, exegetical, and eschatological writings than about the more socially dominant Sadducees and Pharisees, who have not left us any literary works.

A variety of sources testify to the dominance of the third group, the Pharisees, as teachers and authoritative interpreters of the law. Josephus claims that while the Sadducees were able to persuade only the rich, the Pharisees had the multitudes on their side. Jesus traditions portray them as overseeing the observance of the Torah, and Qumran literature recurrently attacks the legal standards of the Pharisees—the "seekers of smooth things" according to the Qumran nomenclature—who have seduced the people of Israel into their liberal ways. Despite their opposing interests, both Jesus traditions and Qumran literature attack the Pharisees' approach to purity, which they deemed to convey a compromising and even hypocritical observance of the law. Considering the prominence of the Pharisees as well as their controversial concept of purity, which they evidently worked to spread, any attempt to understand the role of purity within Judean society in general requires that we obtain an undistorted view of the Pharisees' policy. Unfortunately, however, while the previously mentioned sources seem to agree that the Pharisees were generally considered to be authoritative interpreters of the Torah and that they advocated the observance of the tradition of the elders, they evidently provide only a biased perspective through the eyes of their opponents. No contemporary source voices their religious outlook or their understanding of the law and Judaism. To a large extent, we are dependent on later rabbinic sources to reconstruct the teachings and worldview of the Pharisees, which the rabbis viewed as their predecessors, even though these sources present their own challenges. Paradoxically, if we are to understand the most basic elements of Second Temple Judaism we must turn to the traditions transmitted and reconstructed by those who sought to adjust them to the post-70 CE era.

Toward the end of the first century CE, two major offshoots emerged from the varieties of Second Temple Judaism: Christianity and rabbinic Judaism. Each religion held on to specific facets of the remarkably rich fabric of Second Temple traditions, which they gradually consolidated into two separate ways of life. At the same time, these roots function in each of the two movements in an opposite manner. The Jesus movement consciously renounced the observance of much of the Torah as it spread among gentile communities. At the same time, since this process is transparent within the earliest Christian sources, the careful reader can trace the changing approaches to the law. Consequently, we may discern within the New Testament some original and authentic elements from within the inner-Jewish debate on the Torah in general and on the meaning of purity more specifically. The acknowledged deviation from traditional Judaism retained an exposed view of earlier stages. The rabbis, on the other hand, made every effort to portray themselves and the normative world that they developed as a direct continuation of Second Temple Judaism, thereby concealing their own innovations. Consequently, the rabbis barely refer to the diversity of Jewish practice during the Second Temple period, and they project their own legal views retroactively into the description of the Temple cult and court system. The few historical reflections in early rabbinic sources give the impression that the rabbis are the direct continuation of a uniform chain of traditions from Moses at Sinai through the Pharisaic leaders to their own academies. As a result, the rabbis' strong sense of continuity, whether justified or not, impedes our ability to distinguish the Second Temple roots of the rabbinic movement.

Thus, while literary and historiographical sources allow us to trace the development of the Jesus movement from its Second Temple roots to its later manifestations, the exact relation of rabbinic Judaism to the movements and ideologies of the Second Temple period is harder to assess. The rabbis saw themselves as followers of the Pharisees, and yet at the same time, they also transformed Jewish legal practices and suggested new concepts of Torah in the post-Temple era. Consequently, scholars are strongly divided over the degree of rabbinic revolutionism, and whether the lost world of the Pharisees can in fact be retrieved from the literature of the rabbis. And even more consequentially, to what degree did the rabbis maintain the sectarian characteristics of the Pharisees? This book offers an answer to these questions, which lie at the heart of the study of the early rabbinic movement and the transformation of Palestinian Judaism following the destruction of the Second Temple. It argues that purity discourse not only shaped Jewish society during the Second Temple period but also allows us to trace the changes of religious sensibilities within their wider social matrix during the subsequent centuries.

The rabbinic movement is by and large a product of the political and social reality of the post-70 CE era, which saw the crumbling of Judean political and religious institutions and the integration of Judean society into Roman imperial order in the province of Syria-Palaestina. As scholarly elites, the rabbis substituted the now-defunct Temple cult and judicial institutions with a developed corpus of legal literature that unprecedentedly covered all aspects of the law, ranging from the laws of the Temple and holidays to matters of private and family law. The first literary product of the rabbinic movement, documenting its scholarly activity during the century following the destruction of the Temple, the Mishnah, is the first Jewish composition devoted almost solely to the exposition of law in a systematic manner and covering all fields of law. The Mishnah is divided into six orders: Zera'im (laws of agriculture), Mo'ed

(Sabbath and holidays), Nashim (marriage and family), Neziqin (private law), Qodashim (Temple), and Teharot (purities). Each of these six orders includes multiple tractates pertaining to specific topics. Redacted in the beginning of the third century by R. Judah the Patriarch, it mostly transmits the legal views of second-century rabbis, called *tannaim*. During the first part of this period the tannaim were active mainly in the area of Judea; however, following the defeat in the Bar Kokhba revolt (132–36 CE) the prominent disciples of the rabbis moved to the Galilee, where they continued to expand on the teachings of their masters and develop new legal fields.

The Mishnah was not the only channel for transmitting the teachings of the tannaim. Due to its literary and legal qualities it acquired authoritative status by the later rabbis of the third to fifth centuries, who feature in the Palestinian and Babylonian Talmuds (*amoraim*). Frequently the Talmuds preserve additional or alternative versions of the tannaitic teachings. The most relevant compilation for our study of early rabbinic law is the Tosefta (literally, "the appendix" of the Mishnah). It follows the Mishnaic order of topics in each tractate and adds alternatives formulations of the laws, positions of other tannaim and interpretations of the Mishnah. The Tosefta also includes more nonlegal material than the Mishnah, including stories and historical anecdotes. Occasionally, it reflects an earlier form of the tannaitic ruling, which, later on, is revised into a characteristically precise formulation in the Mishnah. Thus, although the Tosefta was redacted after the Mishnah and includes views of later third-century rabbis, it also preserves earlier traditions and provides an expanded view of the diversity of positions among the tannaim.

Even though the bulk of rabbinic teachings in the Mishnah and Tosefta is either transmitted anonymously or attributed to post-70 CE tannaim, both compositions occasionally allude to figures from the Second Temple period, most prominently Hillel and Shammai and their academies called the House of Hillel and the House of Shammai. Important for our purposes, these texts also include a few debates between the Pharisees and their opponents and they consistently support the Pharisaic opinions. Evidently then, Second Temple traditions are woven into the Mishnah and Tosefta; at the same time, scholars have debated whether it is possible to separate these traditions from their current rabbinic context and reconstruct the original legal world of the Second Temple Pharisees. At the same time, to understand the rabbinic movement, we must also ask to what degree, if any, did these traditions shape rabbinic discourse in later generations.

In this book, I argue that not only can we discern a layer of early rabbinic law that was consolidated already prior to the destruction of the Temple but also that it is possible, through these early laws of purity, to reconstruct central aspects of the specific worldview of the Pharisees, the prominent predecessors of the rabbis. This method provides a deeper understanding of the powers that shaped Second Temple Judaism. Furthermore, comparative analysis of rabbinic sources with Second Temple texts—primarily the legal literature from Qumran and the Jesus traditions—enables us to reconstruct major aspects of the social and religious policies of the Pharisees, as these were shaped in opposition to alternative ideologies. At the same time, since later rabbis continued to engage with these same legal questions and reshaped the realm of purity law on both the ideological and practical levels, we have the means to examine the upshot of one of the central pillars of Second Temple Judaism and its gradual disintegration in the following generations with the rise of new forms of piety and religious experience.

Book Plan

As an introduction to the study of the unique features and message of the Pharisaic tradition, the first section (chaps. 1 and 2) offers a comprehensive survey of purity discourse within Second Temple Judaism. In contrast to the limited biblical purity system, throughout the Second Temple period the impact of purity language spread into multiple realms, from the ordering of daily life and protection from evil spirits, through the determination of social boundaries, to the shaping of eschatological expectations. Alongside new ways of implementing biblical obligations, the first chapter points to the rise of a new conceptualization of impurity, through which one could classify objects, people, and places. The second chapter addresses forms of exclusive purity among different groups during the Second Temple period. Qumran literature testifies to the social and cosmological meaning of the aspiration to purity, and multiple Jesus traditions testify to an attempt to purify creation toward the messianic age. The discourse of purity was therefore shared by many but functioned differently within each ideology.

Against the background of the social and ideological map presented in the first section, in the second section we turn to the Pharisees and examine the role of purity within their own worldview. After surveying the diverse descriptions of the Pharisees proffered by scholars—as a leading religious elite or a separatist sect—we turn to examine their conception of purity, as a standard form of ideological expression. In chapter 3, we focus on two peculiar purity practices vehemently denounced by Jesus, who expressly viewed them as an embodiment of Pharisaic worldview and behavior: handwashing and purification of the outside of the cup. As we learn from Jesus's condemnation, handwashing was intended to protect the body from the penetration of impurity. In stark contrast to biblical conceptions, the Pharisees were primarily concerned with preserving the individual's integrity rather than maintaining the purity of the holy Temple. By introducing new practices, they suggested an alternative mode of religious consciousness, which did not accord with traditional priestly perceptions. Thus also with regard to Jesus's second complaint, regarding the compromising approach of the Pharisees with regard to the purification of eating vessels. In his denunciation of the Pharisees for their neglect in fully purifying their food vessels, Jesus is following a similar complaint of the Sadducees against the Pharisaic practice of separating liquid streams. Both cases reflect different sides of the same compromising approach, in which pure and impure foods and vessels were maintained side by side on the Pharisaic dining table. The Pharisees deliberately implemented a policy of lack of distinction, which became their identifying mark, as a group that offered a path for personal purity within impure surroundings.

In the fourth and fifth chapters, we turn from individual behavior at the dining table to the role of purity practices in the social realm. Here, a comparison of Pharisaic policy to Qumran literature reveals opposing strategies for establishing social order through the laws of purity. At the same time, I will demonstrate that these contradictory approaches in fact emanated from a common legal legacy and sectarian discourse, shared by the Pharisees and the Qumran sectarians.

The fourth chapter compares the attitude of each of these communities toward outsiders, whom they defined as impure. The concept of outsider impurity is rooted in the attitude toward non-Judeans, whom Ezra and Nehemiah termed *ammei ha-aretz* (people of the land). Later on, this notion was turned inward toward other Jews, who did not belong to one's own circle of purity. The underlying tradition shared by the Pharisees and other sectarians viewed group affiliation as a precondition for purity. Based on this shared tradition, each group shaped a distinct social policy. While Qumran law offered a binary model, which identified the outsider with the gentile, in accordance with their separatist worldview, the Pharisees offered a graded system that was careful to distinguish the impurity of *am ha-aretz* from the intrinsic impurity of the gentile. Thus, the legal details served to delineate a complex social system based on a rigid hierarchy between pure and impure while, at the same time, enabling varying degrees of social relations.

The fifth chapter deals with the different strategies in Qumran and Pharisaic law for including those who have incurred impurity, such as the menstruant, the *zav* (one who has experienced abnormal genital secretions), or one who has contracted corpse impurity, within the community. Here, too, a common legal tradition is transformed into two opposing strategies of social engineering. The "first-day ablution" familiar from Qumran law stands against the status of the rabbinic *tevul yom*, who immerses on the last day of the purification process, indicating the different processes the impure person must undergo to return to the community. While Qumran law demanded immediate purification, and left anyone who had not completed the purification process on the social margins, rabbinic law enabled immediate reintegration, thus narrowing the gap between completely pure and partially pure. We see again in this chapter how the Pharisees maintained similar legal structures to those found in Qumran law but denuded them of their attendant social meaning.

The following two chapters, which comprise the final section of the book, address the gradual diminishing of purity observance in the generations following the destruction of the Temple, and the rabbinic attempts to preserve the ancient traditions within changing social contexts. A careful textual analysis of purity laws in tannaitic literature reveals internal gaps and tensions, through which the extent of the reworking of ancient traditions throughout the tannaitic generations is revealed.

The sixth chapter traces the fundamental change in the attitude toward am ha-aretz in the teachings of the second-century rabbis, with the transfer of rabbinic activity to the Galilee. Fundamental differences between the am ha-aretz pericope in Mishnah Teharot and its parallel in tractate Hagigah instruct us on the rise of a new, more suspicious and anxious policy toward am ha-aretz. With the lack of a shared public concern for purity, akin to those measures in place in the Second Temple period, the community could no longer provide support for those who sought to observe purity, and the public sphere was tainted with the impurity of am ha-aretz. Thus, we can trace the process of reinterpretation and reformulation of early traditions in the later Mishnah of the Galilean rabbis.

In the final chapter, we will survey textual testimonies to the diminishing of purity observance in the final layer of tannaitic literature and its continuance in the amoraic and post-Talmudic period in Byzantine Palestine. These sources lead us to the end of our story, whereby purity observance was gradually transformed from a marker of communal identity (as among the Pharisees), through the creation of voluntary associations for promoting the observance of purity, to an expression of religious virtuosity limited to a select few. Finally, a popular form of separation from impurity developed. Complex instructions, intended to prevent indirect contact with impurity, were ultimately abandoned, although the fear of contamination continued to infiltrate through other channels. Eventually, the aspiration to experience some form of purity, which shaped Jewish society for centuries and provided meaning for Jewish daily observances, lost its appeal, and as this powerful language ceased to function, a central component of ancient Jewish culture faded away.

NOTE ON TRANSLATIONS AND EDITIONS

Translations of the Hebrew Bible follow the New JPS translation (1985). Translations of quotes from the Apocrypha and the New Testament follow the New Revised Standard Version Bible (NRSV). Old Testament Pseudepigrapha is quoted from James, H. Carlesworth, *The Old Testament Pseudepigrapha*, 2 vols. (Garden City, NY: Doubleday, 1983–85). Translation of all rabbinic texts are my own.

Editions of other translated works:
Philo: Francis H. Colson, *Philo, With an English Translation* (Cambridge, MA: Harvard University Press, 1929–62). *Josephus*: Flavius Josephus, *Translation and Commentary*, edited by Steven Mason (Leiden, Netherlands: Brill, 2000) [=Flavius Josephus Online]. In books missing in this edition, I followed: Flavius Josephus, *Jewish Antiquities*, edited by H.st.J. Thackray, Ralph Marcus, and Louis Feldman (Cambridge, MA: Harvard University Press; London: Heinemann, 1926–65); *Qumran*: Florentino Garcia Martinez and Eibert Tigchelaar, *The Dead Sea Scrolls Study Edition* (Leiden, Netherlands: Brill, 1999); and Steven S. Fraade, *The Damascus Document* (Oxford: Oxford University Press, 2021).

ABBREVIATIONS

Second Temple Literature

1 En.	1 Enoch
1 Macc.; 2 Macc.	1 Maccabees; 2 Maccabees
1QH	Thanksgiving Scroll (Hodayot)
1QS; 4QS	Community Rule (Serekh Ha-Yaḥad), Qumran cave 1 and 4
1QM	War Scroll
4QD	Damascus Document, from Qumran cave 4
4QMMT	Miqsat Ma'ase ha-Torah
11QT	Temple Scroll
A. Ap.	Against Apion
Ant.	Judean Antiquities
CD	Damascus Document
J.W.	Judean War
Jdt	Judith
Jub.	Book of Jubilees
Life	Life of Joseph
T. Mos.	Testament of Moses
Tob	Tobit

Rabbinic Sources

Rabbinic Literature

m.	Mishnah
t.	Tosefta
y.	Yerushalmi (Palestinian Talmud)
b.	Bavli (Babylonian Talmud)

Talmudic Tractates

'Abod. Zar.	Avodah Zarah	Neg.	Nega'im
B. Bat.	Bava Batra	Nid.	Niddah
B. Meṣ.	Bava Meṣia	'Ohal.	Ohalot
B. Qam.	Bava Qamma	Parah	Parah
Bek.	Bekhorot	Pesaḥ.	Pesahim
Ber.	Berakhot	Qidd.	Qiddushin
Bik.	Bikkurim	Roš Haš.	Rosh Hashanah
'Ed.	Eduyyot	Šabb.	Shabbat
'Erub.	Eruvin	Sanh.	Sanhedrin
Git.	Gittin	Šeqal.	Sheqalim
Ḥag.	Hagigah	Sot.	Sotah
Ḥul.	Hullin	T. Yom.	Tevul Yom
Ma'as. Š.	Ma'aser Sheni	Tehar.	Teharot
		Ter.	Trumot
Mak.	Makkot	'Uq.	Uqtzin
Makš.	Makshirin	Yad.	Yadayim
Menaḥ.	Menahot	Yeb.	Yevamot
Miqw.	Miqva'ot	Zabim	Zavim

PURITY AND IDENTITY IN
Ancient Judaism

Introduction

From Pharisees to Rabbis

Come and see the extent to which purity had spread!
For the earlier sages did not decree that, "a pure man may not eat with a
 menstruant," since the earlier generations refrained from eating with
 menstruants altogether!
Rather they decreed that a *zav* may not eat with a *zava*,
 since it lends occasion to transgression.

(Tosefta Shabbat 1:14)

R. Shimon b. Eleazar is astonished to learn that according to the early teaching of the Houses of Hillel and Shammai, a man who has experienced an abnormal genital discharge (*zav*) would not eat with a woman experiencing abnormal genital discharge (*zava*), and a Pharisee who is a zav would not eat with other *zavim* who are not careful in matters of purity, although both were equally impure. His words express the wide gap between the world of the rabbis in third-century Galilee and that of the rabbinical academies of Jerusalem during the Second Temple period, a century and a half earlier. The gap between the generations is twofold, encompassing both the level of purity observance and the formulation of the law. For Second Temple Jews, the concern for purity was an inherent part of daily conduct, and it had an inevitable impact on social relations. The early rabbis therefore saw no need to mention that one must not eat with a menstruant. They did, however, emphasize that impure persons of different groups should not eat together and must still maintain social separation. However, 150 years later, in R. Shimon b. Eleazar's surroundings, one could not assume even minimal distancing from sources of impurity. R. Shimon is aware that each generation phrases its laws in accordance with the needs of its time and place. Therefore, to learn the level of purity observance of earlier generations, rather than recovering historical memories or testimonies, he points to the style of the legal material from this earlier time period. The formulation of the legal tradition thus serves R. Shimon as a window into the world of the early rabbis, and its phrasing testifies to their practice and to the value system of those who formulated it.

From R. Shimon b. Eleazar's perspective, the historical memory encapsulated in the early legal traditions arouses mostly sorrow for an earlier, better, and purer world that has now been lost.[1] From our perspective, R. Shimon's declaration lays the foundation for a comprehensive examination of the history of Jewish religious culture and the changing societal and ideological contexts that shaped it. The sense of a decline in purity observance from the Second Temple period to the beginning of the third century, alluded to by R. Shimon, is well attested in material findings,[2] but it is only the literary data that reveals the full meaning of this process within ancient Judaism in general and rabbinic Judaism in particular. Behind R. Shimon's statement stands the story of far-reaching changes that took place in the religious culture of Palestinian Jews during the first two centuries CE (equivalent to the period of the tannaim, the rabbis of the Mishnah). From the perspective of a third-century rabbi, this is a clear tale of religious decline. From a scholarly perspective, the realm of purity law, more than any other field, reveals the transformation of traditions, practices, and ideas from the social and religious world of Second Temple Judaism to the world of later rabbis who attempted to hold on to a revered culture that had been marginalized. This book seeks to tell the story of this process as it is illustrated in the legal traditions of the rabbis during the first three centuries.

The Changing Contexts of Early Rabbinic Literature

Rabbinic literature does not lend itself easily to historical exploration, neither of its legal traditions nor of its social and cultural background. The laws of the earlier and later rabbis are woven together side by side in composite texts, thus creating the impression that the concrete historical contexts in which the rabbis operated have been lost to the organized, comprehensive legal system into which the different traditions were woven. Can one, despite this fundamental characteristic of rabbinic legal compositions, pierce the veils of the tightly woven texts and separate the whole into its parts, describing the path trodden by the traditions of the law at its different stages? Can one distinguish between the historical and social world of the early legal traditions and the challenges that faced latter-day tannaim?

As opposed to those that minimize the value of the Mishnah and other rabbinic texts for the historical exploration of this period, viewing it primarily as an ideological expression of the rabbinic worldview,[3] in this book I suggest an essentially positive answer to these questions. The tannaitic legal project responds to wider processes that took place during this period, and these are inevitably reflected in it. As we will see, the complex array of traditions concerning the laws of purity reflects a changing social reality to which the rabbis were compelled to adjust. I should point out that my approach is not based on the assumption that the rabbis necessarily had some leading role within Jewish society—in fact, there is no better indication of the gaps in religious standards within Jewish society than the laws of purity, and rabbinic literature in this field does not make any attempt to represent the prevalent way of life. At the same time, from their very nature, the laws of purity embed the features of social reality, and rabbinic activity in this field was therefore necessarily sensitive to these changing environments. Arguably, then, an analysis of the legal discourse allows us a glimpse into these changing contexts, as well as to the changing forms of rabbinic activity.

As I will demonstrate, the topic of purity, more than any other legal field, reveals early layers of the Mishnah pertaining to the world of Second Temple Jews. To explain the uniqueness of this field and my approach to it, I shall briefly survey attempts by other scholars to establish the antiquity of the Mishnah and the critiques against them. Since the earliest stages of the critical study of the Mishnah, scholars tended to view legal traditions relating to the Temple ritual as authentic documentation from the Second Temple period.[4] However, as more recent scholars have commented, the mere treatment of Temple rituals does not testify to the early arrangement of these tractates. Laws concerning the Temple are for the most part based on the teachings of rabbis of the second century, even when they are formulated as vivid rituals. They combine fragments of earlier traditions from the Temple days with later ideas and exegetical tendencies and should not be viewed as a product of the sages of the Second Temple period.[5]

It is now widely accepted that one must not assume the antiquity of traditions about the Temple in the Mishnah without further evidence. Similarly, discussions of legal institutions, such as the Great Court, the Sanhedrin, do not necessarily testify to their actual activity, and even the inclusion of early traditions within some of these discussions is insufficient to indicate the antiquity of all such discussions.[6] A similar problem exists regarding the historical significance of distinct literary styles within the Mishnah. Previous scholarship tended to assume that traditions using archaic language were necessarily early, but this assumption ignores the rhetorical and ideological value of such archaic language.[7] We have therefore no clear signs, whether relating to content or to style, that aid us in the task of distinguishing between earlier and later tannaitic material.

In fact, a general overview of the Mishnah reveals fairly consistent stylistic unity. One gets the impression that the original language of the rabbis was rearticulated in short, unified linguistic molds, which almost completely concealed a variety of modes of expression under a blanket of unified phraseology. This fact has the potential to discourage us from attempting to trace the developmental paths of this literature and its early roots. Indeed, Jacob Neusner arrived at far-reaching conclusions along this line of thought.[8] In his early work, Neusner sought to systematically describe the history of purity law, and this project served as the platform for his programmatic essays on the Mishnah.[9] Initially, Neusner believed he could separate the laws of every tractate into distinct historical layers, according to the named rabbis included in them—that is, the rabbis of the Second Temple period, the Yavneh period prior to the Bar Kokhba revolt (132–36 CE), and the Usha period following the Bar Kokhba revolt—and to identify each stage with a clear, central legal tendency and set of questions. From the style of the Mishnah, Neusner concluded however that all its laws were edited in such a way as to erase all traces of earlier sources, and therefore, he viewed the differences between the generations of rabbis as a logical-philosophical construct rather than historical documentation.[10] Thus, within the fairly uniform text, which prevents us from accessing the early sources themselves, Neusner allows us to reconstruct only a theoretical history of ideas.[11]

Neusner's approach undermines the possibility of reconstructing the history of rabbinic law on the basis of attribution of specific rulings to named rabbis. Ostensibly, the name of the speaker of a particular ruling testifies to its original temporal and geographical context. But is this indeed a reliable tool for reconstructing the history of rabbinic law? A look at tannaitic literature informs us that during the latter part of the second century CE, the disciples of R. Akiva frequently disputed the wording of a disagreement between the Houses of Hillel and Shammai. As a result, Neusner questioned the value of any kind of attribution to these early rabbinic authorities. Per Neusner, the Mishnah pseudo-epigraphically attributes rulings to early rabbis to ground its own approach and principles.[12]

In spite of the real need for caution and although the wording of citations in rabbinic literature does not comprise a direct quotation, Neusner's conclusion turns a blind eye to the nature of rabbinic study culture, which focused not on the development of a legal-philosophical system but rather on the interpretation of the words of earlier rabbis, through the conservation and processing of their traditions.[13] There is no doubt that the tannaim saw themselves as the successors of the Jerusalem academies and, therefore, produced varied interpretations and formulations of the early legal traditions,[14] but this is not sufficient cause to question the value of the early tradition itself. Instead of viewing the disputes regarding the precise wording of early traditions as evidence for the lack of credibility of the process of transmission, they actually reflect the intense exegesis and reworking of those traditions. The study of the various traditions through philological-historical analysis presents us with adequate tools for tracing their development. On the other hand, ignoring rabbinic commitment to the interpretation and development of early traditions in the different tannaitic works runs the risk of imposing foreign approaches onto the text.[15]

However, even if we accept the possibility of reconstructing specific traditions in principle, we are still faced with the challenge of imposing order on to the presumably jumbled materials of the Mishnah. As mentioned, the Mishnah is usually perceived as a kind of messy collection of traditions from different periods, which the scholar must separate to speculatively create groups of laws, opinions, and stories from different periods. Tannaitic literature in general, and the Mishnah specifically, are largely viewed as an unsteady composite of materials, at the basis of which stand innumerable competing traditions, and the student of this material must leap beyond the text to unravel its sources.

This textual situation engendered a new approach in the study of Mishnah. This more recent trend has been indirectly influenced by Neusner's critical work, thereby recognizing the role of the redactor of the Mishnah in reshaping the various sources it had at its disposal. Current studies do not reject the source-critical methodology and do acknowledge the history of individual traditions, but at the same time, due to the elusiveness of Mishnah source criticism, they tend to focus on the final form of the redacted Mishnah.[16] This tendency is bolstered by the growing occupation with the comparison of the Mishnah to its parallel compilation, the Tosefta. A key feature that has been highlighted in recent research is the extent of literary reworking of the mishnaic text in comparison to its Toseftan parallels. The Mishnah is revealed to be a more tightly knit text, in which effort was invested to fashion a highly stylized text and create a coherent literary product.[17]

And thus, the scholar of early rabbinic literature in general, and Mishnah in particular, finds himself at a crossroad. The focus on the redacted compositions provides important insights into the views, interests, and ideologies of the rabbis during the beginning of the third century, as the earliest rabbinic compilation, the Mishnah, took its final shape. This perspective, however, largely forgoes the voices of earlier sources embedded in the tannaitic compositions, from which arises a dynamic portrait of the legal and historic happenings of the period. Is it possible to bridge the gap between these two methodologies, and may one approach the Mishnah as a redacted text without relinquishing its historical depth?

As mentioned, we do not have clear indications of the antiquity of specific laws, besides cases of explicit attribution to earlier authorities. A careful reading of the Mishnah may reveal, however, traces of legal development. The Mishnah and the Tosefta, similar to other Talmudic sources, do not erase the gaps, contradictions, or tensions between different sources. Gaps are revealed in the content of laws, in their phrasing and stylization, and in the ways in which they are organized. These gaps serve to uncover the ongoing process of exegesis, composition, and weaving together of sources, which may at times represent varying contexts. A careful procedure of discerning and unraveling enables us, in many cases, to separate the different literary strata that comprise these works and attribute them to the various different stages of development of early rabbinic law.[18]

This is a delicate, and at times speculative, work indeed, but in the realm of purity law, we stand on fairly firm ground. This field is not only the most widely discussed topic in the Mishnah (it occupies about a quarter of the Mishnah) but it also possesses the earliest foundations, as is evidenced both by the rulings attributed to the early academies of Hillel and Shammai and through the comparison to other legal corpora of the Second Temple period, primarily that of the Qumran sectarians. The realm of purity law contains a wide layer of early sources that stand against the teachings of later rabbis. Unlike the laws pertaining to the Temple, which ostensibly treat an ancient institution but in fact rest on a thin layer of earlier legal traditions and are discussed primarily by later rabbis, in the realm of purity law one can trace the channels of development, from the teachings of the earliest rabbis of the Second Temple period up to the activity of the last generation of tannaim in the beginning of the third century.[19]

Traces of Pharisaic Law in the Mishnah

Writing a history of the culture of purity in Judaism that stretches for over two centuries is based not merely on the assumption that rabbinic literature reflects a variety of historical contexts but also on the understanding that this literature is deeply rooted in the world of Second Temple Judaism. The analysis of the early layers of early rabbinic literature in comparison to other contemporary sources provides sufficient material to place some early rabbinic purity traditions alongside other, competing perceptions of purity, which occasionally provide the most suitable background for their interpretation. Furthermore, I argue that not only can we discern a layer of early rabbinic law that was consolidated already prior to the destruction of the Temple but also that it is possible, through these early laws of purity, to reconstruct central aspects of the specific worldview of the Pharisees, the prominent predecessors of the rabbis, thereby providing a deeper understanding of the powers that shaped Second Temple Judaism.

The meaning of this claim is twofold: On the one hand, one can produce, from rabbinic literature, a comprehensive picture of the Pharisaic worldview. On the other hand, it is possible to trace the changes that took place in the Pharisaic tradition, as it was transmitted and transformed by the rabbis through later periods and environments. The teachings of the rabbis are rooted in the Pharisaic tradition, but the trajectory of purity laws in rabbinic sources reveals the extent to which this tradition underwent processing and adaptation up to the third century. While Pharisaic law, with its unique characteristics, was part and parcel of the ideology of purity and practice of the Second Temple period, later rabbinic law, which took shape in a new environment, directed purity laws into new realms.

To a large extent, my approach here is based on the work of the late Aharon Shemesh, a prominent scholar of early Jewish law, but adds to it a deeper historical dimension. Shemesh distinguished between a "developmental model" whereby the laws of the tannaim reflect a later stage of legal development in comparison to Qumran and a "reflective model" in which rabbinic law preserves the Pharisees' approach, which competed with other approaches from the Second Temple period. Following this distinction, I seek to demonstrate that tracing the evolution of purity laws within early rabbinic literature enables us, on the one hand, to uncover the early Pharisaic stance, which sought to provide an alternative to the contemporary ideas of purity; on the other hand, this analysis reveals the change in the halakhic and religious discourse of the later rabbis.[20]

My own approach lies, then, in between two opposing scholarly trends with regard to the question of the continuity between Pharisaic traditions and the complex system presented by the Mishnah. On the one hand, there appears to be strong evidence for the link between tannaitic law and the Pharisaic tradition. Both the New Testament and Josephus consider Rabban Gamaliel and Rabban Shimon b. Gamaliel to be Pharisees, and in rabbinic literature they are part of the rabbinic leadership.[21] Furthermore, since the Pharisaic movement was considered a dominant stream during the Second Temple period, as the Gospels, Josephus, and Qumran literature testify,[22] it would seem only natural that they were the ones who laid the foundations for the religious leadership of the rabbis following the destruction of the Temple, whereas their competitors, the priests and the members of the various sects, supposedly disappeared. The overwhelming support of Pharisaic law in the rabbinic sources has also been understood against this background.[23] Furthermore, the commitment of the Pharisees to the tradition of the elders, in addition to the written Torah, seems to be equivalent to the rabbinic principle of the two Torahs given at Sinai.[24]

Several factors, however, have served to undermine this image of continuity, and subsequently, new approaches sought to limit the historical link between the Pharisees and the rabbis. On one level, a critical look at the literature of the period—Josephus and rabbinic literature—raises doubts regarding the dominance of both the Pharisees during the Temple period and the rabbis following it.[25] Both groups are depicted in this literature as sects or separatist associations more than they are described as accepted religious leadership.[26] On the ideological level, too, there is a significant difference between the tradition of the elders in Pharisaic doctrine and the rabbinic notion of Oral Torah.[27] The intensive exegetical activity of the rabbis and the growing tendency to establish rabbinic traditions anchored in scripture also points to an implementation of Saducean tendencies, downplaying the independent authority of tradition.[28]

Against this background, Shaye Cohen suggested a new description of the rabbinic ideology and policy that took root in Yavneh following the destruction of the Temple.[29] In place of the accepted picture of a Pharisaic victory, following the destruction, over other forms of Judaism, Cohen points to a rabbinic rejection of the sectarianism that shaped Jewish society during the Second Temple period and dominated Pharisaic ideology as well. Instead, he claims, the rabbis sought to include all streams within the developing rabbinic movement. In Cohen's opinion, the rabbis who lived after the destruction of the Temple severed their association with the Pharisees, despite their objections to the other sects, the Sadducees and Boethusians, as well.[30] Per Cohen, while the Pharisees operated as a sect with distinct purity practices, the rabbis sought to uproot sectarian consciousness and leave it behind them. Only a few signs remained of Pharisaic practices, but these are marginal when compared to the overall revolutionary stance of the rabbis. Cohen attributes great significance to this shift, which is reflected not necessarily in specific legal stances but rather in the nature of rabbinic discourse, which is characterized by dispute and a multiplicity of opinions.[31] Despite various reservations from Cohen's description,[32] the distinction between the rabbis and the Pharisaic tradition familiar from the literature of the period was adopted by other scholars, and the rabbis are considered the product of the postdestruction reality.[33]

To my mind, any consideration of the degree of continuity between the Pharisees and the rabbis must take into account, first and foremost, the similarity between their legal stances, which shaped the identities of both groups. This is the field in which we have the most data and the clearest chronological documentation. Unlike social policy or ideological stances, about which we have only partial information, clouded by anachronism, legal trajectories, complex as they may be, have the potential to serve as a more precise indication of the changes that took place during this period. Indeed, the starting point for any historical reconstruction is the fact that the rabbis preserved Pharisaic laws. They adopted the legal positions attributed to the Pharisees against the approaches of their opponents, the Sadducees, and one can consistently find reflected in early rabbinic literature the legal policy attributed to the Pharisees and attacked by their sectarian rivals.[34]

As Cohen has noted, the existence of a small number of shared legal positions is insufficient to testify to social or ideological continuity, and Cohen chose to describe the link between rabbinic law and Pharisaic tradition as local and unimpressive.[35] An in-depth analysis of the realm of purity law, however, points to the constitutive role of Pharisaic practices in shaping the more developed rabbinic system, which continued to develop in new directions.

The question is therefore not whether one may find elements of Pharisaic law spread throughout tannaitic sources but rather how the rabbis adapted these legal traditions, as well as the worldview they embodied.[36] While it is difficult to determine the continuity of group identity through periods of historical upheaval, one can attempt to pin down the internal viewpoint of those who were involved in this process and their attitude toward the ancient legacy they inherited. This is particularly true with regard to purity laws: since the observance of purity was the hallmark of Pharisaic practice and worldview, tracing this field and the changes it underwent brings us very close to understanding the ways in which the rabbis managed this rich legacy.

Scholars have indeed attempted to find indications within rabbinic literature of the adoption of the Pharisaic worldview, primarily in the realm of purity observance. In his influential study "The History of the Halakha and the Dead Sea Scrolls," Ya'akov Sussman claimed that behind the many disputes and legal stances among Second Temple sects, one can identify two basic approaches: "It appears that a basic split occurred between the stringent, inflexible and uncompromising [Sadducean] approach, and the flexible, evolving and relatively lenient [Pharisaic] approach, which answered the needs of the general public and sought to enable the people to share in the new spirit."[37] Against this background, the Pharisees were often accused of leniency by their opponents. According to Sussman, behind their lenient rulings stood a desire to democratize ritual practice and allow wider participation in the cult. This turn to the masses was the founding principle of Pharisaic law, and it continued to shape the rabbinic worldview during the generations following the destruction.

This general picture painted by Sussman was elaborated on in additional studies.[38] Notably, however, the examples adduced in these works focus exclusively on polemics relating to the operation of the Temple and the preservation of its purity. As we saw in R. Shimon b. Eleazar's words previously, however, the Pharisees' policy focused to a large extent on the daily observance of purity, and these are the traditions that were later preserved by the rabbis following the destruction of the Temple.

The Pharisees' concern with the daily observance of purity, beyond the realm of the Temple, stands at the center of Neusner's depiction of Pharisaic ideology. According to Neusner, the teachings of the Houses of Hillel and Shammai represent the ideology of the Pharisees, who, from Herod's days onward, abandoned any political aspirations and adopted a separatist, sectarian way of life.[39] From the topics included in the teachings of the houses, Neusner deduces that these Pharisees were mainly concerned with eating unconsecrated foods in the state of purity and that they viewed the dining table as a substitute for Temple holiness. The Pharisees thus presented an alternative to the priests, not in the management of the Temple, but by adopting an equivalent level of purity and holiness. According to Neusner, with the destruction of the Temple, the practical observance of purity as an alternative to the priesthood was annulled, and was subsequently replaced by theoretical discussions and speculative analysis. Notably, then, while Sussman underlines the continuity between the rabbis and the Pharisees, and characterizes them jointly, Neusner's reconstruction suggests a deep revolution in the role of purity between the two phases.

Neusner's focus on daily purity is indeed pertinent to any understanding of the Pharisees; however, the descriptions he offers for the Pharisaic and rabbinic approaches are far from satisfactory. Instead of carefully comparing them with other current practices, Neusner is content with a simplistic image of the nature and role of purity observance in general. In his view, the mere occupation of the Pharisees with purity inevitably points to their separatist and sectarian tendencies. However, among Palestinian Jews of the Second Temple period, minute differences in purity practices created a rich taxonomy of social boundaries and religious ideologies. Within this setting the unique features of the Pharisaic worldview can be revealed only through a detailed examination of their purity policies. Indeed, the scope of purity laws in early rabbinic traditions reflects the general concern for purity during the Second Temple period, and this trend largely continued even after 70 CE independently of the existence of the Temple. At the same time, the distinct features of the Pharisaic purity perception can be identified by setting them alongside alternative approaches that were available in the ideological marketplace of the time. This is the approach I take in this book.

Comparing rabbinic sources with Second Temple texts—primarily the legal literature from Qumran and the Jesus traditions—enables us to reconstruct major aspects of the social and religious policies of the Pharisees, as these were shaped in opposition to alternative ideologies. Since later rabbis continued to engage with these same legal questions and reshaped the realm of purity law on both the ideological and practical levels, we have the means to examine the upshot of one of the central pillars of Second Temple Judaism and its gradual disintegration in the following generations.

Purities: Toward a New Scholarly Approach

Purity observance had a considerable impact on the daily conduct of the Jews of Palestine during the Second Temple period. After all, any attempt to eat in a state of purity required constant awareness of multiple sources of impurity; most importantly, it involved distancing oneself from various "others." The severity of safety measures one chose to apply and the types of foods one chose to protect determined, to a large extent, one's social affiliation and from whom one separated. Purity practices shaped multiple facets of human behavior, and the disputes between the competing ritual systems of the Second Temple period touched on fundamental differences in religious and social worldviews. Most revealing are the differences between the purity laws of the rabbis and those that appear in the Qumran legal corpus.

Many works have been dedicated to describing the uniqueness of the rabbinic purity laws in comparison to those of the Qumran sectarians, and these provide the foundation for my own historical approach to the development of the purity discourse from the Second Temple to the Mishnah. In what follows, I briefly survey three such works, written by Hannah Harrington, Vered Noam, and Mira Balberg, each of which highlights a different aspect of rabbinic purity discourse.

According to Hannah Harrington, the central difference between the rabbis and the Qumran sect in the realm of purity lies in their exegetical approach.[40] Both, she claims, attempted to systematically fill in the exegetical gaps in biblical law, but each group chose opposing methods. In the Qumran sect, the biblical system was harmonized and homogenized toward stringency, whereas the rabbis tended toward leniency. According to Harrington, even terms that make their first appearance in the rabbinic corpus are firmly anchored in biblical interpretation.[41]

While it is justified to take the rabbis' exegetical commitments seriously, even when these are not made explicit, Harrington's approach is insufficient to understand the purity policies of the rabbis. The laws of food purity, in particular, are only loosely linked to biblical precepts. Topics such as hand purity and gentile impurity lack a biblical foundation and were introduced later. The rabbis display a highly developed system of food purity, parts of which have no parallel in Qumran literature, and the rabbis themselves consider some of the laws as nonbiblical innovations.[42] Furthermore, some of these innovations are particularly stringent, and are not in line with the presumably lenient interpretation of biblical law.[43]

Against this background, Vered Noam's comprehensive analysis of the ancient laws of corpse impurity offers a thorough comparison of the rabbinic system of corpse impurity with the one reflected in Qumran literature. Unlike earlier works on this topic, which were limited to select rulings, Noam examines an entire halakhic field.[44] As her work demonstrates, there is a considerable gap between the relatively limited and straightforward biblical injunctions, which are basically maintained in Qumran literature, and the complex system presented in rabbinic literature. From Noam's research, it appears that the laws of corpse impurity from Qumran literature exhibit a strong affinity to the biblical text: "this is a relatively conservative halakha, which does not distance itself much from the plain meaning of the biblical text."[45] Rabbinic leniency, on the other hand, represents a revolution when compared with a straightforward reading of the verses.[46] Several innovative characteristics of rabbinic corpse impurity laws, including what Noam describes as an abstract conception of the "physics" of impurity dissemination, join together to create "a real earthquake."[47] In her view, following Sussman's description, this revolution is not essentially the product of a later rabbinic innovation but rather took place in Pharisaic circles already during the Second Temple period, in opposition to the conservative trend of Qumran law.

Noam argues for an essential contrast between the revolutionary nature of the Pharisaic-rabbinic tradition and the conservative tendency of Qumran law.

Admittedly, however, although she provides an apt characterization of the two legal systems as a whole, when taking a closer look we see that this generalized contrast does not take into account the far-reaching changes that took place within the rabbinic tradition itself. Noam describes the general approach of the Pharisees, and later the rabbis, but does not examine the ways in which rabbinic law developed and transformed. This approach is largely based on the assumption that rabbinic law faithfully followed in the footsteps of the earlier Pharisaic revolutionary approach.[48] Noam therefore seeks to anchor each of the legal revolutions she identifies in the early stages of Pharisaic law, out of which the later rabbinic formulations developed.

In my view, to sufficiently explain the continued dynamics of rabbinic law, we must take into account its internal tensions. Thus, for instance, in the field of corpse impurity, rabbinic law is lenient with regard to the size of bones that confer impurity and, at the same time, considerably extends the dissemination of "tent impurity." This gap raises the question: Was the same group in fact responsible for both tendencies? Is it not reasonable to conjecture that they were created in different environments and reflect changing motivations? And indeed, a look at Qumran literature reveals that the first issue, regarding the size of the bone, fits in within contemporary legal discourse and reflects a dispute between the different traditions, whereas the second tendency, that dramatically extended the spread of tent impurity, has no echoes in early rabbinic law, not to mention in Qumran literature.[49] A comparison to Qumran law therefore not only reveals the contrast between the two legal traditions but it also allows us to trace the changing tendencies within rabbinic law throughout the ages. We must distinguish between legal issues that generated controversy among Second Temple Jews, versus topics that are embedded in later rabbinic legal discourse and indicate the rabbis' new concerns and conceptions.

Once scholars perceive the laws of purity as an evolving and changing system, additional questions arise: What are the forces that drive these legal changes? To what degree is legal development based on an interpretation of earlier traditions, and to what extent is it driven by external forces and contexts to which the rabbis responded? In other words, to what extent can the development of rabbinic law serve as an indication of historical, cultural, and social processes? Without denying the role of exegesis, conceptualization, and unification within rabbinic legal activity, I claim that we must not ignore the weight of other surrounding factors in analyzing the history of rabbinic purity laws.

First, as mentioned, far-reaching changes took place during the first two centuries CE with regard to the material culture that supported purity observance. The archaeological digs of Second Temple–era layers have revealed a substantial number of ritual baths (*miqva'ot*) in Judea, in both private and public domains.[50] Additional findings, such as stone vessels and stamps indicating purity on slay jugs, testify to the spread of purity measures even beyond Jerusalem and the Temple.[51] The material evidence, therefore, aligns with the testimony of cotemporaneous literature, and together they teach us that there was an "outbreak of purity in Israel," as R. Shimon b. Eleazar said. However, with regard to the post-70 CE era, the assessment of the archaeological data has undergone significant change in the last few years. At first it was assumed that there was a drastic decline in the number of miqva'ot following the destruction of the Temple, to the extent that some claimed that in the absence of a Temple, there was no longer any place for purity practices;[52] archaeological findings, however, indicate the continuity of purity routines and widespread use of miqva'ot and stone vessels following the Great Revolt in the years 66–70 CE as well. Purity was, therefore, independent of the existence of the Temple and continued to shape the daily lives of the Jews of Palestine long after its destruction. The dramatic change in archaeological findings comes from the period following the Bar Kokhba revolt, with the transition to the Galilee. At this stage, the number of sites at which miqva'ot were found declined, alongside a steep decline in the evidence of stone vessel usage.[53]

How, then, did the rabbis respond to these changes? From their perspective, the changes in purity practices were not purely a matter of historical inquiry into a remote past. The people of this period witnessed substantial changes in the nature of religious practice and culture, as well as the collapse of traditional social structures, to which the rabbis were compelled to respond. This situation presented them with pressing questions: What was the value of these ancient ritual practices, and in what form should they be preserved? What mechanisms existed for the conservation of the social role of purity observance, and could one continue maintaining those same distinctions between different levels of purity? On the other hand, as the social networks which supported the observance of purity in the past crumbled, the rabbis were required to react to alternative attempts to adopt purity habits.[54] The archaeological findings, therefore, indicate changes in the purity routine, and rabbinic literature instructs us of the mechanisms of response to these changes.

Destruction and migration can indeed serve as a platform for normative change, such as we witness in the rabbinic reshaping of purity practices. At the same time, one must also take into account the role of the cultural exchange underlying rabbinic legal activity. It was not only specific practices (such as handwashing, as we see in chap. 3) that permeated the purity practices of Palestinian Jews from their Greco-Roman surroundings, even well-founded traditions could be charged with new meaning when exposed to contemporary ethical ideals. Thus, for instance, in an attempt to explain the purpose of rabbinic involvement with purity, Mira Balberg suggests that the rabbis were engaged in the technology of self-formation through the establishment of a highly conscious subjectivity, similar to prevalent trends in the Roman world. The conception of the self in the Roman world during the second century was one of vulnerability, and one was expected to constantly engage in practices of self-control and mental attention. These became the cornerstones of the prevalent stoic ideal of self-perfection through mechanisms for the care of the self, which in turn served to transform the very meaning of Jewish concerns for the purity of the self.[55]

From this perspective, the rabbis approached the ideal of purity as an ethical venture, directed at the perfection of the individual (in particular, the Jewish male who adheres to rabbinic instructions). While strongly linking rabbinic purity discourse to Greco-Roman cultural trends, Balberg sets the rabbis' conception of purity at odds with the predominantly social function of purity observance within the world of Second Temple Judaism. As the first chapters of this book exhibit in detail, for the Jews of the Second Temple period, competing forms of purity observance signaled the dividing lines between different worldviews and groups. Accordingly, the study of purity became a central component of the study of Jewish society during the Second Temple period. Therefore, scholars have been drawn to the following questions: Why did the Pharisees observe purity, and what was the attitude toward this practice in wider segments of the Jewish population? What was the nature of Jesus's objection to purity? What are the roots of Second Temple sectarianism?

Evidently, in the world of ancient Judaism *purity shaped community*. Purity observance cannot be understood outside of its particular social setting, and even when it addresses the daily conduct of the individual, purity policy seeks to shape one's space and environment. Arguably, then, this feature governed purity discourse not only during the Second Temple period but also in later rabbinic teachings, as they negotiated the role of purity within changing circumstances. Major facets of purity laws, including those governing the separation from Jews who do not practice the laws of purity (*am ha-aretz*) and those regarding the voluntary association of the pure (*havurah*), directly derive from particular social conditions and serve to implement spiritual ideals within concrete social structures. While Balberg's work provides invaluable insights regarding purity and the self, this book examines the ways in which different Jewish communities in antiquity defined themselves through their unique versions of the purity traditions.

PART I

THE VARIETIES OF PURITY

1

Biblical Foundations, New Conceptions

Introduction: The Multiple Dimensions of Purity Observance

Impurity lurked around every corner for Jews of the Second Temple period. Although not all Jews of the time partook in the culture of purity to the same degree, it nevertheless played a central role in shaping their worldview. Everyday events rendered one impure. Ritual immersion was necessary after sexual intercourse to commence daily activities, and in many families menstruants were separated from the rest of the household for several days each month. Serious illnesses were considered a manifestation of impurity that only miracle workers could banish, and those who came across a corpse were careful to cleanse themselves from the impurity it imparted as soon as they could. Alongside these events, people observed fixed moments of purification: before each meal, before prayer, or in preparation for the Sabbath.[1] All Second Temple Jews purified themselves for a full week before their pilgrimage to the Temple in Jerusalem.

In addition to the shared experience of incidental contact with sources of impurity, concern for purity also regularly divided social groups. Those suffering the impurity of leprosy or abnormal genital discharges (*zov*) were distanced from the city for an undetermined period of time and could not reenter it until they were healed. There were others who were similarly impure but whose presence in the public sphere was unavoidable. Thus, not only was it forbidden to marry gentiles due to their impurity, but some Jews did not even visit their homes. Imported vessels and gentile-produced oil were also considered impure.[2] As a rule, physical touch was never spontaneous or uncalculated, as impurity demarcated Jewish groups from one another.[3] The Pharisees considered other, less observant Jews—whom they called *ammei ha-aretz* (lit., "people of the land"; sg.: *am ha-aretz*)—impure, while the Qumran sectarians considered all other Jews impure.[4] For individuals who did not join the sectarian covenant, sins and impurity were inextricably linked together, and Qumran sources grant the benefaction of purity only to those who obeyed the rule of God and received the gift of the Holy Spirit.

For some Second Temple Jews, purity and impurity were also imbued with cosmic significance.[5] Impurity embodied the satanic control of bodily functions and the power of the evil inclination, and only with its removal could the path toward cosmic renewal be paved. Eschatological groups of this time called for a purification of the world in anticipation of its ultimate redemption. Their acts of purification—whether through use of water or through acts of healing—reflected the nature of the anticipated change. The language of purity therefore expressed the eschatological hopes of Second Temple Jews.

Thus, the perpetual striving toward purity became an important arena of activity that reflected a wide array of views and needs. Yet despite its varied manifestations, the pursuit of purity provided a shared language through which ancient Jewish formulated different and competing worldviews. Within this diversity of discourses regarding purity among ancient Jews, this book offers an in-depth study of one particular strand—namely, the purity of the Pharisees, the dominant movement whose ideology shaped rabbinic Judaism. What was the unique nature of Pharisaic observance of purity, especially when compared to the concept of purity adopted by other groups such as the Essenes, Qumranites, and Jesus followers? What worldview did it reflect and what social politics did it promote?

Indeed, the Pharisees' specific approach to purity can only be understood against the backdrop of contemporaneous purity discourses. To that end, this chapter surveys the concepts of purity among Second Temple Jews by addressing the role of the biblical legacy in shaping popular practices during the Second Temple period, as well as the major innovations that gained widespread acceptance. In the next chapter, I analyze the doctrines of the Qumran sectarians and the Jesus movement who promoted unique forms of purity, corresponding to their eschatological schemes.

In these two chapters, I argue that, despite scholarly opinions to the contrary, the principles of the biblical system of purity provide only a limited foundation for understanding the concern for purity in the Second Temple era. Instead, as a close analysis of the discourse of purity reveals, there was a significant expansion of the role and meaning of purity, even on the level of popular observance, among the Jews of the Second Temple period. As we shall see, Qumran literature and, to a lesser degree, the New Testament provide the richest evidence for the shared processes that lie at the foundation of all conceptions of purity, including that of the Pharisees. At the same time, these sectarian sources provide the backdrop for understanding the unique features of the Pharisees' own ideology of purity.

Tracing the Biblical Legacy of Purity

Basic Features of the Purity System in the Hebrew Bible

The biblical texts present two groups of events that defile the sanctuary and undermine God's holy presence. Leviticus 11–15 and Numbers 19 detail the first group, which is comprised of natural events that produce impurity, such as birth, zov, leprosy, and death, as well as contact with animal carcasses or swarming things. These chapters also establish the processes of purification from these unavoidable situations, which include the removal of the source of impurity and the observance of a waiting period of up to seven days. The purity of the sanctuary is threatened by disregarding, interacting with, or not purifying oneself after contact with these sources of impurity (Lev. 5:2–3). The Israelites are punished for any neglect in this sphere, even if they have not actually entered the Tabernacle (Num. 19:20),[6] which the High Priest annually purifies from the pollution of the Israelites (Lev. 16). Due to the contaminating effect of impurity, both the priests and anyone in the camp who may indirectly pollute the Tabernacle are obligated to observe purity laws.[7] Therefore, those who can severely defile other people are sent out of the camp (Num. 5:1–4; Lev. 13:45–46), and any individuals who become impure must ritually cleanse themselves as soon as possible to prevent the spreading of the impurity to the sanctuary.

The second type of defilement is the result of the grave sins of fornication (Lev. 18:24), murder (Num. 35:34), and idol worship (Lev. 19:31, 20:3; Jer. 2:7–23). This impurity of "idols, abominations, and sins," in Ezekiel's words, banishes the presence of God from among the Israelites and from the land (Num. 35:34) and leads to exile (Lev. 18:28; Ezek. 22:15). Only the actions of God at the End of Days, which include judgment, punishment, and the granting of a new spirit, can purify the sinners and return Israel to its land (Ezek. 20:30–44, 31:16–37).

Although there are significant differences between bodily impurity and sin impurity,[8] both are rooted in a single principle. God can dwell among His people as long as they remove discernible causes of impurity. The Tabernacle must be free of all contamination, even such impurity as is unavoidable in human surroundings, and a lack of meticulousness on this matter inevitably desecrates the sanctuary (Lev. 22:2). Additionally, God cannot dwell in the land contaminated by the most grievous sins. In both contexts, the observance of purity enables humans to exist alongside God's divine presence.

The two central principles of the biblical system outlined here have guided scholars in their attempt to describe the development of different attitudes toward purity during the Second Temple period from the uniform biblical roots. The first principle is the inherent link between purity and holiness. It is clear from the Torah that the concern for the holiness of the sanctuary lies at the center of the purity regulations, yet at the same time, the practical ramifications of these practices spread beyond the holy into the realm of the mundane, including in the Israelite encampment.[9] According to Gedalyahu Alon's seminal article "The Bounds of the Laws of Levitical Cleanness," the various approaches to purity among Second Temple Jews were stimulated by this expansion of the concern for purity from the realm of the sanctuary to outside spaces.[10]

An additional biblical criterion for characterizing the different approaches to purity during this period is the relationship between ritual and moral impurities as described in the Bible. In his book *Impurity and Sin in Ancient Judaism*, Jonathan Klawans suggests that one can map the differences between Second Temple approaches based on the ways they resolved the tension between the two biblical types of impurity.[11] Some sources equate the two types of impurity and consequently impose ritual restrictions on sinners; others prefer one type over the other, while still other groups maintained a clear separation between the moral and the ritual.

Despite their different approaches, Alon and Klawans share the assumption that all notions of purity among Second Temple Jews were anchored in biblical foundations. These biblical principles set the contours for the diverse ideological and halakhic policies of the Second Temple period. In what follows, I examine the claims of Alon and Klawans to demonstrate that, biblical roots notwithstanding, new ideologies and social settings during the Second Temple period generated revolutionary notions of purity.

Purity Observance beyond the Temple

In his article, Alon presents three types of purity observances that are not derived directly from the biblical text but, in his opinion, are rooted in the Levitical tendency toward expansion of the realm of holiness beyond the boundaries of the Temple.

(A) *Purification for the sake of holy practices.* This group of observances includes the Talmudic prohibition to pray or study Torah after a seminal emission and the practice of purification before worship.[12] This latter practice is described in the *Letter of Aristeas*, a Jewish Hellenistic text of the second century BCE (paras. 305–6): "Following the custom of all the Jews, they washed their hands in the sea in the course of their prayer to God and then proceeded to the reading and explication of each point. I asked this question: 'What is their purpose in washing their hands while saying their prayers?' They explained that it is evidence that they have done no evil for all activity takes place by means of the hands."

(B) *The eating of ordinary (unconsecrated) food in purity.* Rabbinic literature mentions the obligation to maintain purity while eating nonsacral everyday foods. For example, the Tosefta refers to the *haverim* (associates) who take it on themselves "to eat *hullin* (ordinary foods) in the state of purity."[13]

(C) *The obligation to maintain bodily purity irrespective of any contact with the holy realm.* This tendency is expressed, for example, in the following comment of the first-century CE Jewish Hellenistic author Philo of Alexandria: "A husband and wife, who have intercourse in accordance with the legitimate usages of married life, are not allowed, when they leave their bed, to touch anything until they have made their ablutions and purged themselves with water" (Philo, *On the Special Laws*, 3.63).

These three types of practices, Alon claims, reflect a shared tendency to expand the realm of purity beyond the Temple and its sacrifices, thereby serving "the extension of priestly sanctity to all Israel and the purity of holy things to common foodstuff."[14] From this monolithic perspective, the different expressions of purity all derive in one way or another from their ties to the holy realm, as it is portrayed in the Bible, but this realm itself is broadened beyond its biblical application to the priests to encompass the entire Jewish people.

Alon's influential article still stands as the basis of any scholarly discussion about purity in ancient Judaism. But a major problem with his method is the mixture of distinct sources, periods, and phenomena. His description merges Palestinian and diasporic sources, Second Temple and later sources, and finally, popular practices and unique sectarian regulations. In his opinion, the practices to which the wider Jewish public adhered were driven by the same motivations as the lifestyle of the Pharisees. According to Alon, while there were some Jews who objected to the Pharisaic tendency to implement purity laws outside of the boundaries of the Temple, generally speaking, the public participated in this trend to some degree or another.[15]

The extent to which people participated in the strict observance of purity laws does indeed indicate the growing significance of purity, but does it necessarily also reflect one distinct approach, as Alon posits? Do the demands for the consumption of ordinary foods in purity and the requirement that one purify oneself in preparation for prayer reflect a similar purpose? It is difficult to consider eating as a holy activity, akin to prayer, and it is doubtful that these different practices belong to a single approach. For instance, the requirement of eating in a state of purity is known to us only from rabbinic literature, whereas purification before prayer is characteristic of Jewish Hellenistic literature.[16] Josephus, as well as archaeological evidence, testify to the custom of building synagogues near the sea, apparently to facilitate personal purification before prayer.[17] In this respect, Jewish purification practices resonate the use of water for purification at the entrances to temples in the Hellenistic world. Philo himself notes the correlation between Jewish and gentile practices surrounding the use of water in preparation for ritual.[18] As E. P. Sanders emphasizes, the practices of diaspora Jews are not necessarily derived from biblical precedents or from Temple purity laws in particular. Therefore, they should not be interpreted against the background of Palestinian notions of purity but rather viewed within their Hellenistic cultural context.[19] At the same time, local purity practices developed in Palestine, which were not characteristic of diaspora Jews. Thus, for instance, Judith's act of purification in a spring every night upon exiting Holofernes's camp and before prayer (Jdt. 12:6–10) would seem to represent the practice of Palestinian Jews to purify themselves after contact with gentiles.[20] Evidently, then, the changing modes of interactions with gentiles created diverse notions and practices of purity in Palestine and in the diaspora.

We should be wary of bunching different forms of purity observance together, like Alon does. While it provides a shared religious language, it does not necessarily represent a unified system of thought. It appears that the scholarly tendency to prove that Jews observed the laws of purity beyond the realm of the Temple colored all manifestations of purity law in one color, without due attention to the variety of meanings this foundational phenomenon took on.

Although research since Alon's classic essay offers a more nuanced portrayal of Second Temple conceptions of purity, largely as a result of the plentiful references to purity in the Qumran library, many scholars still reproduce the basic biblical paradigm of purity as a means for extending holiness,[21] as does, for example, Hannah Harrington's recent comprehensive book entitled *The Purity and Sanctuary of the Body in Second Temple Judaism*.[22] In her view, after the destruction of the First Temple the concept of Israel as sanctuary emerged to replace the holiness of the temple. Consequently, the site of purity was transferred from the Temple to the people of Israel and their bodies. In this sense, Qumran's self-image as a holy house and as a substitution for the Temple worship sets a model for this conception also among diaspora communities who did not have access to the Temple or to rabbinic responses to the destruction of the Temple. According to Harrington, all these diverse forms of purity observances represent various attempts to compensate for the holiness of the Temple.[23]

Against this biblicizing tendency, I argue that a closer look at the various expressions of purity enables us to break this phenomenon down into different processes and to delineate the (limited) role of the biblical paradigm of purity and holiness in the shaping of common practice and conceptions of impurity. I will at first examine the common purity practices, rooted in the Hebrew Bible, and then turn to new conceptions.

The Biblical Foundation of Common Purity Practices

As opposed to locally and culturally bound forms of purity, there are two practices that cross these boundaries and testify to the ways in which biblical purity laws were implemented among wide circles. Different authors share the assumption that the Torah prescribes purification immediately after contact with a dead body and after sexual relations. Josephus addresses both situations in proximity to one another and explains both in a similar manner.[24] Philo, too, set up the two situations as parallel and forbade contact with any object before ritual immersion.[25] Philo clearly bases himself on the biblical verses, and his phrasing implies that the Torah required immediate purification following seminal emission and contact with a human corpse. It appears, from both these authors, that scripture was understood to demand purification from these impurities not only as a preparatory step before interaction with the sanctuary but also as a necessary step before returning to one's daily routine. An additional testimony to the dominance of the notion of immediate purification from corpse impurity is the addition of a "first-day ablution," in the Temple Scroll from Qumran, as a first step in the purification process.[26] The Temple Scroll assumes that one must undertake immediate ritual immersion to return to daily life, in addition to the sprinkling of lustration water on the third and seventh days of purification, necessary for entering the sanctuary.[27] The requirement of immediate purification is, therefore, common to different groups and reflects a shared manner of implementing the biblical tradition.

According to Josephus, anyone who touches a dead body is forbidden from living in their home with other people for seven days. Another witness to this practice is the apocryphal book of Tobit. Not only did Tobit immerse before eating every time he buried a corpse, but even after immersing, he slept outside of his home.[28] Washing itself did not complete the purification process. Although not a historical story, the story of Tobit testifies to the widespread assumption among Jews concerning the need to purify oneself from corpse impurity and to remove those who dealt with dead bodies from their homes. Furthermore, as we learn from Josephus, the preoccupation with corpse impurity was such that at first Jews were not even willing to settle in the city of Tiberias, established in the first century CE, since it was built on grave sites.[29]

In *Judean Antiquities*, Josephus explains, in his treatment of the obligation to distance impure persons from the camp as mentioned in Numbers 5:1–4, that menstruants, like those carrying corpse impurity, were not permitted to live with others, although they were not removed from the city: "He [Moses] expelled from the city both those whose bodies were attacked by leprosy and those with spermatorrhoea. He segregated until the seventh day women whose secretion occurs for them in accordance with nature, after which he permitted them, as already pure, to associate with the community. Similarly, it is prescribed by law for those who have buried the dead to associate with the community after as many days."[30]

This practice does not appear in the Torah but is clearly derived from the attempt to observe its laws. Although the Torah does not mention the distancing of a menstruant, and imposes separation only on those who contract the most serious impurities, Josephus adds this tactic for dealing with the more prevalent impurity of menstruation. Not only was the menstruant distanced from the Temple Mount,[31] but she was also separated within the cities. A similar practice of separation appears in rabbinic literature as well (see chap. 5 in this volume).

Josephus's description therefore indicates how Second Temple Jews implemented the biblical legacy. In accordance with the biblical demand, they established means for distancing individuals from common sources of impurity, determined the degree of separation necessary for safe operation alongside menstruants, and instituted the obligation to immediately remove day-to-day impurities. Although such details do not appear in the Priestly Code, the practices described by Second Temple authors reflect the basic aspiration of the Jews of their time to protect themselves from the impurities against which the Torah warns.

Although Second Temple Jews implemented the biblical laws of purification in their daily conduct, they did not necessarily make a deliberate attempt to, so called, expand the realm of purity beyond the Temple. From their perspective, the Hebrew Bible imposes on all Israelites the obligation of purity; the fulfillment of purity laws does not comprise a broadening of the Temple realm but rather an expression of the fundamental commitment to the commandments of the Torah, through the implementation of additional safeguards against the daily, lurking threats of menstrual and corpse impurity.[32]

It is likely that effort was also made to avoid less severe impurities, such as the impurity imposed by swarming things falling into food (Lev. 11:32–38), but we have no concrete evidence for the implementation of this concern.

From the Desert Camp to the Jerusalem Temple

As we have seen, Second Temple literature reveals specific arenas of private observance of purity practices among Jews who sought to fulfill scriptural purity laws in their personal conduct. At the same time, historical and archaeological evidence testifies to the public role of purity in shaping the urban environment of Jerusalem as the Temple city. This shared purity observance in Jerusalem was of course also rooted in the desire to fulfill the scriptural commandments, but—unlike those observances previously described—it played a central role in the structuring of the public norms of the Temple city. In this situation, the question arose as to how to implement biblical purity principles in the urban realities of Jerusalem. As we will see, a shared public norm that shaped Jerusalem as a pure city generated diverse exegetical and ideological approaches among different groups.

On the exegetical level, the Jews of the Second Temple era needed to determine how to adjust the biblical model, which was intended to protect the purity of the Tabernacle, to the urban realities of the city of Jerusalem in their time. On the practical level, they were compelled to determine how to maintain some form of mundane conduct in the shadow of strict purity laws befitting the holiness of the Temple. Literary testimonies reveal the tensions that arose during the Hasmonean period regarding the appropriate way to realize the biblical model. At the same time, to understand the disputes that split Judean society, it is not enough to be familiar with the underlying exegetical approaches among different groups; one must also take into consideration the unique reality of Jerusalem as the urban space operating in the shadow of the Temple.

In the decree of the Seleucid king Antiochus III, published around the beginning of the second century BCE and posted at the entrance to Jerusalem, we find the following prohibitions:

> It is unlawful for any foreigner to enter the enclosure of the Temple which is forbidden to the Jews, except to those of them who are accustomed to enter after purifying themselves in accordance with the law of the country.

Nor shall anyone bring into the city the flesh of horses or of mules or of wild or tame asses, or of leopards, foxes or hares or, in general, of any animals forbidden to the Jews. Nor is it lawful to bring in their skins or even to breed any of these animals in the city. But only the sacrificial animals known to their ancestors and necessary for the propitiation of God shall they be permitted to use. And the person who violates any of these statutes shall pay to the priests a fine of three thousand drachmas of silver.[33]

The decree is addressed to gentile visitors to Jerusalem, who were expected to adjust their behavior in accordance with Jewish law. The first section expels certain people from the Temple precincts, whereas the rest of the decree addresses the effect that the purity of the Temple had on the daily activity in Jerusalem.

The prohibition on gentiles entering the Temple was unfamiliar in the Greek world, which did not regularly view strangers as intrinsically impure. To soften this inconsistency, Antiochus's decree ties the distancing of gentiles to the fact that impure Jews were also forbidden to enter parts of the Temple grounds.[34] On this point, there is a striking difference between Antiochus's decree and the inscription that was later fixed to the partition separating Temple Mount from the inner precinct. This inscription, dating to the Herodian period, warns gentiles, both in Greek and Latin, not to enter the Temple: "No alien may enter within the balustrade around the sanctuary and the closure. Whoever is caught, on himself shall he put blame for the death which will ensue."[35] The earlier decree of Antiochus, on the other hand, made sure not to discriminate or completely banish gentiles from the Temple. A similar picture is reflected in the Mishnah and in Josephus's writings.[36] Mishnah Kelim 1:8 details the spheres of holiness: "The Temple Mount is holier, for neither zavs nor zavas [men or women who experience abnormal genital emissions] nor menstruants nor women after childbirth may enter it. The rampart is holier, for neither gentiles nor one who contracted corpse uncleanness may enter it." Although impure people are allowed in Jerusalem (with the exclusion of the leper, who is distanced from all settlements), those suffering bodily impurity are forbidden from entering the Temple Mount until they can be purified. The gentile is distanced only from the Temple courtyard like one who has not purified himself from corpse impurity.[37] The Mishnah thus preserves the comparison that appears in Antiochus's decree between a gentile and a Jew who has not yet been purified.[38]

In the same spirit, Josephus writes: "Thus anyone was allowed to enter the outer court, even foreigners; only menstruating women were prohibited entry.

To the second court all Judeans were admitted, together with their wives, if they were free of all impurity."³⁹ Josephus does not mention those suffering from severe bodily impurities, such as the zav, and it is possible that he believed they were completely forbidden from entering Jerusalem (Ant. 3:261). On the other hand, people who had contracted corpse impurity, along with those suffering from less severe impurities, could reenter the Temple courtyard only after undergoing purification.⁴⁰

Entering the Temple courtyard (in contrast to the Temple Mount) did indeed require special preparations, with the standard process being the weeklong course of purgation from corpse impurity. This was particularly relevant for those Jews who came to the Temple from the diaspora, such as Philo and Paul,⁴¹ who wished to display his righteousness by funding Nazirite sacrifices. This attempt ended with a moblike attack on Paul, who, it was claimed, sought to bring gentiles into the Temple courtyard, and finally with his arrest:

> Then Paul took the men, and the next day, having purified himself, he entered the Temple with them, making public the completion of the days of purification when the sacrifice would be made for each of them. When the seven days were almost completed, the Jews from Asia, who had seen him in the Temple, stirred up the whole crowd. They seized him, shouting, "Fellow Israelites, help! This is the man who is teaching everyone everywhere against our people, our law, and this place; more than that, he has actually brought Greeks into the Temple and has defiled this holy place." For they had previously seen Trophimus the Ephesian with him in the city, and they supposed that Paul had brought him into the Temple. Then all the city was aroused, and the people rushed together. They seized Paul and dragged him out of the Temple, and immediately the doors were shut. (Acts 21:26–30)

Nazirites, who vowed not to drink wine or cut their hair until they brought their sacrifice to the Temple, occasionally waited for a donor to fund their sacrifices. Once the donation was allocated, they purified themselves for a week before bringing sacrifices. Paul, their donor, underwent a similar period of purification to enter the Temple courtyard. One could not come from overseas and immediately enter the Temple without a period of purification from corpse impurity. This period of a week provides the dramatic timeframe that explains Paul's tarrying and his presence on the Temple Mount, which ended with an attack that was backed by the decree posted at the entrance to the Temple. Apparently Paul, who was purifying from corpse impurity, and Trophimus the gentile spent time together during that week, thereby arousing suspicion on the part of some of the Jews present. This story illustrates the nature of separation between the different circles of purity in the Temple arena and verifies the testimony of the Mishnah regarding the presence of individuals who contracted corpse impurity on the Temple Mount together with gentiles.

However, the separation schema—developed already in the Hellenistic period and continuing to the last years of the Second Temple period—which allowed the entry of some impure people into the Temple Mount and their participation in the activities therein, is incongruent with the biblical impurity schema. In reality, the Temple Mount served as a middle ground. While certain impure persons were forbidden entry, on the whole it functioned as a public forum (and commercial center) open to all, including gentiles. The Temple Mount, although a holy space, was not off-limits for all impure people. This stands in stark contrast to the biblical schema, which distinguished between two circles of purity: the Israelite encampment and the Sanctuary.

The disparity between the realities of Second Temple Jerusalem and the biblical model engendered different reactions. On the one hand, Qumran literature rejected current practice, which did not fit the principles of biblical law. The utopian Temple Scroll from Qumran named Jerusalem the Temple city and distinguished it from the rest of the cities of Israel. It allowed people who had contracted corpse impurity into the cities, following the first-day ablution, but it removed all impure people from Jerusalem. Thus, it eliminated the middle ground and tensions that characterized Second Temple Jerusalem.[42] The Temple Scroll even distanced from Jerusalem those who had had sexual relations.[43] An alternative implementation of the Pentateuchal camp model is suggested in the epistle sent by the Qumran sectarians to the High Priest, entitled "Some Precepts of the Torah" (Miqsat Ma'ase ha-Torah; 4QMMT). According to this epistle, the Temple corresponded to the Tabernacle, and Jerusalem to the Israelite encampment (2:29–31). Either way, this construction of purity does not allow for such mixture of pure and impure on the Temple Mount.

On the other hand, in contrast to Qumran law, rabbinic literature justifies the complex schema that characterized the activity around the Temple through a reinterpretation of the verses that prescribe the removal of impure people from the camp: "to remove from the camp anyone with an eruption or a discharge and anyone defiled by a corpse," "put them outside the camp so that they do not defile the camp" (Num. 5:1–4). The rabbis interpreted these verses as mandating a distinction between three separate sites in which the leper, the zav, and the one defiled by corpse impurity operated.[44] Through a creative rereading of the biblical commandment, the rabbis delineated three separate arenas, thereby creating a new, artificial middle ground: "As there were three camps in the desert encampment, a camp of the divine dwelling, the camp of the Levites, and the camp of Israel, so was the division in Jerusalem: From the gates of Jerusalem to the gate of Temple Mount was considered the camp of Israel; from the gates of the Temple Mount to the Nikanor gates—the camp of the Levites, and from the Nikanor gates inward (the Temple courtyard)—the camp of the divine dwelling."[45] Paradoxically, then, while menstruants and others with bodily impurity were removed from the Temple Mount, people who contracted severe corpse impurity were permitted. From an exegetical point of view, this represents a revolution in thinking;[46] however, it is clear that this description, preserved in the rabbinic tradition, was more fitting to the complex situation in practice in Jerusalem during the Second Temple period than the more straightforward interpretation that the contemporary sectarian authors proffered.

The Purity of Jerusalem

According to Antiochus's decree, one may not bring the meat or hide of an impure animal into Jerusalem, but only that of a pure animal that is permitted for sacrifice. These prohibitions are understandable, given that activity in Jerusalem complemented Temple rites and sacrifices brought to the Temple could be consumed throughout the city. On this matter, too, a complex norm developed in Jerusalem, which found expression in a range of exegetical strategies of biblical law.

The meat or hide of an impure animal causes particularly severe problems in Jerusalem. For instance, the meat of an impure animal imparts pollution just as an animal carcass does and could potentially defile the pure sacrificial foods found in Jerusalem. Furthermore, even the hides of such animals could convey impurity onto the pure foods in Jerusalem. This fear is expressed in the words of the author of 4QMMT (B, 22–23), which reads, "And concerning the hide of a carcass of a clean animal; he who carries such a carcass shall not have access to the holy food." According to the author of this epistle, this is also the reason that it is forbidden to bring dogs into Jerusalem, "since they may eat some of the bones of the sanctuary while the flesh is still on them" (B, 58–59).

We learn from different sources that the only meat found in Jerusalem was sacrificial meat.[47] This is supported by Antiochus's decree, which prohibited bringing any animal forbidden for sacrifice. However, the texts provide a variety of explanations for the exclusive presence of sacrificial meat. For example, 4QMMT says that it is forbidden to slaughter any meat in Jerusalem unless it is brought as a sacrifice to the Temple, in line with the commandment in Leviticus 17:3–4. The status of Jerusalem is equivalent to that of the Israelite camp in the desert,[48] and therefore, only sacrifices, tithes, and firstborn animals may be eaten in the city. The Temple Scroll likewise forbids bringing unholy meat into Jerusalem, and it adds, as in the decree of Antiochus, that animal hides must come exclusively from sacrificial animals. Any other hide is impure with respect to the purity of Jerusalem.[49] Just as the only meat allowed in Jerusalem is sacrificial meat, so too the only hides that were pure enough to be brought into the city are those of sacrificial animals.

Even the rabbis, who basically allow the consumption of unconsecrated meat in Jerusalem, [50] assume that the commercial activities in the city must serve the needs of the Temple. According to m. B. Qam. 7:7, one may not raise chickens in Jerusalem "on account of the sacrifices"—that is, due to the fear that the chickens will peck at something impure and then defile the sacrificial meat. This fear parallels the aforementioned fear regarding dogs in 4QMMT. Another rabbinic source lists the ordinances intended to limit the spread of impurity in Jerusalem. Among these rules are prohibitions against building balconies in Jerusalem and the use of rubbish disposals (t. Neg. 6:2). Moreover, m. Šeqal. 7:4 assumes that the animal market in Jerusalem was devoted purely to the sale of sacrificial animals: "If cattle was found in Jerusalem as far as Migdal Eder, and within a like distance on any side [of Jerusalem], males [must be considered as] burnt-offerings, but females [must be considered as] peace-offerings." Furthermore, according to the rabbis, a person may, in fact, eat unconsecrated meat in Jerusalem, though every effort was made to limit this type of meat. Mishnah Šeqalim 7:2 teaches that all animals sold in Jerusalem were bought with monies from the tithes that were intended for consumption in Jerusalem (called a "second tithe"), and these were used exclusively for peace offerings. From another source, we learn that even though there was no actual prohibition against buying meat for ordinary consumption with the money from tithes, people who bought meat for ordinary consumption were penalized and their meat was considered impure.[51]

Each of the previously mentioned corpora presents a different set of principles while nevertheless sharing the same practical application. Jerusalem is intended for the consumption of sacrificial meat, and as a result, nonsacrificial meat is impure and forbidden for consumption. The rabbis consider this a nonbiblical ordinance intended to encourage the consumption of sacrificial meat, whereas the Temple Scroll defines this meat as unholy meat that desecrates the Temple. Whereas sectarian literature is based exclusively on the biblical model, the rabbis, supposedly following the Pharisees, turned to nonscriptural decrees. Nonetheless, both reflect the same reality, and this correlation is a strong factor in considering the authenticity of the rabbinic tradition, and the complex legal situation it portrays.

But the fact that Jerusalem served consumers of sacrificial meat created a new problem. On the one hand, there was a lot of sacrificial meat available in Jerusalem that was to be eaten in a particularly high degree of purity; on the other hand, however, this same space included impure persons. How could one navigate this state of affairs?

One possibility was to reject the situation in Jerusalem. For instance, the book of Jubilees, whose stringent laws are similar to those of the Qumran sectarians, limits the consumption of all sacrifices, including the fruit offering, the second tithe, and the Paschal sacrifice, to the Temple courtyard.[52] This position was presumably a polemical response to the accepted practice of the author's time, around the middle of the second century BCE.[53] An alternative solution in the Temple Scroll imposes a severe level of purity throughout the entire city.[54]

The approach reflected in rabbinic literature is more lenient in its purity demands but consequently relinquishes some of the biblical purity system. As David Henshke phrases it, according to rabbinic law, Jerusalem has no special status within the Israelite camp in terms of its purity and is like any other city when it comes to the distancing of impure persons.[55] On the other hand, according to Deuteronomy 12, one may consume the burnt offerings and the peace offerings, the vows and the oaths only in Jerusalem. The fact that Deuteronomy does not address the issue of purity and expands the consumption of sacrifices to all of Jerusalem allowed the inhabitants of Jerusalem to maintain a system that was incoherent and incongruent with the Priestly Code and to permit impure people to reside side by side with those who consumed sacrificial meat.[56]

It is to this complex reality that the author of 4QMMT is reacting. The scroll suggests a norm that is in practice very similar to the Pharisaic one, as maintained by the rabbis, without renouncing the biblical schema. The scroll determines that Jerusalem is also equivalent to the holy camp and the site chosen by God (B, 59–61). One must, therefore, be careful to distance from the city dogs and carcasses as well as isolate those people within it who are impure. The author complains that lepers who were undergoing purification would return to their homes and defile the sacrificial meats consumed in the houses: "But now, while their impurity is (still) with them, lepers enter into a house containing sacred food" (B, 67–68). The author learns of the need to isolate anyone who has not completed the process of purification from the biblical injunction that the lepers remain outside their tents during the seven days of purification (Lev. 14:8). After all, although they are pure with respect to ordinary foods, they still pose a threat to the sacred foods found in Jerusalem.[57] From the author's complaint, we learn of the compromising norms that were in practice in Jerusalem.

Thus, since Jerusalem did not possess a special status with regard to purity, and impure persons remained in the city, special means were required to allow the consumption of the sacrificial meat. In addition to the extensive archaeological findings of ritual baths (miqva'ot) in Jerusalem,[58] public space in the city was adjusted, wherever possible, to the demands of purity. Archaeological findings and literary sources testify to the spatial separation between pure and impure in the city, both around the ritual baths and in the streets of Jerusalem.[59] For example, we read in the *Letter of Aristeas* 106: "There are steps leading to the thoroughfares. Some people make their way above them, others go underneath them, their principal aim being to keep away from the main roads for the sake of those who are involved in purification rites, so as not to touch any forbidden thing." This public norm allowed anyone desirous of it to maintain purity, despite the crowded streets. Rabbinic tradition, too, assumes that pure and impure walked separately throughout the city streets: "At other times of the year [spittle found] in the middle [of the road] is unclean, while [spittle found] at the sides [of the road] is clean; but in the season of festivals [spittle found] in the middle [of the road] is clean, while [that which is found] at the sides [of the road] is unclean, for since [persons who have an issue] are few in number, they betake themselves [in the season of festivals] to the sides of the road" (m. Šeqal. 8:1). Although the urban reality dictated the presence of impure people in Jerusalem, purity was ever-present in public spaces and shaped the behavior of its inhabitants on a daily basis.

The prevalent observance of purity laws surveyed in the last two sections reflects a widespread interest in maintaining biblical purity laws in both the private and the public domains. The scriptural obligation to remove the impurity imparted by sexual relations or a corpse governed daily conduct, irrespectively of contact with the Temple, and had thus become an independent obligation. This does not necessarily reflect a new sensitivity or conception of purity, nor does it reflect a desire to expand the realm of the holy to daily life. Additionally, the maintenance of the purity of Jerusalem in the public arena had become a collective mission and required novel solutions; after all, the urban realities were incongruent with biblical models. Different groups sought to align the public reality with their exegetical approach, but at the end of the day, the public observance of purity law was inevitably incoherent, as they attempted to maintain the purity of the Temple within a complex urban space.

New Dimensions: The Reification of Sin Impurity

While careful to maintain the biblical laws concerning bodily impurities in both private and public domains, at the same time Jews of the Second Temple period radically transformed the biblical concept of sin impurity. These new forms of impurity were incompatible with biblical conceptions, and they reshaped the worldviews of contemporary Jews.[60]

As we have seen, the Torah attributes impurity to grievous sins. For example, it states that fornication and murder defile the Land of Israel and idolatry defiles the Temple (Lev. 18:24, 20:3; Num. 35:34). The prophets further expand on this short list of grievous sins. For instance, Ezekiel bemoans the defiling of Jerusalem through idol worship and bloodshed, including theft and exploitation of the poor as well as illicit fornication. The prophet believes that all these sins have defiled the city (Ezek. 22:1–16). Ezekiel also employs more general language, directed at the overall behavior of Israel: "When the House of Israel dwelt on their own soil, they defiled it with their ways and their deeds; their ways were in My sight like the uncleanness of a menstruous woman" (Ezek. 36:17). The idea that sins defile Jerusalem or the Temple left its traces throughout Second Temple literature as well. Thus, for instance, in the Qumranic interpretation of the prophecy of Habakkuk, known as Pesher Habakkuk, we find:

> And as for what he says: "Owing to the blood of the city and the violence (done to) the country" (Hab 2:17). Its interpretation: the city is Jerusalem in which the Wicked Priest performed repulsive acts and defiled the Sanctuary of God. The violence (done to) the country are the cities of Judah which he plundered of the possessions of the poor. (1QpHab 12:7–10)
>
> And he (the Wicked Priest) robbed and hoarded wealth from the violent men who had rebelled against God. And he seized public money, incurring additional serious sin. And he performed re[pul]sive acts by every type of defiling impurity. (1QpHab 8:11–13)

These and other sources correspond to the biblical notion of sin impurity; at the same time, Second Temple literature revolutionized the biblical tradition, through its consistent tendency to reify it. In other words, the impurity that was originally attached to forbidden actions now came to be identified with the objects involved in those behaviors and became a physical characteristic of any object involved in the act itself. Whereas the Torah associates impurity with forbidden acts, such as idol worship or fornication, Jewish texts from the Persian period claim that ritual impurity is imparted to the objects and people that are identified with this sort of activity. This conceptual development had far-reaching implications.

Whereas earlier sources do not offer any mechanism for ridding oneself from sin impurity other than repentance and hope for divine atonement, the reification of sin impurity in Second Temple sources generated new solutions to the contaminating effects of sin. Since the impurity was embodied in a tangible object, second-order instructions developed regarding separation from the impure object, irrespective of the initial immoral act. Subsequently, it was made possible to avoid contact with the concrete source of impurity and get rid of it. Thus, even though the foundational notion of sin impurity was firmly rooted in biblical notions, Second Temple sources collapse the initial distinction between ritual impurity and its ramifications and sin impurity and the obligations it entailed. This development led to another, in which the concepts of purity and impurity served not only for the defining acts and events, as in early biblical literature, but they also marked and labeled groups of objects and people, which were associated with immoral activity. The most manifest expressions of this process is the creation of two novel notions, idol impurity and gentile impurity, an innovation that has garnered significant scholarly attention. Both innovations, it should be noted, do not reflect any particular concern for holiness, as purity has now become an end in itself.

The demand put forth by Ezra and Nehemiah to separate from the "people of the land" who did not belong to the community of Judean returnees from Babylonia signals the beginning of this process. The list of forbidden relationships in Leviticus 18 concludes with the following explanation: "Do not defile yourselves in any of these ways, for it is by such that the nations that I am casting out before you defiled themselves . . . for all those abhorrent things were done by the people who were in the land before you, and the land became defiled" (Lev. 18:24–28). The forbidden actions defiled those who committed them as well as the land itself. Israel is therefore cautioned against those same actions and the sin impurity they impart, lest they be exiled from the land (Lev. 19:31, 20:3). The prohibition against intermarriage with the inhabitants of the land also derives directly from their dangerous devotion to idolatry (Deut. 7:3). In Ezra, on the other hand, the impurity is associated not with the forbidden actions but with the inhabitants themselves, which results in new forms of separation: "The land that you are about to possess is a land unclean through the uncleanness of the peoples of the land, through their abhorrent practices with which they, in their impurity, have filled it from one end to the other. Now then, do not give your daughters in marriage to their sons or let their daughters marry your sons; do nothing for their well-being or advantage" (Ezra 9:11–12). These verses are inspired by the verses in Deuteronomy but, at the same time, replace the fear of idolatry, not mentioned in Ezra, with the impurity of the gentiles. The warning is therefore directed against contact with the people themselves.[61] The distancing of oneself from all gentiles is perceived as a distancing from the impurity that is embodied in them, as seen in the following phrase: "all who joined them in separating themselves from the uncleanliness of the nations" (Ezra 6:21). And when Nehemiah speaks of the banishment of foreign women with the phrase "I purged them of every foreign element," he implies that gentile women themselves were a source of impurity (Neh. 13:30).

Scholars dispute the extent to which the books of Ezra and Nehemiah represent a new form of impurity in general and gentile impurity in particular. According to Klawans, these works preserve the earlier distinction between ritual and moral impurity. In his opinion, Ezra and Nehemiah only attribute "moral impurity" to the gentiles, as earlier writings do.[62] Their behavior is corrupt, and therefore marriage with them is forbidden. Klawans rejects Alon's understanding, according to which Second Temple Judaism, from its inception, identified gentiles as possessing ritual impurity and viewed physical contact with them as defiling.[63] While this concept appears explicitly in rabbinic literature,[64] Klawans believes that initially it was shared only by separatists such as the Qumran sectarians. In his opinion, any place in Second Temple literature where gentiles are associated with impurity, the impurity in question is moral impurity, which testifies to their moral corruption but does not incur contamination or lead to physical distancing.

Christine Hayes, who takes this approach as well, adds an additional dimension to the discussion.[65] Hayes points to the expansion of the use of impurity terminology in Ezra and Nehemiah. While in the Pentateuch a priest deprives his offspring of the priesthood when he contracts a forbidden marriage (Lev. 21:7, 13–14), Nehemiah believes that the marriage of priests to gentile women *defiles* the priest's offspring ("how they polluted the priesthood," Neh. 13:29). At the same time, Hayes claims, this limited phenomenon touches only on the priestly lineage, which is polluted with "genealogical impurity." Gentile women, however, are not impure and, therefore, marrying them cannot cause defilement. Only the priestly lineage can be genealogically defiled and lose its priestly status. The rest of Israel must preserve "the holy seed" and are warned not to desecrate it, but impurity, according to Hayes, is not the reason intermarriage is forbidden.

In my opinion, both Klawans and Hayes undermine the revolutionary understanding of impurity in Ezra and Nehemiah. In addition to the moral impurity of the gentiles (Ezra 9:11–12) and the genealogical impurity they impart (Neh. 13:30), the banishment of the non-Judean Tobiah the Ammonite from the Temple courtyard (Neh. 13:7–9) indicates that gentiles physically convey ritual impurity: "When I arrived in Jerusalem, I learned of the outrage perpetrated by Aliashib on behalf of Tobiah in assigning him a room in the courts of the House of God. I was greatly displeased, and had all the household gear of Tobiah thrown out of the room; I gave orders to purify the rooms, and had the equipment of the House of God and the meal offering and the frankincense put back." The very presence of Tobiah, despite the fact that he is not an idol worshipper, physically defiled the House of God. This is an early expression of the existence of ritual impurity associated with the physical presence of the gentile; an impurity that is spread through physical contact. Bible scholar Saul Olyan claims that the editors of Ezra and Nehemiah blurred the boundaries between the various types of impurity to present a comprehensive strategy for the banishment of strangers. Following this approach, Hanan Birnboim argues as follows: "One must view this renewed understanding as an initial stage of a prolonged process of the transformation of metaphorical expressions of impurity, which represent the moral corruption of the gentiles, into practically applicable practices which, in their later, crystallized form, appear in rabbinic literature as gentile impurity."[66] According to Birnboim, the exiles in Babylonia developed the concept of gentile impurity to protect their minority identity.

In my view, the emergence of a novel conception of gentile (ritual) impurity was not an isolated phenomenon intended to contend with social threats but rather reflects an overall shift in the perception of the very nature of impurity. The affinity between the emergence of gentile impurity and the creation of idol impurity reveals a shared process of reification that revolutionized the notions of impurity among Second Temple Jews. Many sources from the Second Temple period testify to the regular use of the term *impurity* as a synonym for *idol* and give witness to the practice of purging places where idols were present.[67] Although the notion that idol worship, like other abominable acts, defiles the land appears in the Bible, it is only from the Persian period on that the objects of idolatry themselves become a source of impurity. As Birenboim notes, the contrast between the descriptions of the banishment of idolatry by Hezekiah and Josiah in the book of Kings and the parallel descriptions in the later book of Chronicles reflects the conceptual change that occurred. While in 2 Kings, Hezekiah abolished the shrines and smashed the pillars,[68] in 2 Chronicles 29:5, 15–16, and 18 he commanded the purification of the Temple from the impurity that it contained. The Levites banished the idolatrous objects that imparted impurity and purified the Temple vessels.

Similarly, according to the book of Kings, Josiah ordered the removal of the items dedicated to Baal and Asherah from the Temple and their incineration, and then he "defiled the shrines where the priests had been making offerings" (2 Kgs. 23:8). According to this passage, the vessels used for idol worship were not impure but, on the contrary, were defiled so as to make them unusable. By contrast, Chronicles describes the act of destroying the idols by Josiah as an act of purification: "he began to purge Judah and Jerusalem of the shrines ... at his bidding, they demolished the altars of the Baals ... he burned the bones of priests on their altars and purged Judah and Jerusalem ... In the eighteenth year of his reign, after purging the land and the House" (2 Chr. 34:3–8). The objects of idolatry have thus become in the literature of the Persian period intrinsically impure. In sum, while the Pentateuch and the Prophets offer no solution for the acts of idolatry that defile the land other than divine punishment and atonement,[69] the author of Chronicles suggests a practical possibility for purifying the land and the Temple by banishing the physical sources of the impurity, such as the altars, the idols, and the images built for Baal and Asherah.

Despite the fundamental disagreement between Ezra-Nehemiah and Chronicles regarding the separation from gentiles,[70] these two sources share the tendency to reify sin impurity and attribute impurity to objects that represent corrupt behavior. This tendency directs the struggle against these threatening phenomena toward the objects that embody them—gentiles, on the one hand, and idols, on the other—and requires their physical removal.[71] This understanding informs the different descriptions of the Hasmonean Wars. The second epistle at the beginning of 2 Maccabees names the holiday of Hanukkah a holiday "of the purification of the Temple" (1:18, 2:16–18) and describes the actions of Judah Maccabee in terms familiar to us from Chronicles. Judah demolishes the altars in the marketplace and the holy areas, thus purifying the Temple and making it ready for renewed worship (10:3–7).[72] Furthermore, according to 1 Maccabees, the "desolating sacrilege" (1 Macc. 1:54) has defiled the altar on which it was erected, and Judah not only banished it but was also compelled to destroy the altar, which has been defiled through contact with it: "He chose blameless priests devoted to the law, and they cleansed the sanctuary and removed the defiled stones to an unclean place. They deliberated what to do about the altar of burnt offering, which had been profaned. And they thought it best to tear it down, so that it would not be a lasting shame to them that the Gentiles had defiled it. So they tore down the altar, and stored the stones in a convenient place on the temple hill until a prophet should come to tell what to do with them" (1 Macc. 4:43–46). This is the clearest expression of the defiling effect of the "stones of impurity." Later on the Hasmoneans implement their purification policy throughout the land, and Simon purges the houses in Gezer from the idols they contained and banishes the impurity (13:47–48).[73]

To conclude, the reification of impurity created two new sources of ritual impurity that are not mentioned in the Bible: objects of idol worship and gentiles. The ramifications of contact with these impurities were not uniformly defined and the degree of separation presumably varied among the different groups. Nonetheless, these new sources of impurity were familiar and meaningful to the Jews of Palestine. Beyond the practical consequences previously mentioned, the reification of moral impurity also added a new dimension to the current discourse of impurity. Henceforth, the distinction between pure and impure could serve to classify physical objects, as well as people and groups. Unlike the biblical stance, impurity was now not only the result of events threatening the Sanctuary, whether natural (death, leprosy, or bodily flows) or intentional (murder, fornication, or idolatry), but was also attached to fixed objects that embodied these events until it became synonymous with them. However, this reification of impurity was only the first step in the increasing role of purity discourse in shaping Jewish worldviews. Beyond the popular usage of purity language to distinguish Jews from gentiles, some groups further developed this classificatory role of this new purity discourse. Their members identified themselves with the cosmic forces of purity in their battle against the powers of the impure realities physically embodied in all "others." It is to these particular versions of purity ideology that we now turn to in the next chapter.

2

Exclusive Paths to Purity from Qumran to Jesus

A striking characteristic of purity discourse in the literature of the Qumran sect is the explicit link between ritual and sin impurity.[1] Jonathan Klawans views this feature as a unique and revolutionary aspect of sectarian ideology.[2] In his opinion, while Second Temple texts generally preserve the biblical distinction between the two types of impurity, Qumran ideology merged the two. However, as we saw in the previous chapter, the blurring between sin and body impurity features in multiple nonsectarian sources. On one level, then, Qumran literature reflects the general expansion of purity discourse in the world of Palestinian Jews of the time. At the same time, this corpus does in fact include a distinctive sectarian approach to impurity, although it is not always easy to determine where exactly the elusive boundary between these two aspects lies.

The literature of the early Jesus movement poses a similar challenge. Although it appears to offer a new mode of absolute purification through the eschatological activity of Jesus, it also reflects widespread conceptions of the cosmic role of the battle between pure and impure powers. The Jesus traditions responded to common anxieties, which find expression also in the Qumran library, and both help us reconstruct the deep-seated fear of impure powers among wider circles. Both the Qumran literature and the Jesus traditions offered exclusive paths to purity. Yet, as I demonstrate in this chapter, both drew from popular notions concerning the power of impure spirits, which they integrated into their unique eschatological narratives.

Two Models of Separation in Qumran

The concepts of impurity promoted by the Qumran sect emanated from widespread notions regarding the reification of moral impurity, to which they added a stringent interpretation of biblical law and a separatist ideology.³ Since the Qumran sources implement these elements to differing degrees, I have divided this corpus into two main groups based on the significance that purity plays in organizing their sectarian worldview. All the sectarian sources from Qumran explicitly or implicitly accuse their rivals of causing impurity through their actions, but only some of them see impurity as a constitutional human trait and limit the right to purity to members of the sect. The first group of sources draws from purity notions that I have already discussed, whereas the second group anchors the distinction between pure and impure within the cosmic order, and it is this latter group that reveals a novel dimension of purity language among Qumran sectarians.

Stringent but Not Exclusive Purity

The sheer volume of laws devoted to purity in sectarian literature testifies to the gravity of the observance of purity as seen in the Temple Scroll (11QT), 4QMMT, and the Damascus Document (CD and 4QD).⁴ These compositions reveal a fervently stringent approach that led to the Qumranites' avoidance of the impure Temple in Jerusalem.⁵ This said, in this group of texts, purity did not become an all-encompassing category that draws ontological distinctions between different parts of humanity.

In its discussion of the purity of the Temple city and other cities (columns 45–51), the Temple Scroll reveals a systematic exegetical approach. Jacob Milgrom notes the "homogenizing" tendency of the Temple Scroll,⁶ which combined the purification procedures from all defiling events. Thus, it adds a "first-day ablution" for corpse impurity and extends the purification process until the final evening after the completion of the prescribed term. This exegetical characteristic provides an explanation for the stringency of purity laws in the Temple Scroll, especially when compared to rabbinic law. At the same time, as Vered Noam has emphasized,⁷ this halakhic system is fairly conservative and does not venture far from the simple sense of the biblical text, apart from filling in exegetical lacunae. It appears, therefore, that beyond its utopian approach to Jerusalem as a Temple city—which, as we have seen, deviated from the actual practice there—the general approach toward the laws of purity in the Temple Scroll was not remarkable and did not necessarily reflect a sectarian, or even a particularly stringent, approach.

In its protest against the defilement of Jerusalem and the Temple by the priests who followed Pharisaic legal policies, 4QMMT expresses a similar attitude. Although the letter does not expand the holiness of the Temple to the entire city of Jerusalem, it shares with the Temple Scroll a consistent and stringent exegetical policy with respect to maintaining the purity of food in the city.[8] Beyond that, the letter emphasizes the obligation to prevent "mixture," which it considers a source of impurity. Two laws of this nature appear in this letter one after the other: Blind and deaf people are not permitted to partake of the sacrifices, since they cannot be responsible for their actions and cannot "beware all (impure) mixtures."[9] Additionally, since the water pipes in the city "do not distinguish between impure and pure" (B 49–58), they fail to comply with Leviticus 10:10 that commands, "For you must distinguish between the sacred and the profane, and between the unclean and the clean." According to 4QMMT, physical distinction is a precondition for maintaining purity, and this principle was neglected in the urban environment of his time.

Furthermore, according to 4QMMT, the defiling threat of mixture is the source of the warning against gentile impurity, and it also threatens Jerusalem.[10] The author cautions against defiling the seed of holiness by mixture (B 75–81). He explains the prohibition against intermarriage based on the prohibition of *kilayim*, forbidden mixtures in agriculture and clothing, but his wording is directly based on Ezra's familiar language regarding the mixing of the holy seed with the nations of the land (Ezra 9:2). Mixing with the gentiles is considered fornication and is a central cause of impurity.[11]

In short, then, both the Temple Scroll and 4QMMT exhibit a strict approach toward the observance of purity laws. At the same time, they do not imply an exclusive right to purity. This is also the case with respect to the Damascus Document.

According to the Damascus Document, those entering the covenant of the sect accept the instruction "to separate themselves from the sons of the pit and to refrain from wealth of wickedness, which is impure. And they must separate between the impure and the pure, and to make known (the difference) between the holy and the profane ... And let them separate themselves from all impurities according to their law. And let not any of them defile his holy spirit, for God has set them apart" (CD 6:14–7:4). All Jews must distance themselves from impurity, including stolen property, which, through the reification of sin impurity, has itself become impure. But evidently only some people are capable of this. The sectarian organization aids its members in fulfilling this obligation. Therefore, the Damascus Document provides detailed instructions regarding the sources of impurity, which correlate to what we have found in other compositions.[12] This work, too, assumes that gentiles are impure.[13]

Despite the volume that purity laws take up in this text and their central place among the duties of the members of the covenant, who consequently avoided the Jerusalem Temple and severed their social connections with other

Jews, the Damascus Document does not formulate the difference between members and others as a contrast between pure and impure, as do other Qumran compositions. The communities of the Damascus Document provided a haven for distancing oneself from the dominion of Belial, who seeks to entrap Israel into acts of impurity (4:13). Life within the sect offered the possibility of observing purity, without identifying oneself as essentially pure and others as essentially impure. The prevailing impurity, according to the Damascus Document, is a result of a defined set of sinful acts, which one can avoid with the correct instruction and social support. The Damascus Document describes these sins as the three nets by which Belial entraps the people of Israel and incur impurity: fornication, wealth, and the defilement of the Temple (4:17).[14]

The first of the three nets is fornication. Following Leviticus 18, the author claims that the sins of forbidden relations defile the land;[15] however, he significantly expands the cases included in this category. The author blames the Judeans for taking two wives in their lifetime, as well as failing to observe the laws of menstrual impurity and marrying the daughter of one's sister. Israel transgresses serious prohibitions on forbidden relations and, as a result, defiles the Temple (CD 4:20–5:11).

The Damascus Document levels an additional accusation against those who "polluted their holy spirits and with tongue of blasphemies they opened their mouth against the laws of the covenant of God, saying 'they are not right,' and abominations they speak against them.... Their webs are spider webs; their eggs are vipers' eggs" (5:11–14). This charge recurs later on, this time explicitly against the leaders of the people who have led them astray: "And the land was desolate, for they spoke rebelliously against the commandments of God" (5:21). Finally, when discussing the corruption of the priests who defile the Temple, the author returns to the theme of the impurity of wealth. The covenanters accept on themselves not to enter the Temple of corrupt priests to avoid their impure riches: "To separate themselves from the sons of the pit and to refrain from wealth of wickedness which is impure due to vows and dedication and to the wealth of the sanctuary" (6:15–16).

Unlike the author of 4QMMT, who bemoans the leniency in matters of ritual purity, the Damascus Document accuses the people, the leadership, and the priesthood of spreading moral impurity. From its sectarian perspective, the only solution is to separate from the sources of these impurities, the Temple, the leadership, and the rest of the people.[16] We should note, however, that each of the three types of impurities is anchored in the biblical perception of sin impurity. As mentioned in Leviticus 18:25 and 20:3, grievous sins, such as forbidden relations and idolatry, defile the land and the Temple. Accordingly, incorrect interpretation of the laws of forbidden relations also leads to the defilement of the Temple. The treatment of the "wicked wealth," derived from the oppression and murder of widows and orphans, hints at Ezekiel 22:1–16, where the prophet castigates Jerusalem, which has become defiled through these same acts.[17] In contrast to these two forms of defilement, it seems at first that the third accusation, concerning those who defiled their "holy spirits" by blasphemous language, represents a new and unfamiliar notion of impurity. A closer glance, however, reveals that this form of impurity, too, is rooted in biblical exegesis.

The accusation that "they polluted their holy spirits and with tongue of blasphemies they opened their mouth against the laws of the covenant of God" seems to assume that every Jew possesses a holy spirit, and that sinful acts, and even improper speech, can defile this spirit.[18] We can derive the precise meaning of the phrase from a comparison to a similar one: "And let him separate himself from all impurities according to the law, and let him not defile his holy spirit, for God has set them apart" (CD 7:3–4). Here, too, we hear that negligence on matters of impurity leads to the defilement of the holy spirit that resides in man. In this case, the biblical source of this notion is quite straightforward: "You shall not draw abomination upon yourselves [lit. upon your soul, *nefesh*] by means of animal or bird or anything that swarms, that I have set them apart as unclean."[19] Evidently, the Damascus Document replaced the word *nefesh* (soul), which initially referred to the entirety of the person, with a particular part of his self, the "holy spirit." The Damascus Document then isolates the part of the person that is vulnerable to defilement, which is distinct from his self as a whole. In his opinion, all Jews have a "holy spirit,"[20] and they are commanded to maintain its integrity. But while the majority of the people of Israel have defiled this precious part of their selves through their transgressions, the covenanters of the Damascus Document have succeeded to protect it. Evidently, there is no ontological difference between different groups of Israel according to the author of this text. Anyone who defiles himself through sin injures the holy spirit that resides within him.

Against this background, we can also uncover the scriptural foundation of the claim against those who defiled their holy spirits by blasphemous words. This notion is the result of the merging of distinct biblical statements into a unified concept of purity of the self. Blasphemy is the most serious accusation, carrying with it the punishment of being cut off from life, as seen in Numbers 15:30–31: "But the person, be he citizen or stranger, who acts defiantly reviles the Lord; that person shall be cut off from among his people. Because he has spurned the word of the Lord and violated His commandment, that person shall be cut off—he bears his guilt." Several traditions develop the notion that there is no atonement for blaspheming God and the Holy Spirit.[21] These include Jesus's statement in Mark 3:28–29: "Truly I tell you, people will be forgiven for their sins and whatever blasphemies they utter; but whoever blasphemes against the Holy Spirit can never have forgiveness, but is guilty of an eternal sin."[22] This idea of the ultimate unforgivable sin of blasphemy against the Holy Spirit resonates with the language of the Damascus Document, which accuses Israel of annulling the laws of the Torah and of blasphemy, through which they defile their own "holy spirit." Both texts then associate blasphemy with sinning against the "Holy Spirit," but the Damascus Document transforms this notion into that of defiling one's own internalized holy spirit.

What is the basis for this transformation? According to Leviticus, certain grave sins lead to a dual result: the person defiles himself with the sin, and as a result he is "cut off." This is the case, for instance, with respect to one who turns to ghosts or familiar spirits. On the one hand, Leviticus 19:31 cautions: "Do not turn to ghosts and do not inquire of familiar spirits, to be defiled by them," but on the other hand, Leviticus 20:6 imposes an unprecedented punishment: "And if any person turns to ghosts and familiar spirits and goes astray after them, I will set My face against that person and cut him off from among his people."[23] The combination of these two verses suggests that the soul is cut off as a result of its grave impurity and cannot exist when it is mortally injured. According to the Damascus Document, the vulnerable part of the person, called nefesh in the Torah, is his holy spirit, and a grievous sin that results in "cutting off" (*kareth*) injures this holy spirit to the effect that the holy spirit itself is irrevocably defiled. Sinners who blaspheme the laws of the Torah have caused intrinsic defilement to their holy spirit, and this condition inevitably results in their eternal cutting off from life.

The Damascus Document suggests a sophisticated mechanism for the workings of divine judgment through the category of impurity. The stance articulated by Jesus, as a paraphrasing of the biblical punishment of "cutting off" (Num. 15:30), according to which God may forgive any sin other than the blasphemy of the Holy Spirit, is hereby radically reimagined. According to the Damascus Document, we are not speaking only of a grave act, which receives unprecedented punishment by an external divine force but rather of an inherent outcome of the act. The sinner defiles the holy spirit that resides in him, and as a consequence, it is cut off. In accordance with the tendency to reify impurity, this sin impurity cleaves to the person and determines one's status and fate.

At the same time, despite the novelty in this interpretation, the Damascus Document preserves the biblical perception, which views impurity as a result of the actions of some people, not as an intrinsic and fundamental characteristic of them. Despite the extensive treatment of impurity and the decision to separate from the impurity of the Temple and from the "sons of the pit" within the supportive framework of the sect, the Damascus Document does not set a essential contrast between the pure members of the sect and all others. Impurity is not an inherent part of human identity, despite the fact that the people of Israel have transgressed and defiled themselves through their grave sins. Consequently, the Damascus Document does not envision the process of joining the sect as a purification procedure, in contrast to other Qumran texts.[24] Belial misleads people and causes them to defile the Temple and themselves, including their own "holy spirit," but this behavior is not rooted in a cosmic picture of the battle between purity and impurity, such as we encounter in the second group of Qumran sources.

Constitutional Impurity and the Right to Purity

Several Qumranic works, including the Community Rule (1QS), the Thanksgiving Scroll, and 4QRitual of Purification (4Q512), intensify the language of impurity to unprecedented heights. Nonetheless, scholars should exercise caution and aim for precision when delineating the precise innovations of these texts. These compositions explicitly blur ritual and sin impurity, which some scholars, as we have mentioned, understand to be the central innovation of the sect.[25] However, in this respect the sectarian sources are rooted in biblical foundations, a phenomenon that we have already exposed in other sources. At the same time, a feature that is unique to this corpus is the transformation of purity and impurity into constitutional human qualities. In other words, the state of impurity is not the result of human determination and behavior but rather an essential feature of the human condition and its status within the cosmic order.[26] The reification of impurity achieves its most developed expression in these sources.

This group of texts views all sins as "menstruous paths in the service of impurity" (1QS 4:10). God, for his part, has the power and mercy to purify humans from their sins: "For the sake of Your glory, You have purified man from offence, so that he can make himself holy for You from every impure abomination and guilt of unfaithfulness" (1QH 19:10–11). This language is familiar from the prophets. For example, according to Ezekiel 36:16–25, sins defile the land ("their ways were in My sight like the uncleanness of a menstruous woman") and God is destined to purify Israel of all their sins ("I will cleanse you") and place his spirit within them.[27] Jeremiah 33:8 likewise prophecies that in the End of Days, "I will purify them of all the sins which they committed against Me." The language of impurity and purification supplies the imagery for sin and atonement, and it is only by the grace of God that cleanses humans of their sins. There is, however, a fundamental difference between the biblical sources and their application in these sectarian works.

Let us compare, for example, Psalm 51 to a prayer that appears at the end of the Community Rule. In verse 4, it requests that God purify him of his impurity: "Wash me thoroughly of my iniquity and purify me of my sin." The psalmist is aware of his sinful nature, adding, "Indeed I was born with iniquity, with sin my mother conceived me" (51:7), but relies on God's generous spirit to purify him: "Hide Your face from my sins; blot out all my iniquities. Fashion a pure heart for me, O God; create in me a steadfast spirit" (51:11–12). Similar expressions appear in the Community Rule regarding the baseness of the human body and the grace of atonement and purification (see 1QS 11:9–15). "In His justice He will cleanse me from the uncleanness of the human being and from the sin of the sons of man, so that I can give God thanks for His justice and The Highest for His majesty" (14–15). Although these ideas present a similar hope to the one expressed by the author of Psalms, their context reveals the unique privilege granted to the members of the sect alone. According to these Qumranic texts, only the chosen ones, "those whom God has selected and has given them an inheritance in the lot of the holy ones," (lines 7–8) are rescued by God from bodily events and the impurity inherent in the human condition. Therefore, the author does not ask God to purify him but rather thanks God for electing him and transforming his condition.

The Qumranic work 4QRitual of Purification (4Q512) reflects a parallel process, whereby the biblical language of purity is associated exclusively with the privileged sect. This collection contains blessings recited after completing the process of purification in different circumstances: in preparation for holidays or upon purification from the impurity of bodily flows or corpse impurity. It expresses the notion that purification is intrinsically tied to redemption from sin through divine atonement.[28] One sees this, for example, in the following quote: "May You be blessed, [God of Israel, who] [forgave me al]l my sins and purified me from impure immodesty / and atoned/ so that I can enter [...][29] purification" (1:29–32). And elsewhere: "[Blessed] [be yo]u, God of Israel, [who commanded the tempo]rarily [impure] to purify themselves from [the impurity of] [...] the soul with the atone[ment...]" (1:1–3, lines 2–3).

There is room to debate the extent to which expressions such as "the shamefulness of the menstruant," "the blemish of the menstruant," or "the shamefulness of our flesh" are laden with the notion of sin. Do they signal a feeling of bodily wretchedness, or are they synonymous with impurity?[30] In either case, the strong sense of atonement in the process of purification is not unique to the sect but is anchored in the laws of the Torah, which demand atoning sacrifices from those suffering bodily impurity (Lev. 12:7; 14:31; 15:15; 15:30). In accordance with the tendency of the sectarians to homogenize the purity system, atonement became a permanent fixture of all processes of purification. As a result, the sprinkling of water of lustration on those who incurred corpse impurity was also an act of atonement. Qumran law therefore commands that only an adult priest sprinkle the water, so he could atone for the person undergoing purification.[31]

Thus, while association of purity and atonement is not a sectarian innovation, limiting the right to purity to an elect few embodies the unique sectarian approach: "God of Israel ... because from what issues from Your mouth [the purification of all] has been [defined ...] men of impurity ... shall not be purified by all the water of ablution" (4Q414 2ii 7–8).[32] Purity, as an expression of God's grace to his elect, does not exist outside of the sect. This idea is expressed in the clearest language in a famous passage of the Community Rule: "And anyone who declines to enter [the covenant of Go]d in order to walk in the stubbornness of his heart shall not [enter the Com]munity of His truth.... He will not become clean by the acts of atonement, nor shall he be purified by the cleansing waters, nor shall he be made holy by seas or rivers, nor shall he be purified by all the water of ablution. Defiled, defiled shall he be all the days he spurns the decrees of God, without allowing himself to be taught by the Community of His counsel" (1QS 2:25–3:7). Sinners who are not members of the sect are considered impure, and they impart their impurity through physical contact: "he should not go into the waters to share in the pure food of the men of holiness" (5:13).[33] Consequently, in the Community Rule, the initiation into the sect entails a process of gradual purification.[34]

In conclusion, the idea that sinners are impure is not a sectarian innovation and is a direct result of the general tendency among Jews of the Second Temple period to reify sin impurity. Any outsider, be it a gentile or someone who is not a member of the sect, is impure. Thus, despite the far-reaching social ramifications of the isolationist sectarian stance, the treatment of a sinner as physically impure was not in and of itself innovative. In this case, too, the novelty of the Qumranic approach is not its blurred distinction between sin and impurity but rather in the transformation of purity and impurity into basic, intrinsic qualities that establish the binary opposition between the "sons of the pit" and the members of the Yaḥad. Outsiders not only brought impurity on themselves through the sins that they committed, as described in the Damascus Document, but according to the Community Rule and similar texts, the basic human condition is one of impurity, from which only the members of the sect have been freed by the grace of God. Membership in the sect therefore not only guards one from the dangerous hazards of impure actions and choices but it also transforms one's very nature.

The Spirits of Impurity and the Redeeming Power of Purity

Some sections of Qumran literature transform impurity into a constitutional trait and view purity as a privilege granted to a chosen few. As we will now see, this process is anchored in a cosmic-eschatological worldview that provides an image of the demonic powers of impurity confronted by the divine forces of purity. On this matter, too, the notions developed in Qumran literature were not created in isolation but rather rested on popular views regarding the power of evil spirits and their role in spreading bodily defects, sins, and impurity in the world. Like the Qumran sectarians, Jesus and his disciples strove to surrender the spirits of defilement to the divine power of purity. However, each of these groups followed a different course of action in pursuit of this ultimate goal.

The notion that evil (demonic) spirits lead people astray and cause them to sin is prevalent in Second Temple literature.[35] In the book of Jubilees, the evil spirits are descendants of the angelic Watchers that rebelled against God, and under the leadership of Mastema, misled humans during Noah's generation. These creatures are named "impure spirits" (10:1). A more detailed picture is found in 1 Enoch 6:6–15, where the presence of evil spirits is the result of forbidden copulation between the Watchers and mortal women. The Watchers were defiled through these acts, and their mixed-race descendants, who contribute to the destruction of the land, are considered impure bastards (10:9). These "bastard spirits" are thus associated with "the spirits of impurity."[36]

The evil spirits cause people to sin and current sources testify to a variety of techniques for banishing these spirits and evading sin. Thus, for instance, Abraham in Jubilees turns to God in an apotropaic prayer and requests protection from these forces: "Save me from the hands of evil spirits which rule over the thought of the heart of man, and do not let them lead me astray from following You, O my God."[37] The poet of the Psalms Scroll also enjoins God to save him from sinning but adds a reference to the evil spirit that controls him: "Forgive my sin and cleanse me from my iniquity. Bestow on me a spirit of faith and knowledge. Let me not stumble in transgression. Let not Satan rule over me, nor an evil spirit; let neither pain nor evil purpose take possession of my bones" (11QPs^a 19 ll. 14–15). The poet combines two types of appeal: purification from sin and delivery from evil spirits.[38] A request for purity appears already in Psalm 51, but the poet here adds a request for the banishment of various forces, including the impure spirits.[39] Through this combination, the author transforms what were initially abstract acts of sinning into tangible demonic forces which exert control over humanity. Thus, purification is accomplished only through their banishment rather than through an internal change of heart. The reification of sin impurity described in the previous chapter is thus personified through the embodied presence of the evil and defiling spirit, which must be banished from the body.[40]

The path for banishing evil spirits offered in Qumran literature include oaths and magical recipes (4Q560; 8Q5; 11Q11), as well as songs of praise (4Q510–511). The purpose of the songs appears at the head of one of the copies of the document: "And I, a Sage, declare the splendor of his radiance in order to frighten and terr[ify] all the spirits of the ravaging angels and the bastard spirits, demons, Lilith, owls and [jackals...] and those" (4Q510 1 I ll. 4–6). In the eyes of the poet, the destructive power of the demonic forces is limited to the current period of strife in which sins hold sway over people: "And you have been placed in the era of the rul[e of] wickedness and in the periods of humiliation of the sons of lig[ht], in the guilty periods of / [those] defiled by / iniquities; not for an everlasting destruction [but ra]ther for the era of the humiliation of sin" (ll. 6–8). It is promised, however, that on the final Judgment Day, God will vanquish the bastard spirits, which will no longer be able to mislead and harm humans.

An interim solution for protecting oneself from the evil spirits is initiation into the Qumran sect, as the Damascus Document declares: "And on the day on which one takes upon himself (an oath) to return to the law of Moses, the angel Mastema will turn away from following him, if he fulfills keep his words" (CD 16, 4–5). This procedure reflects the idea that the observance of the commandments protects one from the deceiving spirits of Belial. Joining the sect is therefore a form of exorcism.[41] The sect describes itself as a group from which evil spirits have been banished even during the reign of the government of evil: "[Bles]sed be Your name, God of mercies, who guards the covenant with our fathers, and during all our generations You have wondrously bestowed Your mercies to the rem[nant of Your inheritance] during the empire of Belial. With all the mysteries of his enmity, they have not separated us from Your covenant. You have chased away from [us] his spirits of [de]struction, [when the m]en of his dominion [acted wickedly] You protected the soul of Your redeemed ones" (1QM 14:8–11). Qumran literature thus offers several strategies for dealing with the power of the evil spirits over humans. On one level, people can hold back the immediate effects of the evil spirits through prayer and incantation. Beyond that, sectarian literature presents these spirits as governing humanity under the leadership of Belial and posits that one may seek protection from their control only within a sectarian haven. "The Treatise of the Two Spirits" in the Community Rule transfers the opposition between the impurity of the people of iniquity and the purity of the members of the covenant to the cosmic realm, under the control of the two ruling spirits of the "sons of justice" and the "sons of deceit," respectively.

Furthermore, the members of the sect perceived themselves not only as released from the influence of the evil spirits but also as being transformed through the purifying power of the holy spirit.[42] As we read in the Thanksgiving Scroll: "For the sake of Your glory, You have purified man from offence, so that he can make himself holy for You from every impure abomination and guilt of unfaithfulness, to become united wi[th] the sons of Your truth and in the lot with Your holy ones" (1QH 19:13–15). The person is, due to his material nature, a sinner, but at the same time: "I know that there is hope for someone You fashioned out of dust for an everlasting community. The depraved spirit You have purified from great offence so that he can take a place with the host of the holy ones, and can enter in communion with the congregation of the sons of heaven" (1QH 11:21–24).[43] A powerful image of the transformation of human nature through the forces of purity appears in the description of the Final Days, when God himself will remove the control of the spirits of Belial once and for all:

> Then God will refine, with His truth, all man's deeds, and will purify for Himself the structure of man, ripping out all spirit of injustice from the innermost part of his flesh, and cleansing him with the spirit of holiness from every wicked deeds. He will sprinkle over him the spirit of truth like lustral water (in order to cleanse him) from all the abhorrences of deceit and (from) the defilement of the unclean spirit, in order to instruct the upright ones with knowledge of the Most High, and to make understand the wisdom of the sons of heaven to those of perfect behavior. (1QS 4:20–22)

With the removal of the spirit of iniquity, the human body is possessed by the power of the holy spirit, which purges it of sin and merits the person the wisdom of the sons of heaven.

There is therefore a strong connection between this cosmic worldview and the legal stance expressed in the Community Rule regarding the impurity of nonsectarians. One must distance oneself from them not only because of their sins but also because they are, by their very nature, subject to the control of the impure spirits. The possibility of purification is dependent on a complete transformation of the self, which one may achieve only through the grace that God grants to those capable of becoming members of the sect.

The Baptism of John

A clear trajectory connects the removal of the impure spirits from humanity at the End of Days in the Qumran sect and the activity of Jesus as purifier of the world, releasing the cosmos from the grip of the demons. Between these two phases stands the purification activity of John the Baptist in preparation for the Kingdom of God. Despite the fact that we have limited information about this figure and the doctrine he espoused, it is well established that his model of purity appealed to many in Judean society. Both Josephus and the Gospels attest to his public standing in narratives about his execution by Herod Antipas.[44] John's practice of purification exhibits, again, the blurred boundaries between sin impurity and ritual impurity familiar from other contemporary sources and groups. Although John's language of purity shares some of the elements featured in Qumran literature, unlike the sectarian approaches, John granted everyone immediate purification in preparation for the Kingdom of God. This act supplied the foundation for Jesus's ultimate act of purifying the world.

There are different and even contradictory descriptions of John's message regarding purity.[45] In the Gospels, John preaches a "baptism of repentance," though each of the Gospels formulates this message in a different way.[46] According to Mark and Luke, John declared "baptism of repentance for the forgiveness of sins," whereas in Matthew he only called for repentance. Mark and Matthew mention that the people whom John baptized in the Jordan River confessed their sins. By contrast, Luke makes no mention of confession but says that John preached for the amelioration of the baptized way of life. All three Gospels, on the other hand, mention the contrast between John, who baptized people with water, and the baptism of the Holy Spirit—or even, according to Matthew and Luke, of the threatening fire of coming judgment. The eschatological purpose of John's onetime baptism is therefore unmistakable. Repentance and forgiveness of sin prepare Israel for the approaching divine judgment.[47]

According to this account, the baptism of John prepared the people for God's future revelation. Yet it is unclear what mechanism this baptism provided. What is the relationship between the act of repentance, divine remission of sin, and ritualized purification through baptism? Peter suggests baptism is comparable to the falling of the Holy Spirit. Thus in Acts 11:15–18 the audience praised God who granted even gentiles "the repentance that leads to life" through the Holy Spirit. Both baptism and the Holy Spirit give life to those who were previously considered dead due to their sins.[48]

The Gospels view baptism within the framework of the eschatological transformation of humanity. Baptism for the sake of repentance facilitates the change of human nature, and it could be accomplished only by God's emissary, such as John himself.[49] Josephus, on the other hand, took John's message in the opposite direction. He ignored the messianic nature of the baptism and, at the same time, focused John's message on the distinction between physical immersion and repentance: "For Herod had put him (John) to death, though he was a good man and had exhorted the Jews to lead righteous lives, to practise justice towards their fellows and piety towards God, and so doing to join in baptism. In his view this was a necessary preliminary if baptism was to be acceptable to God. They must not employ it to gain pardon for whatever sins they committed, but as a consecration of the body implying that the soul was already thoroughly cleansed by right behaviour."[50] In the eyes of Josephus, only righteous acts can purify the soul, whereas the immersion that follows is limited only to bodily purification. Admittedly, Josephus's words conceal more than they reveal, for if this is so, then why did John's message attract so many, and why did Josephus feel the need to specifically disagree with the same interpretation of baptism for the sake of remission of sins that surfaces in the Gospel tradition?

Scholars take three basic approaches to explain John's message within the context of first-century Judaism.[51] According to David Flusser, John's baptism reflects the notions of purity that we find in the Community Rule, according to which sin defiles the body and the sinner is incapable of purification. Repentance is, therefore, a necessary precondition for the achievement of ritual purity through baptism (as in Mark and Matthew's versions).[52] This interpretation is largely based on Josephus, according to whom the immersion itself did not achieve atonement. However, despite the fact that both John and Qumran literature tied repentance to purification, it is doubtful that John was as invested in physical purity as were the Qumran sectarians, who practiced immersion regularly and maintained bodily purity on a daily basis.

John's baptism, therefore, does not appear to have been integrated within a regular observance of bodily purity but rather offered onetime purification for the sake of repentance. Thus, other scholars suggested that this ritual was inspired by the prophetic descriptions of purification: "I will sprinkle clean water upon you, and you shall be clean; I will cleanse you from all your uncleanness and from all your fetishes" (Ezek. 36:25). The prophet uses metaphors of purification to describe the expiation that will pave the way for redemption, and John provides an actual realization of these expressions of atonement.[53] But the shift from divine acts of purification to a physical practice of purification, such as that offered by John, requires a fundamental transformation in the perception of impurity. He is not merely performing Ezekiel's prophecy.

Hence, I suggest a third explanation for John's practice. The prevalent tendency in Second Temple sources to obscure the distinction between ritual and moral impurity provides the background for John's baptism for the sake of atonement. As we saw in the previous chapter, even those outside the sect shared the notion of the reification of sin impurity. The popular practice of physical distancing from gentiles reflected the notion that they physically embodied sin and were, therefore, a source of defilement. To a certain degree, this type of impurity could cling to any sinner. Furthermore, many Jews would have identified the defiling power of sin within themselves as being under the dominion of demonic forces in a concrete manner, with these forces causing them both to sin and to suffer. One could not shake off these forces of impurity that nested in the human body without external intervention. In this sense, many Jews might have shared the eschatological hope quoted previously from the Community Rule: "Then God will refine, with His truth, all man's deeds, and will purify for Himself the structure of man, ripping out all spirit of injustice from the innermost part of his flesh, and cleansing him with the spirit of holiness from every wicked deed."

Here, then, lies the essential difference between the perceptions of impurity prevalent in the world of John the Baptist and the earlier language of Ezekiel. Reified sin impurity was transformed from an abstract concept into an actualized entity, which many Jews imagined in the form of demonic powers that held control over them. This embodied image of reified impurity also led to the creation of new ritualized methods for the banishment of impurity. Purification was no longer understood to be a metaphor for a person's change of behavior and internal consciousness but rather a ritualized model for banishing those spirits that resided within his bodily members ("ripping out all spirit of injustice from the innermost part of his flesh"). Although God himself, or someone operating under his authority, executed the change that came with the Holy Spirit, a physical purification technique was necessary for the banishment of the spirits of impurity, the elimination of the power of sin, and the transformation of one's nature, within a unified image of flesh and spirit.[54]

The Purifying Force of Jesus

The impure spirits that occupy Qumran literature and operate under the rule of Belial lead people astray, and the final battle against them is intended to emancipate the world from the power of sin. In this body of literature, the role of the spirits in spreading illness and physical deformities appears in the margins, if at all.[55] Jesus traditions also express the eschatological aspiration to cleanse the world of impure spirits in expectation of the imminent revelation of God and the coming of the Kingdom of Heaven. As opposed to Qumran literature, however, the Jesus traditions associate these spirits primarily with illness and bodily disfigurement, not only with sins. Nonetheless, both traditions link the struggle against these harmful spirits with the purification of the world of both ritual and sin impurities. Both corpora testify to the central role of purity in the messianic consciousness of the time, albeit in different ways.

The issue of Jesus's attitude toward purity appears in three distinct contexts in the Gospels. The first relates to Jesus's explicit statements concerning the observance of certain purity laws and customs. Scholars have frequently understood Jesus's polemics against the Pharisees concerning matters of purity and his preference of moral over ritual purity as reflecting his critical approach toward the law. Jesus rejected the practice of handwashing (Mark 7:1–23) and attacked the Pharisees for the way they purified their food utensils (Matthew 23:25–28; Luke 11:38–41).[56] However, as we shall see in the next chapter, contrary to accepted interpretation, these cases do not demonstrate that Jesus rejected purity laws specifically, or the Torah in general; rather, they testify to a specific objection to the ways in which the Pharisees handled the day-to-day business of purity. Rather than revealing Jesus's attitude toward purity, these cases in fact testify to the nature of Pharisaic purity observance and to the widespread objections to their practices. These served Jesus, who chose to join in such disputes, in exposing the moral shortcomings of the Pharisees.[57]

The second group of sources describe Jesus as one who freely comes into contact with impure persons and uses his power to purify them. These healing stories involve three types of ritual impurity. First, Jesus heals a leper by touching him, and he instructs him to go to the priest, who will deem him pure, and bring the required sacrifice.[58] In another case, a woman who had been hemorrhaging for twelve years (a zava) and was incurable touches Jesus's cloak, hoping to be healed. Jesus senses the effect of her touch, feeling the power leave his body, and she is immediately healed. The woman is frightened by her action, but Jesus reassures her of her faith.[59] In an adjacent story, Jesus brings back to life the daughter of the local *archisynagogos*, after entering her room and declaring that she is not dead but only sleeping.[60] These stories demonstrate Jesus's fairly free contact with those suffering from severe impurity. He touches the leper and entered a house that contains what is presumably a corpse.[61] At the same time, in the story with the zava Jesus is horrified by the forbidden touch and feels that he has lost his power as a result of this contact. Jesus is willing to forgive the woman for her touch due to her faith.

How should we understand Jesus's reactions? It is clear that his actions do not express an outright rejection of biblical purity laws. Jesus even instructed the leper to undergo the priestly purification procedure, as required. The healing stories are also not indicative of Jesus's deviation from the accepted norms around him, in a manner that would arouse the wonderment of others. Only in apocryphal sources is Jesus known as one who ate with lepers.[62] Otherwise, Jesus comes in contact with impure people only to heal those who approach him. Thus, even if Jesus was careful to distance himself from impure people, as others around him were, he was willing to defile himself to help the ill and impure. These actions, therefore, do not testify to the regular level of purity observance practiced by Jesus but rather illustrate the efforts he made to overcome impurity through his power to heal with his divine powers of purification.[63] This is the third and primary context in which purity concerns Jesus and the Gospels.

From his first appearance, Jesus sought to purify the world of impure spirits in preparation for the coming of the Kingdom of God. The basic narrative framework in Mark reveals the stages of this eschatological purification. Mark's Gospel opens with John the Baptist's declaration of a baptism of repentance for the forgiveness of sins and his announcement of the coming of a more powerful purifier than himself: "I have baptized you with water; but he will baptize you with the Holy Spirit" (1:8).

Fittingly, Jesus's first public action is to banish an impure spirit from a man in the synagogue of Capernaum (Mark 1:21–28). Jesus's authority over the impure spirits arouses wonder, and he becomes famous among the sick and those possessed by spirits (1:34, 39). This is the background for the two stories that end the first set of purification stories, in which Jesus cures the leper and then heals a paralyzed man by forgiving his sins (1:40–44; 2:1–12).

The gospel describes a gradual process: Jesus first exorcises impure spirits, then purifies someone from a ritual impurity (e.g., leprosy), and finally remits the paralytic of his sins, which had brought on him his physical disability in the first place. Jesus claimed to possess the authority not only to banish impure spirits but also to forgive sins. In the eyes of the scribes, it was a blasphemous pretension, but it is in the forgiveness of sins that Jesus's purifying activity reaches its peak, as John the Baptist had foretold. While John baptized people with the purpose of expiating sins, Jesus, using his authority, uprooted the forces of impurity and, following from this, also the power of sin over humanity. One by one, Jesus banished the various impurities in order of their severity: from impure spirits and demons to leprosy to the reified sin impurity.[64]

The second set of wondrous deeds is based on the same structure (chap. 5). Here, too, the stories begin with the banishment of impure spirits. Jesus expels a legion of impure spirits from a man who has been living among graves and transfers them to a herd of pigs, who leap to the sea. Later, Jesus purifies a woman with unusual genital discharge and then brings a dead girl to life. Again, Jesus's authority over the impure spirits, which allows him to heal those who are made miserable by the demons who have overtaken them, also gives him the power to banish the ultimate sources of bodily impurity, including death.[65] Jesus even grants the authority over the impure spirits to his disciples, who go out and call for repentance, drive away demons, and heal illnesses (6:7–13). The actions of the disciples pave the way to a new, pure world, and this eschatological reality, similar to what we found in Qumran literature, ties together repentance, transformation of bodily members, and the banishment of evil spirits in preparation for the coming of the Kingdom of God.[66]

* * *

According to a tradition shared by Matthew and Luke, Jesus acknowledged the challenges facing him on his way to purifying the world from the control of impure spirits: "When the unclean spirit has gone out of a person, it wanders through waterless regions looking for a resting place, but it finds none. Then it says, 'I will return to my house from which I came.' When it comes, it finds it empty, swept, and put in order. Then it goes and brings along seven other spirits more evil than itself, and they enter and live there; and the last state of that person is worse than the first."[67] Exegetes agree that the spirit leaves the person having been exorcised by Jesus himself, as described in detail in the stories attributed to him. Surprisingly, however, Jesus addresses the possibility that the spirits he has exorcised might return and reinhabit people. His actions are not final and may be influenced by additional factors.[68] It is difficult to know what Jesus meant in describing the body as "empty, swept, and put in order." Possibly, he was referring to the Pharisee practice of maintaining the purity of the inside of the body.[69] In any event, it appears that Jesus was referring to the possibility that inappropriate conduct and interference of other forces, would attract the impure spirit back into the person, along with other spirits. Judging by its context in the Gospels, Jesus directed this charge against those who questioned his authority, and Matthew even adds: "So will it be also with this evil generation."

These traditions thus present Jesus's purifying acts as competing with other norms of purification, which detract from his own efforts and allow impure spirits to reign over people. Despite Jesus's authority over the defiling spirits during the era of the Kingdom of God, Jesus traditions point to the actual tension between the methods of purity he offered and other techniques of managing daily life in purity. Of all the alternatives, the most accessible, and at the same time the most contentious, was the ideology of purity offered by the influential Pharisees, to which we turn our attention now.

PART II

COMMUNAL IDENTITIES

3

The Purity of the Pharisees

Who Were the Pharisees?

Like the Qumran sectarians, John the Baptist, and Jesus—all of whom offered different paths for achieving purity—the Pharisees, too, were active in spreading their own doctrines regarding purity. Although the Gospels, Qumran literature, and Josephus testify to the dominant status of the Pharisees, in reality we know much less about them than we would like. As I show in this chapter, one productive angle into learning more about the ideology of the Pharisees is to analyze the role that purity played in their daily lives and social identity. Arguably, the debated question of whether the Pharisees ate ordinary foods in a state of purity is intrinsically tied to the nature of their activity and relationship with other segments of the Jewish population in Palestine.[1] Did the Pharisees observe purity laws to form a sectarian mode of association or to compete with the priests? Were they maintaining an exceptional level of piety, or were they partaking in the popular observance of purity practices? The wide range of answers that scholars have offered to these questions reflect the diverse image of the Pharisees in current scholarship.

Based on references to the Pharisees in Josephus's writings, the New Testament, rabbinic literature, and Qumran writings, scholars believe that the Pharisees were active from the beginning of the Hasmonean period to the end of the Second Temple period.[2] However, these sources do not reveal the nature of the Pharisees' organization. It is unclear whether they should be viewed as an educated elite, a political party or religious movement, a social class into which one had to be born, or a sect with its own protocol of initiation.[3] The extent to which the Pharisees were embedded within Palestinian society at large—or, conversely, distinguished themselves from it—is also uncertain. On the one hand, according to Josephus, the general public supported the Pharisees. They achieved the height of their public authority during the reign of the Hasmonean queen Salome (76–67 BCE), who sought popular support. In addition, the Pharisees disseminated their legal interpretations and traditions, much to the chagrin of the authors of the Qumran literature and the Jesus traditions.[4] On the other hand, early rabbinic literature implies that the Pharisees—as their Hebrew name, *perushim* (i.e., "those who have separated themselves"), indicates—were careful to distance themselves from the rest of the population, whom they considered ammei ha-aretz (lit., "people of the land"), particularly through their observance of purity laws. In an attempt to solve these tensions, scholars offer conflicting descriptions of the Pharisees.

Some scholars describe the Pharisees as popular teachers of Torah, who had the capacity to shape the worldview and practice of the majority of Palestinian Jews during the Second Temple period. For example, according to Elias Rivkin, one must distinguish between the Pharisees, the loyal representatives of Jewish tradition who were the arbiters of Jewish law for the general public, and a small group of "associates" (ḥaverim), who were stricter in their purity observance and separated themselves from other Jews.[5] Rivkin argues that the Pharisees basically practiced the same laws that they transmitted to their followers. Following Adolf Büchler, Rivkin sought to save the Pharisees from the separatist image and therefore rejected the reliability of rabbinic sources, according to which the Pharisees were careful not to mingle with other Jews.[6]

Other scholars are more moderate in their description of the Pharisees, maintaining the role of purity in their identity while still describing them as closely associated with other Jews. For instance, Gedalyahu Alon believes that the Pharisees represented the majority of Palestinian Jewry, even though there were inevitable differences of practice between the Pharisaic scholars and the masses that followed them who naturally maintained a lower degree of purity observances. Alon avers that the aspiration to maintain purity in daily life was shared by the associates, Pharisees, and the general public, as the testimony in the Gospel of Mark indicates: "For the Pharisees, and all the Jews, do not eat unless they thoroughly wash their hands, thus observing the tradition of the elders; and they do not eat anything from the market unless they wash it; and there are also many other traditions that they observe, the washing of cups, pots, and bronze kettles" (Mark 7:3–4). According to this approach, the strict observance of food purity was anchored in tradition and common among wide circles. At the same time, because it could not reach absolute consensus, Alon concludes: "But the halakha as such, which calls for Levitical purity when eating unconsecrated food, was left undecided from the outset, for others ruled that uncleanness applies only in the sanctuary and to holy things. Hence the halakha could not be firmly established and applied to all things, but remained for many 'a precept of piety' and succeeded in being firmly applied in given cases only."[7] The Pharisees embodied the full implementation of the biblical commandments and observed fully what others managed to perform only partially.

Even scholars who take into account the sectarian tendencies of the Pharisees maintained that their religious outlook was the most faithful representation of common Judaism. For instance, Emil Schürer and Geza Vermes believe that Pharisaic separatism justifies their categorization as a sect (*hairesis*) by ancient authors, although they chose for themselves the term *associates*. They distanced themselves from ammei ha-aretz and fiercely criticized Jesus for consorting with them. At the same time, they implemented the religious ideology common among Jews of the time, even if this required them to live in separate associations.[8] They were, therefore, also able to represent the religious and political interests of the general public before the Hasmoneans. Along the same lines, Roland Deines describes the Pharisees as "a separate movement within the nation for the nation," who sought to influence prevalent religious practice, not through formal institutional means, but rather through their religious prestige. They served as models for their fellow citizens of what a life according to God's will looked like, thereby gaining growing influence and social power.[9]

Other approaches tend to disassociate the Pharisees from the general public and to describe common Judaism on its own terms. Morton Smith has undermined the dominance of the Pharisees, as described in Josephus and tannaitic literature, and described them as a separatist sect. In their stead, he posits the Hellenized am ha-aretz as the true representatives of Palestinian Judaism, although this group did not bequeath any written testimony and are largely unknown to us.[10] According to this approach, even the presumed adherence of the marginalized Pharisees to the "tradition of the elders" was in fact no more than an empty slogan.[11]

The separatist image of the Pharisees gave rise to new possibilities for understanding their scrupulous purity practices. Jacob Neusner explains Pharisaic purity practices against the changes in their public standing. While Josephus's descriptions of the Pharisees during the Hasmonean period portray them as a politically active group that advocated the authority of tradition, in the Gospels and tannaitic literature they are presented as occupied with the implementation of their own pious form of living. Neusner thus argues that the Pharisees abandoned their political aspirations during Herod's rule and focused on sanctifying their daily lives, as if they were priests, mainly through table fellowship, and thereby transferring Temple purity to daily eating practices. They strove to implement the biblical injunction, "But you shall be to Me a kingdom of priests and a holy nation" (Ex. 19:6) through strict adoption of purity laws.[12] Other Jews (ammei ha-aretz), on the other hand, adhered to the simple meaning of the biblical commandment, which demanded purity only with relation to the Temple. In Neusner's view, the Pharisees, similar to the Qumran sectarians, invented a new type of purity to fulfill their own religious aspirations. Within this framework, the idea of eating daily food in the state of purity defined the Pharisaic way of life.

Against the backdrop of Second Temple sectarian environment, Albert Baumgarten provides a sociological framework for the Pharisees' ideology of purity.[13] Baumgarten outlines the processes that led certain groups to congregate in sectarian enclaves due to their opposition to Hellenism around the Hasmonean period. The mechanisms that initially served to separate Jews from gentiles were now turned inward and used to distinguish between faithful Jews and those who threatened the safe boundaries of Judaism. The sects, including the Pharisees, considered the food of nonsectarians to be impure, similar to gentile food, and thus established boundaries between themselves and other Jews. Baumgarten emphasizes that as a reformist sect, seeking to spread its influence, the Pharisees were more lenient than the Qumran introversionist sectarians regarding contact with outsiders. Nonetheless, the Pharisees were careful as well to eat only among themselves, thereby preserving their group boundaries through purity laws.

Toward a New Model

Different scholarly descriptions of the Pharisees' social standing, therefore, entail contradictory views of their ideology of purity and its underlying motivation: to expand the realm of purity to all Jews, an aspiration for sanctified daily life similar to the priestly order, or a mechanism for separation from the masses. However, one crucial factor must be taken into consideration when deliberating these diverse images. Arguably, the Pharisaic choice of purity observance should be understood first and foremost within the wider purity discourse of Second Temple Judaism and against the ideological variety of the period. We should not interpret the Pharisees' approach in isolation, since they shaped their approach to a pure life in opposition to other alternatives within a shared discourse of purity.[14] The Pharisaic approach cannot be reduced to the prevalent practice as if there were a uniform norm observed by a majority group, nor can it be boiled down to the adoption of a separatist approach. As we saw in the previous chapters, purity supplied the Jews of the Second Temple period with a practical and ideological vocabulary for an array of distinct approaches and a rich grammar for formulating competing worldviews one against the other. The details of Pharisaic law, as well as their purity system as a whole, are best understood in dialogue with competing purity approaches.

In their portrayals of the Pharisaic worldview, scholars tend to view purity as a fundamentally uniform phenomenon, not as a language through which different worldviews confronted each other. Thus, Neusner's explanation that the Pharisees attempted to achieve holiness by adopting a priestly way of life assumes one basic type of purity—namely, that of the Temple and the priests— which provided an exclusive model for those adopting a life of purity. However, as E. P. Sanders has pointed out in his criticism of Neusner's argument, rabbinic literature distinguishes between the purity of unconsecrated food, priestly tithes, and the purity required for sacrifices. From this perspective, one cannot assume that the Pharisees' simply sought to replicate the purity of the Temple, and therefore, Sanders prefers to characterize their approach as "minor gestures" toward purity.[15] However, Sanders's objection to Neusner's thesis led him to make the opposite mistake. Sanders assumes that the Pharisees sought to maintain biblical purity laws, which in their own interpretation pertained to daily foods. Although the Pharisees were simply more careful to follow these laws than others, they did not hold to an alternative conception of purity. According to Sanders, Pharisaic purity observance was not distinct from its surroundings in any way other than its level of scrutiny, since all Jews shared the general desire to be pure and to observe scriptural law. Even though this approach acknowledges some differences between priests and laypeople (as implied in the Torah itself), it also assumes a monolithic purity and disregards the far-reaching developments in the purity culture of the period.[16]

As we have seen, Alon's attempt to tie Second Temple purity practices to the framework of the biblical approach toward maintaining Temple purity also brought him to blur the lines between fundamentally different phenomena. Among other things, he ignored the difference between observing biblical law and practices that had no anchor in scripture, such as the consumption of ordinary food in the state of purity. In fact, while early Pharisaic traditions broadened the observance of purity to the realm of the mundane and even added central sources of impurity, such as liquids and hands, they intentionally refrained from anchoring these practices in scripture.[17] It is no wonder then that, as we shall see, with regard to one of the central aspects of their way of life, the scrupulous observance of the purity of ordinary foods, the Pharisees explicitly based their practice not on biblical exegesis but rather on "the tradition of the elders."

At the same time, just as we cannot interpret the purity approach of the Pharisees directly on the basis of its biblical underpinnings, so too must we not be satisfied with explanations that perceive purity as a uniquely Pharisaic phenomenon and ignore the centrality of purity observance among general Jewish society at the time.[18] As described previously, impurity shaped the extent to which Jews separated from gentiles as well as the Hasmonean battle against idolatry. Many people were careful to distance themselves from physical causes of impurity on a daily basis, and they struggled against real threats of impurity, spirits, illnesses, and sins. Within the space in which different groups offered paths to purity and salvation, the Pharisees, too, offered a doctrine of purity that deviated from biblical exegesis and reflected current tendencies. Alongside the disputes between the Pharisees and their opponents, it appears that Pharisaic law shared some basic principles with other approaches, and at the same time, they adapted the halakhic structure to their own particular religious and ideological tendencies.

Controversial Purity Practices

Anyone attempting to characterize the purity doctrine of the Pharisees and its purpose through an examination of rabbinic literature faces a twofold challenge. The first challenge, which I discussed at length in the introduction, is how to isolate the early strata embedded within the developed rabbinic legal system, as it appears in tannaitic sources. Even if we manage to overcome this difficulty by isolating traditions that are attributed to early rabbis, we must still face a second challenge: how to interpret the intention of Pharisaic purity practices independently without relying on the meaning they later acquired within the developed rabbinic legal system. Since we generally encounter Pharisaic traditions within rabbinic compilations, there is reason to suspect that the general picture that emerges from the developed legal system of the rabbis will determine our interpretation of earlier legal traditions as well. On the other hand, the earliest traditions in and of themselves are too meager to provide an adequate image of the Pharisaic system of thought. How then can we understand the intention of Pharisaic laws without imposing later rabbinic notions? In the case of purity, there is a particular difficulty due to the changing contexts of these laws and their reinterpretation in later tannaitic strata.

In light of these challenges, scholars are fortunate to be able to turn to the Jesus traditions in the Gospels, which play a crucial role in our reconstruction of prerabbinic attitudes. These nonrabbinic sources on purity explicitly address the intention and purpose of the Pharisees' observance of purity laws, and at the same time, they allow us to compare to rabbinic sources and suggest new interpretations of these early legal traditions.

Handwashing

The ritual of handwashing before the meal, common among observant Jews up to this day, originated as a unique Pharisaic practice and, as such, was rejected by other groups. In this section, I argue that this practice, which significantly shaped daily life, encapsulates the role of eating in a state of purity for the Pharisees and their adherents. Here, as in other cases, Jesus's external point of view on this practice reveals the foundations of the Pharisaic tradition, which we could have deduced only indirectly from some rabbinic legal details. The dialogue between the Pharisees and Jesus reveals that the practice of washing hands before eating was not intended to protect foods from impurity, and certainly not to protect the purity of holy foodstuff, but was rather introduced to protect the bodies of those who sought to distance themselves from impurity. The Pharisees thereby created a new arena of purity observance that was independent of the Temple realm. The case of handwashing demonstrates the strong link between the Jesus traditions and early rabbinic sources, especially when contrasted with the later Talmudic sources that were unfamiliar with the Pharisees' worldview and were therefore surmised that hand purity was somehow related to the purity of the sancta.

THE PHARISAIC TRADITION AGAINST THE TORAH

The polemic between Jesus and the Pharisees regarding handwashing before eating appears in both Matthew (15:1–20) and Mark (7:1–23). The Pharisees express wonder at the fact that Jesus's disciples contravene the tradition of the elders by eating without first washing their hands. Jesus, in turn, attacks the "tradition of the elders" in general and specifically the practice of handwashing before eating. In both versions of the story, there is a literary distinction between Jesus's denouncement of the "tradition of the elders," addressed directly to the Pharisees (Matt 15:3–9; Mark 7:6–13), and his lecture to the audience and his disciples regarding the nature of impurity. This literary complexity indicates that several different traditions and textual sources were incorporated in this pericope.[19] Here, we will focus only on the section that deals directly with the issue of handwashing:

Mark 7

[1] Now the Pharisees and some of the scribes who came from Jerusalem gathered around him.
[2] And they saw that some of Jesus's disciples ate their bread with impure hands, that is, unwashed. [3] For the Pharisees and all the Jews do not eat unless they thoroughly wash their hands, holding fast to the tradition of the elders. [4] And when they come from the marketplace, they do not eat unless they wash. They hold fast to many other traditions: the washing of cups, pots, kettles, and dining couches.
[5] The Pharisees and the experts in the law asked him, "Why do your disciples not live according to the tradition of the elders, but eat with unwashed hands?"
...
[14] Then he called the crowd again and said to them, "Listen to me, everyone, and understand. [15] There is nothing outside of a person that can defile him by going into him. Rather, it is what comes out of a person that defiles him."

[17] Now when Jesus had left the crowd and entered the house, his disciples asked him about the parable. [18] He said to them, "Are you so foolish? Don't you understand that whatever goes into a person from outside cannot defile him? [19] For it does not enter his heart but his stomach, and then goes out into the sewer." Thus he made all foods clean. [20] He said, "What comes out of a person defiles him.
[21] For from within, out of the human heart, come evil ideas, sexual immorality, theft, murder, [22] adultery, greed, evil, deceit, debauchery, envy, slander, pride, and folly. [23] All these evils come from within and defile a person."

Matthew 15

[1] Then Pharisees and scribes came to Jesus from Jerusalem and said,

[2] "Why do your disciples break the tradition of the elders? For they do not wash their hands before they eat."
...
[10] Then he called the crowd to him and said to them, "Listen and understand: [11] it is not what goes into the mouth that defiles a person, but it is what comes out of the mouth that defiles."
...
[15] But Peter said to him, "Explain this parable to us." [16] Then he said, "Are you also still without understanding? [17] Do you not see that whatever goes into the mouth enters the stomach, and goes out into the sewer? [18] But what comes out of the mouth proceeds from the heart, and this is what defiles.

[19] For out of the heart come evil intentions, murder, adultery, fornication, theft, false witness, slander. [20] These are what defile a person, but to eat with unwashed hands does not defile."

There are a number of differences between the two versions.[20] For instance, Mark alone mentions that the disciples ate "with impure hands" and clarifies that this refers to "unwashed hands." Mark also adds a note here regarding the purity practices of all Jews, which include regular ritual immersion and vessel purification. In addition, Jesus phrases his parable differently in each of the gospels: While Matthew focuses on what comes in and out of one's mouth, Mark relates to the body as a whole, that which enters a person and comes out of him. The conclusion of both authors from the parable is different as well. In Mark, we find a comment, according to which Jesus has made all foods clean; Matthew, on the other hand, summarizes Jesus's approach by saying that eating with unwashed hands does not defile.

In general, one can attribute these differences to the different audiences of the two evangelists. Given that Mark is speaking primarily to a gentile audience, he specifies the purity practices of the Pharisees and the Jews in general. This may also be the background for his comment: "and thus he purified all foods" (v. 19).[21] This comment, which ostensibly renders any food pure for consumption—including foods forbidden by biblical dietary law—is unparalleled in the Jesus traditions. Scholars have already noted that despite the fact that the question of Jewish dietary laws was at the heart of the conflict between the different factions within the early church, this verse did not play a role in the dispute. It therefore appears that this statement was added by Mark, who reached this radical conclusion within his gentile community.[22] Matthew, on the other hand, who is speaking to a Jewish-Christian community, was concerned mainly to resist the influence of the Pharisees/rabbis.[23]

Although Mark adapts the story to a gentile audience, there are internal indications that his version of the story actually preserves original elements of the tradition, including the phrasing of Jesus's central statement (Mark 7:15; Matt 15:11).[24] It appears that the original statement focuses on what enters and exits the body, as in Mark, which Matthew then adjusted so that it relates to the question of eating without washing one's hands—and in the end, changed it to "that which comes in and out the mouth." As a result of this revision, however, the following claim became convoluted. In lieu of Mark's conclusion, according to which whatever emerges from a person's heart—such as bad thoughts—defiles her, Matthew describes a more complex process: things that emerge from the mouth contaminate the person because they originate from the heart. Accordingly, other things that come out of the heart, even if they do not necessarily exit through one's mouth—such as bad thoughts—defile.

At first glance, Jesus's reply does not match the claim made by the Pharisees. This raises a set of important questions, such as: What is the connection between the Pharisees' requirement of handwashing, which is supposedly meant to protect the purity of the food, and the fear, rebuked by Jesus, of contaminating one's body? Why does the claim that things entering the body do not defile it lead to the conclusion that handwashing is unnecessary? Arguably, the answers to these questions are the keys to understanding the purpose of Pharisaic handwashing and, more broadly, their controversial conception of purity.

As mentioned, the earliest interpretation of Jesus's words is found already in Mark's comment, "and thus he purified all foods" (v. 19). According to this radical interpretation, Jesus permitted the consumption even of impure animals and replaced the observance of ritual purity with internal, moral purity of the heart.[25] This interpretation of Jesus's words vexed more recent scholars, who sought to avoid having Jesus reject explicit biblical commandments, and they offered minor adjustments to it. For example, some scholars interpret Jesus's statement as a rhetorical device. Jesus opens with a declaration that sounds as though he is undermining the Torah, thus shocking the Pharisees, before then transferring the notion of purity to a higher ethical plane.[26] Another similar interpretation suggests that the contrast between ritual and moral purity is relative. Jesus did not question the importance of biblical dietary or purity laws, he only placed moral purity above them, as if to say: "nothing outside of a man can defile him halakhically to the same degree that those things that come from the heart can defile him morally."[27] Jesus did not abolish purity laws altogether but simply stated that they have no effect on a higher moral plane.[28]

Although these latter scholarly interpretations absolve Jesus of antinomianism, they do not provide an accurate interpretation of his statement, which does not contrast internal and external impurity but rather the movement of impurity in and out of the body.[29] Furthermore, according to these explanations, Jesus ignored the particular question that he was asked regarding hand purity. Should we assume that Jesus took advantage of this situation for an attack on purity laws, perhaps to justify his unrestricted contact with lepers and other impure people?[30] Is it possible to maintain a coherent narrative and understand Jesus's statement as a direct response to the specific question of handwashing?[31]

In my opinion, the best way to interpret Jesus's words is to contextualize them within the legal realities of his time. When Jesus says that food does not contaminate the people eating it, he is not referring to the swarming things and other forbidden foods listed in Leviticus 11. After all, these were not suitable for consumption. Rather, he is discussing kosher food that has been defiled.[32] Once read within the context of first-century law, Jesus's words can be understood against a set of purity principles formulated in early rabbinic sources which reflect Pharisaic practice. While the Pharisees believe that eating with defiled hands actually leads to contamination of the body, Jesus holds on to the biblical position, according to which food never transfers impurity to the person eating it.

To help clarify this point, let us turn to the relevant rabbinic sources. At the end of Mishnah Zavim (5:12), the rabbis state that one is defiled by eating impure food: "The following render heave-offering [terumah] unfit: one who eats foods of first or second grade uncleanness, and who drinks unclean liquids." These cases relate to a person who has eaten or drunk impure food or drink. These foods are not impure in and of themselves, like a carcass or a swarming thing, which are considered first-grade uncleanness but rather have been defiled through contact with a source of impurity. The Mishnah thus teaches that a person who has consumed such foods contracts a lower degree of impurity. This ruling is already familiar to R. Joshua and R. Eliezer, tannaim of the first century, who dispute its details: "R. Eliezer ruled: he who eats food of first [grade uncleanness contracts] first [grade uncleanness]; [he who eats food of] second [grade uncleanness contracts] second [grade uncleanness]; [if it was] third [grade uncleanness, he contracts] third [grade uncleanness]. R. Joshua ruled: he who eats food of first [grade] or of second [grade uncleanness contracts] second [grade uncleanness]; [if it was] third [grade uncleanness, he contracts] second [grade uncleanness] in regard to holy things but not in regard to terumah" (m. Tehar. 2:2). In contrast to the biblical notion that only forbidden animals defile through touch or consumption (Lev. 11:40),[33] these two early rabbis share the assumption that the impurity of defiled foods disseminates into the body of one who consumes them.

In light of the disparity between scripture and rabbinic law, we can understand why the practice of handwashing spurred Jesus's response.[34] First, already according to the laws of the Houses of Hillel and Shammai, and in contrast to biblical law, hands can be defiled independently of the body.[35] These impure hands further contaminate food and unconsecrated foods that come in contact with fluids (m. Tehar. 1:14). Next, as we previously saw, in the eyes of the early tannaim, impure foods contaminate people who consume them. Thus, when eating with impure hands, they transmit defilement to the food, which is later digested into the body. In response to this opinion, Jesus argues, "There is nothing outside of a person that can defile him by going into him" (Mark 7:15). In other words, it is as though Jesus says: as opposed to your approach, Pharisees, according to which one must remove hand impurity before eating to prevent this impurity from clinging to the food and thus penetrating one's body, I say that according to the biblical conception of impurity, consumption (of permitted food) does not defile. For Jesus, the expansion of purity laws according to the "tradition of the elders" and the addition of the requirement of hand purification, out of a fear that defiled food will enter a person and contaminate him, contradicts the biblical principle.

Jesus contrasts the Pharisees' perception of purity with the biblical one regarding the role of human agency in the process of spreading impurity. As the Priestly Code makes abundantly clear, people are superspreaders of impurity. The Torah categorizes leprosy, genital discharges, and corpse impurity as "human uncleanness," and as such, they may spread to others (Lev. 5:3). Impurity can also transmit from a person to vessels and foods (Lev. 7:19), but not in the opposite direction.[36]

By contrast, in Pharisaic law—which includes the ordinance on hand purity and their ruling that impure foods defile the body—we encounter a different dynamic. Here, food takes an active role in spreading impurity by transmitting it back to the person. Jesus's depiction of this approach implies that the Pharisees were not simply widening the realm of contamination, but they were actually transforming the intention of purity laws. Rather than being concerned with contaminating their surroundings, the Pharisees were concerned to protect the purity of their own bodies. At the heart of these novel purity practices lies the fear of being contaminated by defiled foods.

Such a claim might have been voiced by others besides Jesus. For example, it is fair to assume that the Essenes or Qumran sectarians—whose laws do not acknowledge hand impurity or the fear of consuming contaminated food—would have responded similarly to the Pharisees. From this perspective, Jesus represents a conservative halakhic position that views the Pharisaic tradition as uprooting the law of the Torah. Indeed, he accused them of abandoning the commandment of God and holding to human tradition (Mark 7:8). But, as is characteristic of the Jesus traditions, his sayings extend the purely legal argument to the moral conclusion. Since humans spread impurity more than they absorb it, they are responsible not to contaminate their surroundings.

In contrast, the Pharisees—like many others—feared that by ingesting defiled food they allowed impurity to invade their bodies.[37] Similar to the fear of impure spirits taking control of people, the consumption of something impure made the body vulnerable to demonic forces. The force of this popular belief drove the creation of a new focal point for purity, and handwashing became, among adherents of the Pharisees, the definitive action that protected them from the threat of contamination through ingestion. Thus, handwashing has come to represent the nonbiblical character of the practice of eating unconsecrated foods in purity.

Later Talmudic exegetes assume that the rabbis originally instituted the notion of hand impurity to protect the purity of sacred foods and the Temple and only secondarily expanded it to daily foods.[38] Scholars have generally followed this assumption that hand impurity was first instituted in the context of the priestly heave offering and sacrifices and only later was extended to unconsecrated foods.[39] A different picture arises, however, from the early sources regarding handwashing. As we saw, Jesus's statement implies that the observance of hand purity was oriented toward the purity of the self, regardless of what sort of food one was eating. Furthermore, the earliest layer of rabbinic teachings mentions hand washing with respect to the consumption of unconsecrated food.[40] A clear testimony to the widespread practice of hand purity specifically for the consumption of unconsecrated foods is seen in the disputes between the Houses of Hillel and Shammai regarding the details of handwashing (m. Ber. 8:2–4). The two houses debate the details of this practice within the context of a nonsacrificial meal and in accordance with Roman dining etiquette.[41] Within this cultural and legal context, handwashing was not intended to secure the purity of holy foods but rather to protect the diners from contamination penetrating their bodies.

Purification without Separation

In addition to handwashing, the Gospels testify to another controversial Pharisaic practice: the purification of the outside of vessels (Matt 23:25–26; Luke 11:39–41). As in the case of hand purity, Jesus's attack reveals the idiosyncratic features of the Pharisaic approach to purity. In his rebuke of the Pharisees, Jesus did not intend to reject the observance of purity in and of itself; rather, his statement represents a widespread refutation of the Pharisees for their permissive approach and their disregard of the obligation to separate pure foods from impurity. In this case, too, the Jesus tradition and early rabbinic law, in addition to Qumran literature, illuminate each other and together provide a full image of the competing purity practices.

A survey of early rabbinic laws regarding food purity reveals that many of them deal with partially impure foods and vessels. A considerable amount of energy, already in the earliest layers of rabbinic law, was directed at drawing artificial boundaries between pure and impure parts within the same objects. Other groups rejected these distinctions and accused the Pharisees of not maintaining adequate separation between the pure and the impure. The Saducean claims against the Pharisees, preserved in the Mishnah, as well as multiple rulings of early rabbis, reveal the extent of this controversial Pharisaic approach.

It is no coincidence that it was this group of laws that raised such vehement opposition. In a world of competing concepts of purity, one's level of piety was evaluated, to a large extent, through the means used to distance, distinguish, and protect against impurity. The methods of separating meat and milk in kosher kitchens provide an apt illustration of this mindset. The observance of kashruth laws in the modern kitchen is most evident in the creation of two separate sets of dishes, above and beyond what the law requires. The possession of two or three sets of dishes and sinks facilitates a worry-free routine. Therefore, the main concern of Jews who maintain a kosher kitchen is not the fear of disqualifying their food for consumption but rather the creation of a supporting apparatus for ensuring the separation between meat and milk. Accordingly, the degree of separation and the effort expended to maintain it supply the clearest indicator of the level of kashruth observance. The technology of prevention shapes the nature of observance, and the same is true regarding purity. It is here where we may see most clearly the substantial difference between the Pharisees and their opponents.

Both internal and external evidence presented in this section reveal a consistent Pharisaic policy of nonseparation, which became their identifying mark. Thus, instead of creating sterile spheres, which would secure a safe realm of purity, the Pharisees acted to purify even parts of things that came into direct contact with impurity.

Purification of the Outside of the Cup

In his scathing litany of "Woe Sayings" against the Pharisees (Matt 23; Luke 11), Jesus exploits the legal positions of the Pharisees to expose what he believes to be their most offensive moral flaws.[42] In addition to issues concerning oaths and tithes, which exhibited the Pharisees' distorted value system, he attacks a specific purity practice that has puzzled scholars. By carefully comparing Matthew 23:25–26 with Luke 11:39–41, we can come close to reconstructing the original form of this tradition:

Matt 23:25–26	Luke 11:39–41
Woe to you, scribes and Pharisees, hypocrites! For you clean the outside of the cup [*potērion*] and the plate [*paropsis*], but inside [*esōthen*] they are full of greed and self-indulgence. You blind Pharisee!	Now you Pharisees clean the outside of the cup [*potērion*] and of the dish [*pinax*], but inside you [*esōthen humōn*] are full of greed and wickedness. You fools! Did not he who made the outside make the inside also?

First clean the inside of the cup and the plate, so that the outside also may become clean.	So give for alms those things that are within, and see, everything will be clean for you.

Our analysis begins with the text of Luke, which is difficult in a number of respects. The contrast between the "outside" of the two vessels and the "inside" of the Pharisees ("inside you") distorts the symmetry of the second part of Jesus's statement in which he contrasts the two surfaces of the vessels. In the final sentence, Jesus even talks specifically about the vessel's inner surface. We can thus hypothesize that the original statement related only to the inside and outside of the vessels.[43] Indeed, in his final statement Jesus contrasts partial and total purification. In other words, the Pharisees performed a partial cleansing that only purified the outside of vessels, whereas Jesus offered complete purification through the giving of alms.

But if the major opposition in Luke pits ritual against ethics, how are we to understand the distinction between partial and total purification?[44] Jesus must have been familiar, to some degree, with a graded system of ritual purification, one that is only implied in Luke but is more visible in Matthew, in which Jesus's entire criticism is more consistent: "You blind Pharisee! First clean the inside of the cup and the plate, that the outside also may be clean."[45] Like Luke, Matthew contrasts ritual purification with moral blindness, as the vessels are full of "greed and self-indulgence," but he draws on norms from the world of ritual cleansing: purification of the vessel's exterior alone as well as purification of the entire vessel by cleansing its interior surface.

Many modern commentators have not been able to make sense of this partial, exterior purification, so they have clung to its metaphorical meaning.[46] However, a parable is rhetorically compelling only if it draws its symbols from actual practice. Moreover, one must admit that most of these vessels are poor choices for representing Pharisaic superficiality. While the cup may symbolize the difference between a visible exterior and a dark, shadowy interior, what can we say about the plate or dish? With them, the "inside" is precisely what is visible, while the "outside" is the underside, hidden from view. If we do not assume that Jesus was referencing some common practice related to the ritual purification of vessels, it would be difficult indeed to make sense of what he was trying to convey.

Therefore, departing from the metaphorical interpretation, I would argue that the distinction between the exterior and interior surfaces of vessels in rabbinic law provides the key for understanding Jesus's statement.[47] Thus we read in m. Kelim 25:6:

If a vessel's exterior was ritually contaminated through liquids, its exterior is impure, [but] its interior, rims, loop handles, and lug handles are pure.

If it became impure from its interior, it is entirely impure.

Jesus and the rabbis agree that the interior surface of a vessel is of greater importance in determining the status of the entire vessel. To purify a cup in its entirety, it is insufficient to cleanse just the outside; one must purify the inside as well.[48] However, early rabbinic traditions introduce us to the special rules applying to a vessel whose exterior surface becomes impure. In this case, the vessel's exterior can only render foodstuffs impure by way of a liquid medium. There was a consensus about this among first-century rabbis, although they disputed the details and consequences of these laws: "[Concerning] the exterior of vessels that became impure through liquids—R. Eliezer says: They render liquids impure, but do not render foodstuffs unfit. R. Joshua says: They render liquids impure and render foodstuffs unfit. R. Simeon brother of Azariah says: Neither this nor that; rather, liquids which became impure through the exterior of vessels render one [degree] impure and render one [degree] unfit."[49] Since the outside of a vessel contaminated by impure liquids could transmit impurity to the foodstuffs around it through a liquid medium, the rabbis devised ways to prevent the spreading of impurity.[50] Aside from designating particular external parts of the vessel as separate entities,[51] the rabbis offered a practical solution for vessels with an impure exterior:

A basket into which [impure] liquid fell is entirely impure.

If it fell on its exterior, its exterior is impure, [but] its interior and loop handle are pure.

If it fell on the loop handle, One may wipe it and it is pure.

However, the priests had the practice of not leaving the [exterior] sides impure because [of the possibility] of offense.[52]

The Tosefta alludes to the conflicting policies of the rabbis and the priests. The priests did not want to leave the exterior in an impure state, because doing so could lead to a problematic situation in which impure liquid would touch it and transmit impurity to other objects. They therefore insisted on immersing even a vessel whose exterior alone was impure, so as to cleanse it entirely. According to the rabbis, it was enough to wipe away the impure liquid and dry the exterior of the vessel. Like the Mishnah, the Tosefta implies that one could continue using a vessel with an impure exterior, because after wiping away the impure liquids there would be no concern about the vessel contaminating surrounding foodstuffs.

As it turns out, Jesus described accurately how serving utensils and drinking vessels were handled in his time. Jesus, like the Tosefta, contrasts two methods of purifying tableware. The optimal one, which the Tosefta attributes to the priests, entails cleansing the entire vessel: "First cleanse the inside of the cup and the plate, that the outside also may be clean." Jesus goes on to denigrate the alternative superficial method: "Woe to you, scribes and Pharisees, hypocrites! For you clean the outside of the cup and the plate" (Matt. 23:25). Jesus refers to the Pharisees' satisfaction with simply wiping any impure liquids off the outside of vessels. And indeed, from the various mechanisms presented in the tannaitic sources, such as wiping the outside of a vessel or establishing an artificial separation between the handle and the vessel itself, it is clear that the Pharisees took pride in maintaining the ritual purity of their food, even though their tableware was not actually free of impurity. After all, they allowed partially impure vessels to mingle freely with sacred food. Jesus criticized the Pharisees for being complacent with a superficial cleansing of the exterior, which could only check the spread of impurity temporarily, rather than eradicating it and consequently allowing excessive proximity between pure and impure.

Jesus likely was not the only one to find fault with the Pharisees on this issue, as the priests also demanded complete immersion of vessels and viewed the Pharisaic norm as unduly lenient. This complaint led Jesus to accuse the Pharisees of hypocrisy (Matt. 23:28): "So you also on the outside look righteous to others, but inside you are full of hypocrisy and lawlessness." Here again the legal argument served Jesus as a springboard for a moral attack on the Pharisees, and it resonates with the accusation, found in Qumran literature, that the Pharisees "chose the lenient way."[53]

The Law of "Liquid Flow" and the Policy of Nonseparation

Jesus's claim against the Pharisaic leniency on matters of purity: "Woe to you, scribes and Pharisees, hypocrites! For you cleanse the outside of the cup and the plate" is parallel in both format and content to one of the complaints of the Sadducees against the Pharisees in m. Yad. 4:6–8:[54] "The Sadducees say: we complain against you, o ye Pharisees, that you declare an uninterrupted flow of a liquid to be clean" (m. Yad. 4:7). The parallel complaints of Jesus and the Sadducees against the Pharisees expose the typical technique the Pharisees applied to maintain purity in an unclean environment.

According to the Pharisaic view, when liquid flows downward and encounters something impure, whether on a slope or when poured into a receptacle, the upper portion of the liquid and the upper vessel do not contract impurity. The Mishnah formulates the following rule: "The stream of liquid, the slope, and moisture do not constitute a connection (*ḥibbur*) for either impurity or purity, but the collection of water does constitute a connection for impurity and purity" (m. Tehar. 8:9). The underlying principle is that impurity located at a lower point within the water stream cannot contaminate that which is above it. This ruling, which was, according to rabbinic tradition, known already to the Houses of Hillel and Shammai (m. Makh. 5:9), allayed the concern that something impure located at one end of the water supply would contaminate the entire system.

The dissent attributed to the Sadducees in the Mishnah also appears in the polemical letter 4QMMT from Qumran: "and also that liquid streams cannot separate impure from pure, because the liquid of the liquid streams and their vessels is alike—the same liquid."[55] According to the sectarian author, the entire system is a single unit whose parts cannot be differentiated, so it is defiled in its entirety even when the impurity is located at its end. This formulation echoes the Torah's command to the priests to "distinguish between the sacred and the profane, and between the unclean and the clean" (Lev. 10:10). The order to distinguish entails a physical separation of the sacred from the profane and the impure from the pure. Although the liquid flows downward, the uninterrupted flow means that the whole network is viewed as a single system, and seeing as it contains both the impure and the pure, everything becomes impure.[56]

While the sources provide a clear reasoning for the Sadducean stance, there is no clear explanation of the Pharisaic approach, the one under attack. From this mishnah, it appears that the Pharisees are willing to turn a blind eye to the presence of impurity within the stream of liquid. Yet how can this approach, which contradicts the biblical imperative to separate the pure from the impure, be sustained?[57] Since the Mishnah in tractate Yadayim offers no solution to this conundrum, we are forced to search for additional sources that might explain the Pharisaic stance. As a first step, we must place the law of pouring within its wider halakhic context. While it appears, from Mishnah Yadayim, that the law of pouring was one of a few laws that the Pharisees' opponents criticized harshly, a comprehensive look at the laws relating to purity reveals that this ruling was actually characteristic of the earliest layer of the laws of food purity in general. Evidently, the early rabbis consistently sought to limit and decrease impurity, both in their food and drink and in their vessels, through artificial means of separation, precisely as the Sadducees and Jesus accused them.

Limiting Impurity in Early Rabbinic Law

The tannaitic units that relate to food impurity, including the early traditions from the Houses of Hillel and Shammai, deal with two major questions: (1) When is food rendered fit to receive impurity? And (2) What constitutes a connection with regard to food; that is, what part of the food is impure and what part is pure? The discussion regarding poured liquids is one expression of this issue, and it is included in the same textual units. Both these issues that comprise the laws of food impurity are clustered together already in the earliest strata in all the tractates that discuss the matter: Teharot, Uqtzin, Tevul Yom, and Makhshirin.[58]

The laws attributed to the Houses of Hillel and Shammai within these units also relate to these two core issues. Alongside their occupation with determining when foods become susceptible to impurity,[59] the Houses of Hillel and Shammai discuss the issue of connections between different parts of foods. For instance, at the beginning of tractate Tevul Yom, the Houses discuss the level of linkage between different types of baked goods:

> If one had collected dough-offering [portions] with the intention of separating them afterwards again, but in the meantime they had become stuck together—
> the House of Shammai say: they serve as connectives in the case of a tevul yom. But the House of Hillel say: they do not serve as connectives.
> Pieces of dough that had become stuck together, or loaves that had become joined, or a batter-cake that had been baked on top of another batter-cake before it could form a crust in the oven, or if there was froth on the water that was bubbling, or the first scum that rises when boiling groats of beans, or the scum of new wine (R. Judah says: also that of rice)—the House of Shammai say: all serve as connectives in the case of the tevul yom. But the House of Hillel say: they do not serve as connectives.

In these cases, baked goods or cooked grains are stuck together. According to the House of Hillel, these food units are connected, and therefore if one part is defiled, it renders the rest of the dish impure. However, in the case of a tevul yom, whose impurity is relatively light and only renders terumah impure, the various foods are not considered one unit. Therefore, a tevul yom who touches one of the loaves will not render the remaining loaves impure. The question of the connectivity of the different units of the same foods is raised time and again, from different perspectives, in the discussions of the early rabbis. This group of laws, many of which were transmitted in the name of the Houses of Hillel and Shammai and the rabbis of Yavneh, is aimed at limiting the scope of impurity within those foods and is based on a routine halakhic mechanism—the division of each food into subunits, so as to limit the spread of impurity to one part of the food and saving other parts.

The attempt to define the connection between different units is characteristic also of the laws of vessel impurity, and there, too, the rabbis break down the vessels into their components and impurity is limited to one "section" of the vessel.[60] Even the famous dispute between R. Eliezer and the rabbis regarding the Oven of Aknai (m. Kel. 5:10) is predicated on the question of whether the various units of the oven are part of one whole vessel or whether the impurity can be prevented by separating the oven into subunits. R. Eliezer, like the House of Hillel, is lenient on the issue of connectivity. Similar discussions appear regarding wooden vessels, such as the parts of a chest (m. Kel. 18:2) or the parts of a bed (m. Kel. 19:2–3). Later, in chapter 25, the Mishnah also addresses the separation between the internal and external parts of a vessel, which, as we have seen, Jesus harshly denigrated.

Evidently, then, the Sadducees' statement "we complain against you, o ye Pharisees, that you declare an uninterrupted flow of a liquid to be clean," and Jesus's claim "Woe to you.... For you cleanse the outside of the cup and the plate" are emblematic of a wide realm of laws, in which the Pharisees employ the same mechanism toward foods and vessels. The Sadducees attacked the Pharisees for the fact that they kept pure and impure next to one another, even though they were present in the same water system. Following the Priestly Code, they claimed that one must "separate between the impure and the pure," and the entire system is contaminated once impurity is present in any component. Jesus also criticized Pharisaic eating practices, where impure and pure vessels were placed alongside one another, and even the very same vessel might contain a pure liquid while its outside is impure. All these sources amount into a comprehensive and consistent Pharisaic approach, which sought to enable purity observance within an impure environment. Evidently, the Pharisees were willing to pay a significant legal and ideological price to advance the observance of food purity within their daily conduct.

Conclusion

Recent scholarship on Jewish law during the Second Temple period has succeeded in outlining some defining features of Pharisaic law and exposing its underlying religious ideology and social policy, thereby distinguishing it from other systems of law.[61] As we saw in the introduction, scholars focused on the Pharisaic attempts to undermine the priestly status and to allow wider participation in the Temple worship. They were scandalously lenient about entry into the Temple during the festival pilgrimage, to the point that they were prepared to allow the Temple itself to be defiled.[62] In addition, they insisted on preparing the red heifer—whose ashes were a sine qua non for attaining the ritual purity necessary to enter the Temple—at the lower level of purity governing nonsacred items rather than at the level required for the Temple.[63]

At the same time, Pharisaic purity ideology sought to extend their alternative beyond the realm of the Temple and transform the meaning of purity as an accessible normative ideal. In contrast to Neusner's conception, according to which the Pharisees sought to appropriate priestly purity and holiness, they were, in fact, more concerned to create a new conception of purity, serving new objectives through new practices that directly undermined the basic features of purity, as these were formulated in the biblical Priestly Code. These features are best expressed, as we have seen in this chapter, in the sweeping onslaught against Pharisaic purity practices carried out by their opponents.

Beyond the dominant presence of purity discourse and practices within Second Temple Judaism, the particular interest of the Pharisees in developing a systematic ritual construct pertaining to daily practice, rather than the Temple, entailed two major innovations that were unique to their own concept of purity. First, they viewed the self rather than the Temple as the ultimate arena of purity. Within this framework, the daily concern to eat unconsecrated foods in a state of purity was not a derivative outcome of the biblical command to ensure the purity of the Temple and holy foodstuff, as part of Temple ecology, but as a self-standing ideal drawing from popular sensibilities concerning the preservation of human integrity.[64]

In addition, to facilitate the possibility to go about one's day-to-day life in a state of purity, the Pharisees adopted a seemingly scandalous policy of nonseparation. To make ritual purity more accessible, they purified even those objects that came into close contact with sources of impurity. Through artificial legal distinctions they promoted a lenient and compromising policy which enabled them to maintain a sense of purity within the complex reality of social and physical contact. Thus, the development of this new system, directed toward a new focus of purity observance, not only expanded biblical notions of purity in the ways outlined in the first section of the book but also, in fact, distorted the priestly order of hierarchy and separation.

Purity, then, had a paradoxical role in shaping the Pharisaic worldview and identity. It served as a major channel for spreading their ideology to wider circles, undermining priestly approaches and offering an accessible form of religious excellence. At the same time, in contrast to the image suggested by Alon and others, they were not just exercising popular forms of purity practices. They held on to distinct customs, which set them strictly apart from others and reflected their learned form of purity knowledge. In the next two chapters, we turn to examine the social implications of the Pharisaic purity policy.

4

Outsider Impurity and the Forms of Judean Sectarianism

Purity observance has generated much interest among historians of Second Temple Judaism, largely due to its crucial role in setting both internal and external boundaries of the Judean society. Different groups—Pharisees, Sadducees, Essenes, and Qumran sectarians—perceived the social relations between themselves and others through the language of purity, and they shaped this distinction through the concept of "outsider impurity." Accordingly, the observance of purity determined the social relations between the Pharisees and other less observant Judeans, whom the rabbis termed am ha-aretz (lit. "people of the land,").[1]

In this chapter, I analyze the earliest references to am ha-aretz, which go back to the earliest stratum of rabbinic literature and arguably reflect the world of the Second Temple period. I will argue that the earliest laws relating to am ha-aretz in rabbinic literature represent Pharisaic social policy and are rooted in the legal tradition regarding "outsider impurity" that was prevalent among different groups during the Second Temple period. A comparison between the laws of am ha-aretz in early rabbinic literature and the impurity of those outside the sectarian covenant in Qumran literature reveals the high degree of similarity between the traditions and testifies to their shared foundations. We will trace the gradual development of the notion of "outsider impurity" from its early roots in Judean society in the Persian period to its diverse representations within the different sects. At the same time, this comparison will also reveal the uniqueness of Pharisaic policy and the alternative it offered to more isolationist tendencies. The Pharisees reshaped ancient legal structures in accordance with their own social and ideological outlook.

The Study of Am Ha-aretz

The term am ha-aretz as indicating a class of less observant Judeans appears only in rabbinic literature, and it is therefore possible to ascertain its social meaning only through this body of literature and within the framework of rabbinic halakhic discourse.[2] More than any other halakhic realm, the laws relating to am ha-aretz impurity are the product of specific historical and social circumstances. One cannot discuss the status of am ha-aretz without taking into account its particular social reality. Tannaitic literature, however, includes guidelines grounded in a variety of social contexts that assume differing degrees of social separation. One who seeks to determine the identity of am ha-aretz in the eyes of the early rabbis, the degree of impurity attributed to them and the means one must employ against them, therefore, must distinguish between different groups of texts and isolate the policy of the sages of the Second Temple period from that of the later rabbis. Even if one assumes that later rabbis followed in the footsteps of earlier ones, it is unlikely that the essential social changes that took place during this period, from the Jerusalem of the Temple period to the Galilee of the early third century, did not affect the phrasing of later halakhah and the attitude toward people who did not properly observe the laws of purity.[3]

Admittedly, any attempt to historicize rabbinic sources relating to am ha-aretz raises difficult methodological issues, and earlier attempts to describe the figure of the am ha-aretz testify to the difficulty of pinpointing each individual source to a distinct social context. Severe critiques of the am ha-aretz, bordering on expressions of hatred, appear only in the Babylonian Talmud.[4] Various laws of separation from the am ha-aretz and processes for initiation into the "association" (havurah) of the pure appear primarily in the teachings of the late second-century rabbis, but they are similar in some ways to the laws of initiation to the Qumran sect and would therefore appear to be of earlier provenance. And we have only a few early mishnaic traditions concerning am ha-aretz attributed to the Houses of Hillel and Shammai. This complex textual situation led scholars to contradictory assessments of this social phenomenon and its historical contexts. The following two works on am ha-aretz in tannaitic literature represent two diametrically opposed approaches regarding these questions.

In his 1906 monograph, *Der galiläische 'Am-ha'Ares*, Adolf Büchler rejected the portrayal accepted by New Testament scholars of his day, according to which there was deep animosity between the Pharisees, on the one side, and the ammei ha-aretz, under the leadership of Jesus, on the other.[5] In Büchler's opinion, the Pharisees did not physically distance themselves from ammei ha-aretz and did not adopt a unique practice of eating daily food in purity. The apologetic motivation that led Büchler to eliminate any confrontation with ammei ha-aretz from the earlier sources, as well as from Jesus's sphere, comes through clearly in his writing. At the same time, his claim seems to be rooted in solid textual grounds, for many laws in the Mishnah and Tosefta regarding separation from am ha-aretz are in fact attributed explicitly only to later rabbis, from the second half of the second century. Büchler therefore claims that the rabbis formed the laws of separation from am ha-aretz only after moving to the Galilee following the Bar Kokhba revolt, in an attempt to improve the religious standards of Galilean Jews. To that end, they enacted ordinances that would aid in the observance of priestly practices, in particular, separation of tithes and observance of the purity of priestly gifts. Büchler repeatedly emphasizes that these rabbis were concerned only for the purity of the priestly gifts and not that of daily foods, which in his view was inconsequential. The term am ha-aretz in the Mishnah therefore denotes the Galilean commoners, and the laws of am ha-aretz reflect the social reality of the Galilee during the second half of the second century. In Büchler's opinion, even laws that the Mishnah attributes to the Houses of Hillel and Shammai belong in fact to this later historical context.[6]

Aharon Oppenheimer, on the other hand, suggested that the am ha-aretz phenomenon was a salient and continuous feature of Jewish society that spanned from the Hasmonean period through the end of the tannaitic era.[7] Unlike Büchler, Oppenheimer believes that the named authorities that transmit specific rulings are not necessarily those who first formulated it, and therefore, even a late rabbi might transmit an early legal tradition. On the heels of this assumption and due to the lack of clear indications for the correlation between a specific ruling and a particular social context, Oppenheimer paints a fairly generalized and unified portrait of the attitude toward am ha-aretz during the long and unstable period under discussion, with small changes from one period to the other. Thus, instead of a historical description that anchors the development of legal policy in social changes, Oppenheimer offers a harmonizing description of the general attitude toward am ha-aretz throughout the entire period.[8]

Against the background of the differing approaches to the historical study of am ha-aretz, I argue that it is possible to distinguish between the different stages of tannaitic material that deals with this topic. By isolating early traditions concerning am ha-aretz and his social setting and comparing them to other concomitant approaches, I describe the nature of the Pharisaic observance of purity, its social ramifications, and the place it occupied in the sectarian discourse of Second Temple Judaism. Later on, in chapter 6, I compare this image of the am ha-aretz to that proffered by later Galilean tannaim. Thus, in addition to featuring the history of purity practices and their development within Pharisaic and rabbinic circles, the case of am ha-aretz impurity offers a salient example of the ability of rabbinic sources to reflect historical realities and the changing circumstances of rabbinic legal activity.

The Roots of the Rabbinic Am Ha-aretz

Following tannaitic literature, scholars regularly characterize am ha-aretz by his lack of observance in two primary realms: tithes and purity. However, it is unclear what makes these specific halakhic fields so unique in this respect and why they are particularly relevant for the designation of am ha-aretz.[9] Furthermore, do both issues figure to the same degree in rabbinic discussions of am ha-aretz? As we shall see, the key for reconstructing the history of this term is to separate the different literary strata that include references to am ha-aretz.

In the earliest layers of tannaitic literature, am ha-aretz always appears with respect to purity observance. Thus, for example, the term appears already in the dispute between the Houses of Shammai and Hillel, where it is set up in opposition to the Pharisee: "The House of Shammai says: A Pharisee suffering abnormal genital discharge may not eat with an am ha-aretz suffering abnormal genital discharge" (t. Šabb. 1:15). Already in early tannaitic tradition the am ha-aretz is presented as impure, as opposed to the Pharisees or the rabbis, who are pure.[10] This characteristic of am ha-aretz, as one who does not observe purity law, is familiar throughout the tannaitic period. The term am ha-aretz, on the other hand, does not appear in the context of tithing law before the second half of the second century. Although early tannaim were already concerned by the fact that some people were not careful to tithe their produce, this topic was not framed through the opposition between am ha-aretz on the one hand and the Pharisee or associate on the other.[11] At first, the term *am ha-aretz* appears exclusively in the context of separation from impurity, and only later, toward the end of the tannaitic period, with the diminishing in the general observance of purity laws, did the rabbis add a new concern for the untithed fruit of am ha-aretz.[12]

The initial association of *am ha-aretz* specifically with the issue of impurity goes back to the biblical roots of the term. We find a variety of uses for the terms *am ha-aretz/ammei ha-aretz* in the Hebrew Bible.[13] In some places *am ha-aretz* appears to indicate the general population (Lev. 4:27, 20:20; 2 Kgs. 15:5), while in others, it relates to a smaller, ruling class (Gen. 23; Jer. 1:18). There were therefore scholars who deduced that the term *am ha-aretz* in rabbinic literature relates to all of the people of Israel.[14] However, in rabbinic Hebrew am ha-aretz never corresponds to the neutral term *Israelite*;[15] rather, the term always functions as the negative corollary to the Pharisee, the associate, or the rabbi. *Am ha-aretz* appears in this negative meaning only in Ezra and Nehemiah, and it is from these texts that one must examine the development of this literary term.

As mentioned, in its earliest attestations in rabbinic literature, the impure am ha-aretz appears in opposition to the pure Pharisee. This opposition corresponds to the exact same contrast embedded in the phrase "one who has separated [*nivdal*] oneself from the people of the land [*ammei ha-aratzot*]," which is repeated in Ezra 9:1 and Nehemiah 10:29. These two sources employ the same verb to denote separation and segregation from am ha-aretz, since the root p.r.š. in Mishnaic Hebrew is the Aramaic equivalent to the biblical verb b.d.l employed in Ezra and Nehemiah.[16] The linguistic link illustrates that the rabbinic notion that the Pharisee separates from am ha-aretz was shaped in this particular biblical mold. In addition, a third component complements the correspondence between the two pairs—that is, Pharisees versus am ha-aretz, separated versus the people of the land—and this third component forms the foundation for both sources: impurity as the root of separation. Ezra and Nehemiah present a complex system of paths for distancing oneself from ammei ha-aretz, due to their impurity.[17] Thus, for instance, the officers tell Ezra that "the people of Israel and the priests and Levites have not separated themselves from the peoples of the land [ammei ha-aratzot], whose abhorrent practices..." (Ezra 9:1, cf. 9:11). Accordingly, the separation from the peoples of the lands enables a life of purity: "The children of Israel who had returned from the exile, together with all who joined them in separating themselves from the uncleanliness of the peoples of the lands, to worship the Lord God of Israel, ate of it" (Ezra 6:21).

It therefore appears that the opposition between the pure Pharisee and the impure am ha-aretz in the teachings of the early rabbis emanated from the notion of separation from the impurity of ammei ha-aratzot in the book of Ezra.[18] The terms were borrowed into tannaitic literature from this literary context. Qumran literature reveals a similar phenomenon. Similar to the terminology renewed by Ezra, and due to their complete identification with "the returned exiles,"[19] the sectarians saw themselves as separate from all impurity and from the "sons of the pit."[20] They possibly even called themselves *prushim* (separatists).[21] The obligation to separate oneself from the impurity of am ha-aretz formulated by Ezra and Nehemiah was, therefore, the ideological and terminological basis for both Qumran literature and early Pharisaic tradition.

The terminological composite reveals a strong link between the impurity of ammei ha-aratzot that troubled Ezra, the impurity of the men of injustice from whom the Qumran sectarians distanced themselves, and the impure ammei ha-aretz from whom the Pharisees separated.

Presumably, these would appear to belong to completely different phenomena: Fear of intermarriage in Ezra, sectarian isolationism accompanied by a hefty dose of blame in Qumran, and the physical distancing from those who are not strict on all purity laws in early rabbinic literature. However, as we will see in what follows, there are clear terminological and practical continuities between early tannaitic law and the separatist tradition found in Second Temple literature. The separation of the Pharisees from am ha-aretz, similar to the distancing of Qumran sectarians from noncovenanters, is at its core rooted in a worldview that ties purity to social affiliation and takes its inspiration from the notion of gentile impurity. Evidently, there were fundamental differences between each of the channels that implemented the notion of "outsider impurity," but early rabbinic law assimilated some major aspects of this concept shared with Second Temple literature.

From Gentiles to the Men of Injustice

The Qumran sectarians viewed themselves as the "true Israel," and therefore compared the legal status of anyone outside the sect to the that of a gentile. As Aharon Shemesh demonstrates, this perception is reflected, among other things, in the correlation between the laws of gentile impurity and the impurity of nonsectarians.[22] However, as we shall see, the implementation of the laws of gentile impurity on various groups within Jewish society was not unique to members of the sect. As I show in the following discussion, Qumran literature and early Pharisaic law belong to a shared tradition regarding outsider impurity and the ways of distancing oneself from it.

Josephus, in his description of the Essenes, already features an explicit comparison between gentile impurity and the impurity of nonsectarians: "They are divided into four groups, according to the period of their training; and so far are the juniors inferior to the seniors, that if by chance they touch them, they (the seniors) wash themselves, as if they had intermixed with a foreigner" (Josephus, J.W. 2.150). Josephus is referring to the internal stratification of the sect, but we can learn from this that those outside the sect also defiled upon touch, as if the member of the sect had intermixed with a foreigner.[23]

It is difficult to determine, from Josephus's own words, the severity of gentile impurity and the extent to which all Jews distanced themselves from them.

Nonetheless, they do point to the public significance of gentile impurity, which served as a model for sectarian separatism.[24] Notably, Josephus does not state that contact with a candidate is comparable to physical contact with gentiles but rather compares it to mingling with gentiles, which leads to impurity. Josephus's language presents physical contact as the manifestation of broader social contact and cultural influence, which threaten the isolating group. It appears from his words that when the sectarians sought to shape the methods of separation from nonsectarians, they followed the familiar model of gentile impurity, with the gentile serving as the ultimate outsider. The gentile and the candidate for entry into the sect are similar in one essential aspect: the very fact of their foreignness, be it small or great, has the power to defile. Other texts, which set gentile impurity as a model for separation within Jewish society, further confirm this principle.

The tendency to reify impurity—which led to an understanding whereby sin impurity became a physical trait (see section 1 of this volume)—is particularly marked with regard to the laws of separation from a gentile. A close look at sources that address gentile impurity reveals the process through which warnings regarding the gentile's impure actions eventually transformed into a fear of their own ritual impurity, which led to a refraining from physical and social contact with them. We can trace this development by comparing two texts that address the issue of social contact with gentiles: The book of Jubilees and the later Acts of the Apostles. The following is Abraham's testament to Jacob in Jubilees 22:16–20:

> And you also, my son Jacob, remember my words and keep the commandments of Abraham, your father. Separate yourself from the gentiles and do not eat with them, and do not perform deeds like theirs. And do not become associates of theirs; Because their works are defiled, and all of their ways are contaminated, and despicable, and abominable ... and all their works are worthless and vain. Be careful, my son Jacob, that you not take a wife from the seed of the daughters of Canaan.

Unlike the prohibition on marrying a Canaanite woman, which is anchored in biblical law, the first part of the testament presents a new realm of prohibitions regarding all gentiles. This includes sharing meals with the gentiles, emulating their behavior, or fraternizing with them. Notably, although these specific prohibitions are new, they are based on the biblical understanding that sins are a source of impurity. Consequently, also the works and ways of the gentiles are considered impure. We will note that, despite Jubilees' negative attitude toward gentiles and the obligation to distance oneself from them, it does not consider them to be impure in body.

On the other hand, the story of Cornelius and Peter in Acts 10 reveals that many Jews of the first century considered gentiles to be immanently impure.

The centurion Cornelius, who is a pious and God-fearing man, sends emissaries bidding Peter to appear before him. Before the emissaries reach him, Peter—in a state of hunger—has a vision (Acts 10:9–16), of a sail full of all manner of animals, insects, and birds, and he is commanded to slaughter and eat them. Peter is horrified by the idea of eating impure (*koinon*) or defiled (*akatharton*) food,[25] but he is told, "What God has made clean, you must not call profane." Immediately following this, Peter receives a sign that he must go to Cornelius's house. The vision would appear to indicate the abolishing of biblical consumption law, permitting Peter to eat anything in Cornelius's home. But Peter himself suggests a different interpretation of the vision; after entering Cornelius's house, while the latter is prostrating himself before him, the story continues (Acts 10:27–29): "But Peter made him get up, saying, 'Stand up; I am only a mortal.' And as he talked with him, he went in and found that many had assembled; and he said to them, 'You yourselves know that it is unlawful for a Jew to associate with or to visit a Gentile; but God has shown me that I should not call anyone profane or unclean. So when I was sent for, I came without objection.'" The key to understanding the story lies in the gap between the vision and its interpretation. In the vision, Peter sees impure animals that he is ordered to eat, since "what God has made clean, you must not call profane." However, he interprets the vision as signifying that he may enter Cornelius's house, since one must not call another person "profane or impure." Many New Testament exegetes were uncomfortable with this gap between the vision and its interpretation, and concluded that the tradition regarding the story underwent several revisions. They believed that the proclamation in the vision annulled the laws of kosher eating for the Christian communities.[26] Later on, the author of Acts employed the vision to provide an explanation for the practice of mixing with gentiles.[27] In my opinion, however, the story as it currently appears is coherent, and it reflects the familiar stance among Jews of this period: that gentiles carried ritual impurity. Peter and the other members of the church never considered eating forbidden foods, and they would not imagine interpreting the sentence "What God has made clean, you must not call profane" as permitting the consumption of all creatures, which is explicitly forbidden in scripture. While Peter was wondering what this sentence meant, messengers arrived to invite Peter to Cornelius's house, and it became clear to him whom he may not term impure or defiled. The impure animals remain impure and forbidden, as the Torah itself states, and the heavenly voice came to instruct Peter that he must not consider the gentiles, who are pure in God's eyes, to be impure.

According to the testimony of the author of this story, Jews do not enter gentiles' homes because they believe they carry ritual impurity, and they are therefore compared to impure animals, birds, and insects. While for Jubilees the impure behavior of the gentiles was the source of the prohibition against friendly relations with them, Acts reflect the notion that the gentiles themselves were physically impure. Even though this text does not address all the ramifications of gentile impurity, there is no mistaking the analogy established by the vision between the impure gentile and any impure animal. Peter learns that he may not apply the adjectives used to define animals and foods, impure and defiled (*koinon e akatharton*), toward foreigners, thereby disagreeing with the common practice among other Jews of the time, who tended to expand the realm of impurity not only to gentiles' food but also to the gentiles themselves.[28] It is reasonable to assume that Jews of the time practiced a wide range of measures of separation, and there were certain circumstances in which they were particularly careful not to contract impurity from gentiles, such as the arena of table fellowship.[29] However, the comparison between Jubilees and Acts testifies to the gradual development of the concept of gentile impurity into a physical quality of the gentiles, which entailed practical ramifications.

A parallel process is reflected in the sectarian sources that address the social distancing from nonsectarians. If we trace the textual development of these sources, we will find that the impurity that was originally attributed to the sinful behavior of the sons of injustice was eventually attached to their bodies and entailed physical separation from them.

From Jubilees to the Community Rule

In his description of the Essenes, Josephus associates the impurity of the young candidate with the prohibition of mixing with gentiles. This comparison is well grounded in sectarian literature itself, as we can see from a comparative examination of the Qumran Community Rule and Jubilees. As Shemesh demonstrates, Qumran literature applied toward nonsectarians the same expressions that appear in Jubilees regarding the distancing from gentiles, due to their sinful way of life. In what follows, I trace, in greater detail, the stages through which the separation from the sinful and impure ways of the gentiles came to include physical distancing from the impure Jewish nonsectarian. This development is revealed in the textual reworking of the laws of distancing from Jubilees through the early version of the Community Rule from cave 4 (=4QS) to the redacted form of the Community Rule found in cave 1 (= 1QS).[30]

The requirement of separation appears in Jubilees and in 4QS in a similar context. In Jubilees, following Abraham's blessing of Jacob (22:11–15), Abraham sums up ("and may He renew His covenant with you") and then turns to command Jacob as to the major components of this covenant. He begins by enjoining Jacob to "remember my words and observe the commandments of Abraham" and, immediately after this, spells out what this directive includes, with the emphasis being on separation from the gentiles. This is also the essence of what is demanded from one who joins the Qumran sect. According to the Community Rule, the candidate who desires to join "the council of the Community" is required to take an oath that he will return to the Torah of Moses with his entire heart and soul, and this is immediately explained as "to be segregated from all men of injustice." Both texts present a similar framework for entering the covenant, at the heart of which is the obligation of separation.[31] This shared structure is directly based on the ceremony of the covenant in Nehemiah 10:29–31, in which we hear:

> And the rest of the people, the priests, the Levites, the gatekeepers, the singers, the Temple servants, and all who separated themselves from the peoples of the lands to [follow] the Teaching of God, their wives, sons and daughters, all who know enough to understand, join with their noble brothers, and take an oath with sanctions to follow the Teaching of God, given through Moses the servant of God, and to observe carefully all the commandments of the Lord our Lord, His rules and law, namely: We will not give our daughters in marriage to the peoples of the land, or take their daughters for our sons.

Already in Nehemiah, then, the central and basic content of the pact and oath to follow God's commandments consists of separation from ammei ha-aretz. It is against this background that we will compare the details of the commitment undertaken in Jubilees and in the early version of the Community Rule from cave 4:

Jubilees 22:16–17	**4QS^d i 5–10**
And you also, my son Jacob, remember my words and keep the commandments of Abraham, your father.	And everyone who enters the council of the community shall take upon himself with a binding oath to return to the Torah of Moses with all his heart and with all his soul . . .[32]
Separate yourself from the Gentiles,	to be separated from all the men of injustice Furthermore, they shall not touch the purity of the men of holiness.[33]
and do not eat with them,	and he shall not eat with him in community.

and do not perform deeds like theirs.	Furthermore, no man of the men of the community shall give answer in accordance with their opinion relating to any Torah or judgment.
And do not become associates of theirs	Furthermore, he shall not be associated with him in possessions or in work, and no man of the men of holiness shall eat from their possessions nor take from their hand anything. And they shall not depend on the people of vanity.

Later on we find the same threefold series of identical explanations:

[A] For their works are unclean, And all their ways are a pollution and an abomination and uncleanness. They offer their sacrifices to the dead And they worship evil spirits.	[A] For futility are all those who do not [know his covenant].
[B] And all their works are vanity and nothingness...	[B] [And all those who scorn] his word, shall be obliterated from the earth;
[C] And all his seed shall be destroyed from off the earth	[C] their works are unclean[ness] be[fore him, there is uncleanness in al]l [their possessions.]

This unit is divided into three sections. At the beginning we find a general warning that one must observe the laws of the Torah; the second section details demands of separation; and the final section presents the fate and future of the sinners. The unmistakable link between the two texts is present in all three sections but is particularly noticeable in the second one. In both texts the demand for distancing appears beside the prohibition on shared eating. The second prohibition in Jubilees is "do not perform deeds like theirs," while the third forbids social contact. The prohibitions in 4QS appear in the same order and are linked with the same activities. The member of the sect is required to abstain from learning the teachings and way of life of nonsectarians, a warning that is parallel to the prohibition "do not perform deeds like theirs" in Jubilees. Following this, the members of the Community are forbidden to take part in shared activities, primarily in a business context, and this prohibition is similar to the enjoinder in Jubilees "do not become associates of theirs." Following the presentation of the three prohibitions, which in the Community Rule are more detailed and are adjusted to the sectarian situation, appear the explanations, which include the three aspects, albeit in a different order: Their actions are both impure and futile, and they will ultimately be destroyed.

Both texts declare that the actions of the outsiders are impure and an abomination, and therefore one must distance oneself from them. Notably, as in the book of Jubilees, the author of this sectarian text avoids the attribution of impurity to the physical touch of the sons of injustice. All the prohibitions relate to social activities with the outsiders, whose actions are impure and who are destined to devastation. Only at a later stage, an additional regulation was added to the text, which transfers us to new halakhic territory: "Furthermore, they shall not touch the purity of the men of holiness." In its present context, this addition does not affect its surroundings, and stands out as a secondary insertion. On the other hand, in the Community Rule from cave 1 (1QS), which at this point represents a later and redacted version of the rule, we see that this secondary addition in the earlier version has transformed into the grounding principle for the separation requirements:

The Community Rule 5, 7–20
(the words in bold appear in the earlier version of 4QS as well):

(7) ... **Whoever enters the council of the Community** (8) enters the covenant of God in the presence of all who freely volunteer.
He shall swear with a binding oath to revert to the Law of Moses, according to all that he commanded, with whole (9) **heart and whole soul**, in compliance with all that has been revealed of it to the sons of Zadok,[34] the priests who keep the covenant and interpret his will and to the multitude of the men of their covenant (10) who freely volunteer together for this truth and to walk according to his will.
He should swear by the covenant **to be segregated from all the men of injustice** (11) who walk along the path of wickedness. For they are not included in his covenant since they have neither sought nor examined his decrees in order to know the hidden matters in which they err (12) by their own fault, and because they treated revealed matters with disrespect; this is why wrath will rise up for judgment in order to effect revenge by the curses of the covenant, in order to administer fierce (13) punishments for everlasting annihilation without there being any remnant.
He should not go into the waters **to share in the pure food of the men of holiness**, for one is not cleansed (14) unless one turns away from one's wickedness, for there is impurity among all the transgressors of his word.
No one should associate with him in his work or in his possessions in order not to encumber him (15) with blameworthy iniquity; rather he

should remain at a distance from him in every task, for it is written as follows: "You shall remain at a distance from every lie."

None of the men (16) of the Community should acquiesce to their authority in any law or regulation. No one should eat of any of their possessions, or drink **or accept anything from their hands,** (17) unless at its price,

for it is written: "Shun the man whose breath is in his nostrils, for how much is he worth?"

For (18) all those not numbered in his covenant will be segregated, they and all that belongs to them.

No holy man should support himself on any deed of (19) **futility, for futile are all those who do not know the covenant. And all those who scorn his word he shall cause to vanish from the world; all their deeds are uncleanness** (20) **before him, and there is uncleanness in all {his} their possessions.**

As shown, 1QS offers an extended version of 4QS, with many additions: explanations, biblical proof texts, and even legal revisions.[35] At various points it is clear that 1QS represents a redacted version of the shorter wording of 4QS, and on this basis, we can resolve difficulties with the more complex and redacted version of 1QS. As we have seen, 4QS inserted a note that interrupts the textual sequence and prohibits the men of injustice to touch the pure foods of the members of the Community. The author of 1QS took advantage of this addition and used it as a hinge to develop his words of reproach and to present a cohesive and detailed claim regarding the essence of the impurity of the men of injustice. The author recounts the sins of the men of injustice, who walk in the path of wickedness and do not seek out God's word. As a result, they are destined to be tried and sentenced to destruction, and their inherent impurity cannot be purged. Unlike 4QS, 1QS is not concerned here with physical contact with pure foods in and of itself but rather uses it to express the view, which is characteristic of the Community Rule, according to which the men of injustice are incapable of purification due to the baseness of their existential state.

According to the adaptation of the author of 1QS, the impurity of the men of injustice embodies their fate, since their wicked ways bring them great punishment, as a result of which they are also denied purgation. He sums up the situation thus: "for there is impurity among all the transgressors of his word." In the adaptation of 1QS, the weakly linked addition in 4QS, "Furthermore, they shall not touch the purity of the men of holiness," turns into a hinge on which to hang the rebuke of the men of injustice, which reaches its peak in their inability to be purified. The adaptation thus adds a new notion of reified "outsider impurity," which was not present in the earlier version. Further, 1QS declares the men of injustice to be ritually impure: "for there is impurity among all the transgressors of his word." This statement, which justifies the prohibition against touching the pure foods of the men of holiness, stands in contrast to the concluding statement of the original unit: "all their deeds are uncleanness before him and there is uncleanness in all their possessions." According to this sentence, derived, as noted, from the book of Jubilees, impurity cleaves to the possessions and the actions of the men of injustice, and one must distance oneself from these. On the other hand, 1QS ties the impurity to the men of injustice themselves, and it determines their status.

Tracing the textual and conceptual development of the Community Rule reveals the process of reification of the notion of outsider impurity. In the earlier sources—namely, Jubilees and the initial version of 4QS—there was no expression of the physical impurity of the stranger, only a demand that members of the Community distance themselves from him due to his impure behavior. At a later stage, a comment was inserted into 4QS, demanding the distancing of the stranger from pure foods. Finally, according to 1QS, the fate of the men of injustice is the result of their intrinsic bodily impurity, and they are therefore denied the right to purification.

To sum up, Josephus compares the defiling touch of nonsectarians to defilement through social contact with gentiles. This comparison assumes that the impurity of the gentile derives from his otherness, and he therefore serves as the model of separation from anyone who is not a member of the community. Qumran literature itself confirms this conception, as the Community Rule derives the laws of separation from nonmembers from the laws concerning gentiles in the book of Jubilees. Furthermore, a comparison between Jubilees and Acts illustrated the process of reification of gentile impurity during the Second Temple period. The different stages of Qumran literature reflect this type of development also with regard to the impurity of nonsectarians. By tracing the development of the language of the Community Rule, we learn that its authors were not content with warning against the sinful and defiling ways of those outside the covenant but rather considered them ritually impure, to the degree that they even impart their impurity on the pure foods of the men of holiness.

Outsider Impurity in Early Rabbinic Traditions

Against the background of the reification of outsider impurity, whether with respect to gentiles or to those outside the sectarian community, we can now turn to describe the impurity of am ha-aretz in early rabbinic law. It is common among scholars to contrast two opposing approaches toward outsider impurity. On the one hand, the Qumran sectarians attribute impurity to sin,[36] and therefore, the sinful stranger who does not follow the laws of the Community cannot be purified. The rabbis, on the other hand, did not attribute any defiling power to sin and were only afraid that those who did not properly observe purity laws might spread their bodily impurity onto others. According to this approach, if one could safely determine that the am ha-aretz had indeed removed the sources of impurity from himself, the rabbis would consider him pure.[37] In what follows, however, I will question this dichotomy and argue that the two legal systems in fact exhibit a surprising degree of overlap. Furthermore, the rabbinic attitude toward the am ha-aretz and the approach of Qumran literature towards the men of injustice, who did not enter the covenant, are based on shared foundations and rely on the same legal tradition, which each group adjusted to its own worldview.

The Community Rule famously presents the immanent impurity of he who "declines to enter [the covenant of Go]d in order to walk in the stubbornness of his heart" (1QS 3:3–9):

> In the source of the perfect he shall not be counted. He will not become clean by the acts of atonement, nor shall he be purified by the cleansing waters, nor shall he be made holy by seas or rivers, nor shall he be purified by all the water of ablution. Defiled, defiled shall he be all the days he spurns the decrees of God, without allowing himself to be taught by the Community of his counsel. For it is by the spirit of the true counsel of God that are atoned the paths of man, all his iniquities, so that he can look at the light of life. And it is by the holy spirit of the community, in its truth, that he is cleansed of all his iniquities. And by the spirit of uprightness and of humility his sin is atoned. And by the compliance of his soul with all the laws of God his flesh is cleansed.

In the eyes of the members of the community, the path of sin has rendered Jews outside the community ritually impure, and therefore acts of purification cannot change their status. Entry into the sect, which is the only avenue for abandoning the paths of evil, is a necessary condition for purification. As we have seen, Josephus provides another expression of the same approach. According to his description of the Essenes, if a young novice touches a senior member of the sect, this senior member must purge himself as if a gentile had touched him. Despite the fundamental differences between the gentile and the young candidate, from the perspective of the older member they are equally impure. This stance derives from a binary contrast between the insider and the outsider, no matter how close he might be. There is therefore no fundamental difference between gentiles and fellow Jews who come closer to the path of the sectarians but are not yet full members—they all carry severe impurity.

The rabbis do not attribute wickedness and sin to those who are not strict in their purity observance, and the only sin of the am ha-aretz seems to lie in the fact that he is not careful to distance himself from the physical sources of impurity. Presumably, the separation from am ha-aretz is proportional and practical. We would therefore expect that according to rabbinic law an am ha-aretz would be able to purify if he so wishes, as opposed to sectarian law. And yet the laws of am ha-aretz in tractate Hagigah are surprisingly close to sectarian law. The same principles we encountered in the Community Rule and in Josephus and that reflect the notion that anyone outside the sect is impure by dint of his otherness find clear expression in these early rabbinic rulings as well.[38]

Hagigah 2:6: "If One Bathed without Being Held to Be Fit, It Is as though He Has Not Bathed"

The second chapter of tractate Hagigah presents the different degrees of purity, which correspond to the varying levels of holiness. First, the Mishnah presents the necessary conditions for achieving each level of purity (m. Hag. 2:6):

> If one bathed for unconsecrated food, and is held to be fit for [Heb., *huhzak*] unconsecrated food, he is prohibited from partaking of second tithe.
>
> If one bathed for second tithe, and is held to be fit for second tithe, he is prohibited from partaking of terumah [heave offering].
>
> If one bathed for terumah, and is held to be fit for terumah, he is prohibited from partaking of hallowed things.
>
> If one bathed for hallowed things, and is held to be fit for hallowed things, he is prohibited from touching the waters of purification.
>
> If one bathed for something possessing a stricter [degree of sanctity], one is permitted [to have contact with] something possessing a lighter [degree of sanctity].
>
> If one bathed without being held to be fit, it is as though he has not bathed.

This mishnah teaches that immersing for one level of purity is insufficient purification for a higher level of purity and establishes two conditions for the achievement of a certain level of purity: (1) immersion for the sake of that same level of purity; (2) being "held [to be fit]" for that level. The commentators of this mishnah agree on the interpretation of these conditions, believing that one's level of purity is determined solely based on his own intentions at the time of immersion. Following the Talmuds, they understand that "held [to be fit]" (*muhzak*) signified the immerser's intention. This approach, in fact, can be identified already in the Tosefta, which interprets the mishnah as follows:

> If one bathed in order to rise from impurity to purity, he is pure for all.
> The bather—if he has the [proper] intention he is pure; if he does not, he is impure. But he who dunks his hands, either way, his hands are pure. (t. Ḥag. 3:1–2)

However, the common assumption that the level of purity depends solely on one's intention is hard to maintain. If the only condition for the determination of the level of a man's purity is his intention at the time of immersion, and he is free to choose as he wishes, how should we explain the gap between the different levels of purity? Should we assume that the decision during immersion influences the level of caution the immerser accepts on himself? Thus, for example, although those who partake of the priestly heave offering (terumah) and those who partake of sacrificial meat are both careful regarding contact with an impure person or a menstruant, we must assume that one who decided, at the time of immersion, to partake of sacrificial meat will be more careful to avoid indirect contact with the impurity of the eater of the priestly terumah. In light of this, it is clear why the Tosefta believes that a simple intention of purification aids all level of purity. However, this interpretation erases the complex set of differences between the two levels and leaves only a general requirement of intent.

Already, then, the Tosefta explained the term *held* in the mishnah as relating to intention. But actually this is never the meaning of the verb *to be held* (*huhzak*) in rabbinic literature. This verb is always linked to social recognition of one's personal status.[39] Remarkably, if we follow the usual meaning of this verb, we will arrive at a completely different understanding of the mishnah, which curiously lines up with the approach to purity that characterized the Jews of the Second Temple period. Presumably, since this approach was unfamiliar to later rabbis, they reinterpreted the mishnah. According to the original meaning of the mishnah, then, a person's immersion counts only if one is already "held," that is, already known publicly as one who observes that level of purity. A person who is "held" for eating ordinary food in purity, cannot partake of pure terumah even if one so desires. Furthermore, the mishnah in its final clause also says that one who is not "held" for anything—that is, one who is not known publicly to eat any of his foods in a state of purity—remains impure despite immersing himself and despite his desire to be purified. This person is "as though he has not bathed."

This interpretation of the mishnah has far-reaching implications. In opposition to the approach that claims that "rabbinic halakhah would undoubtedly permit an ʿam ha-ʾareṣ to eat with ḥaverim, provided that he was willing to undergo a ritual cleansing of his body and of his clothing,"[40] the mishnah in fact states that the am ha-aretz is not permitted to share in the associate's meal and to purify himself for that purpose. For "if one bathed without being held to be fit, it is as though he has not bathed"! In other words, one cannot be purified unless he is associated with those who eat in purity—or, to put it another way, unless he has ceased to be an am ha-aretz![41] Every person is held to be of a certain level of purity and remains at that level unless he has publicly joined one of the groups of pure persons mentioned in the mishnah: Pharisees, consumers of terumah, or consumers of hallowed things.

In fact, the following mishnah supports the same position: "the garments of an am ha-aretz possess *midras* uncleanness for Pharisees; the garments of Pharisees possess midras uncleanness for those who eat terumah," and so on. To maintain purity, one is inevitably required to be constantly aware of the purity status of those surrounding him. A person's group affiliation must be transparent. Otherwise, one is in constant doubt regarding whom he may be in contact with and the ramifications of his own contact for others. Clear group affiliation, which is determined by public awareness ("being held," hazaqah), is essential for regulating behavior in the social arena. Surprisingly, then, the notion of affiliation and the way in which it is presented in the Mishnah are quite close to the language of 1QS column 3.

Arguably, m. Hagigah 2:6 and 1QS 3:3–12, quoted previously, present the same concept, according to which outsiders are precluded from purification despite all their efforts! And in both sources, this stance is presented in rather sharp terms. Of those outside the community, 1QS states that they "shall not be purified by all the water of ablution"; in the Mishnah we hear that "if one bathed without being held to be fit, it is as though he has not bathed." These two statements reflect the same essential tradition, albeit couched in different terms and carrying a different ideological weight. According to both sources, the stated and recognized affiliation with the group of pure persons is a prerequisite for purification.[42] Both sources agree that there is no act of purification that stands alone, without a clearly defined group affiliation. Evidently, then, the source that is considered to most patently represent the unique association of sin and impurity in the worldview of Qumran is strongly tied to the early strata of the Mishnah and its approach toward outsider impurity.

Despite the ideological disparities between them, both texts share the notion that outsiders, by dint of their foreignness, are bound to be impure. In truth, this stance may take root within different worldviews. Alongside the strong claim that any outsider is a sinner and impure, for he does not act according to sectarian laws, a weaker version may claim that one must suspect the ability of the outsider to live a life of purity, for he does not act according to the purity practices of the Pharisees. Nonetheless, the structure of the claims is essentially identical, and despite the different overtones of the two sources, they share the basic view that purity is contingent on group affiliation and not on personal desire.

Arguably, the halakhic norm that distances the outsider from purification predated the ideological schism between the tradition of the Pharisees embedded in the Mishnah and the author of 1QS (supposedly sometime during the early Hasmonean period). Each of these groups assimilated the same principle of outsider impurity, whose early roots can be found in Ezra and Nehemiah, but it assumed a different meaning for each of the groups.

Hagigah 2:7: Relative Impurity

The notion that affiliation determines purification is also reflected in the principle of relative impurity. As we have seen, this idea appears in Josephus's description of the Essenes: "and so far are the juniors inferior to the seniors, that if by chance they touch them, they (the seniors) wash themselves, as if they had intermixed with a foreigner." According to this approach, the members of each group, including those who observe purity, defile the members of purer groups to the same degree. In other words, anyone who is outside of one's own circle is an absolute outsider, and there is no difference between a gentile and a younger member of the sect. This system therefore directly derives from the immanent impurity of the outsider, regardless of his specific level of purity observance. Here again we discover that the Pharisees share this approach, as evidenced in m. Hagigah 2:7:

> The garments of am ha-aretz possess midras uncleanness for the Pharisees;
>
> The garments of Pharisees possess midras uncleanness for those who eat terumah;
>
> The garments of those who eat terumah possess midras uncleanness for [those who eat] hallowed things;
>
> The garments of [those who eat] hallowed things possess midras uncleanness for [those who occupy themselves with the waters of] purification.

Yose b. Yo'ezer was the most pious in the priesthood, yet his napkin was [considered to possess] midras uncleanness for [those who ate] hallowed things.

Yohanan b. Gudgada used all his life to eat [unconsecrated food] in accordance with the purity required for hallowed things, yet his napkin was [considered to possess] midras uncleanness for [those who occupied themselves with the water of] purification.

According to this mishnah, all Jews on a lower level of purity share the same status. Their clothes are midras (i.e., a garment that conveys severe impurity even through indirect shifting) compared to those who are purer than them. In other words, the clothes of those in a lower level are treated as if they were defiled by indirect contact with a zav or with a menstruant, and these clothes defile others through physical contact. But why is everyone impure on the same level? How can one compare the impurity of an am ha-aretz to that of the Pharisee who keenly attempts to distance himself from any impurity and particularly from severe impurity? How can we explain this rigid model, which relates identically to all, from the am ha-aretz up to one who eats hallowed things? Commentators suggest that in all of these cases the purer individuals are concerned with the menstruation impurity of the wives of the less pure.[43] Such a concern accords well with the impurity of am ha-aretz, whose clothes carry midras impurity out of a fear that his wife touched them while menstruating. But this cannot be said of a Pharisee, even if he is not as strict as a priest. And what shall we say of a priest, who is clearly pure enough to partake of the holy terumah—how can his clothes be considered to possess midras impurity with regard to those who are purer than him? Evidently, the uniform rule—that the clothes of one who is less pure convey midras impurity to those who are more pure—blurs a complex reality in which different degrees of observance exist.

It appears, therefore, that Mishnah Hagigah chose one definition and applied it to the other cases, even if it does not necessarily line up with the actual diversity of purity observances. According to the Mishnah, am ha-aretz supplies a fixed model of separation, even for the higher levels of purity. Thus, from the perspective of one who is pure with regard to hallowed food, anyone outside his own group is like an am ha-aretz, and he must maintain the same degree of separation from all other Jews. This system creates a binary distinction between one's own group and all groups of lower purity. The Mishnah therefore reveals the same strain of thought that features in the description of the Essenes. Both traditions agree that anyone who is not in your circle is considered completely impure, regardless of their precise degree of purity observance.

Again we find that the different movements drew from a shared legal tradition while disputing its specific details. These differences between the practices of the Essenes, as documented by Josephus and Mishnah Hagigah, reflect the nuanced ideological distinctions between the two movements. According to Josephus, the young Essene defiles the more senior one as if he were a gentile. In Mishnah Hagigah, on the other hand, the impurity of the "other" is modeled after the am ha-aretz, rather than the gentile. This is a crucial distinction. The gentile defiles like a zav, who is considered a primary source of impurity,[44] whereas the am ha-aretz is only a carrier of impurity. He is defiled by his clothes, which convey midras impurity, but he himself is not considered to be a source of impurity.

Various rabbinic sources assume that the gentile defiles like a zav: "Even though they do not incur the impurity of zov, they are considered as impure as though they have experienced zov with regard to all things."[45] The meaning of this precept is that the gentile defiles both people and foods through indirect contact, even if they are contained in closed vessels. Furthermore, his saliva and urine also defile.[46] Due to this ruling one must always fear in an urban space lest he steps on the urine or saliva of a gentile.[47] Furthermore, if a gentile steps on one's clothes, they are also considered impure with midras impurity and, therefore, also defile the person wearing them.[48] These laws neatly align with the common conception that the body of the gentile was considered a source of impurity, and the genital discharge provides the ultimate model for a human bodily source of impurity.[49]

The rabbis do not consider the am ha-aretz, on the other hand, as a source of impurity but rather as a carrier of midras impurity. This means that his clothes defile foods and vessels only if they come in direct contact with them, and he defiles others only when he interacts with them in some significant way: for example, if he touches them directly, or if the majority of his body weight is on them, or if he moves them.[50] Unlike the gentile, who is impure like a zav and therefore defiles even through indirect shifting of an impure object, it is not enough to sit by an am ha-aretz on a bench to be defiled by his clothes. Accordingly, an associate may not host an am ha-aretz only if he is wearing his own clothing (m. Demai 2:3). The am ha-aretz leaves no imprints of impurity in the public space, and although his clothing transmits midras impurity, he is permitted to carry clay vessels containing pure foods, and even terumah.[51]

From a rabbinic perspective, while a gentile is considered a source of impurity, the Jewish outsider, modeled after am ha-aretz, is a perpetual carrier of impurity but not intrinsically impure. According to Essene law (following Josephus's testimony), any outsider is as impure as a gentile. It appears, therefore, that on this matter, too, rather than diametrically opposed perceptions of impurity, we encounter here two approaches that organize the difference between pure and impure according to the same principles but that lend different weight and content to these distinctions. In the social worldview of the period, there is only one group of pure people—that is, one's own group—whereas anyone outside it is completely impure. There is, however, a clear ideological difference between the Essenes and Qumran sectarians who take the gentile as the model of outsider impurity and the rabbis who model it after the am ha-aretz.

According to the Community Rule and the Essenes, the gentile is the model for outsider impurity. This is a distinctly sectarian perspective, which views the members of the sect alone as the "true Israel" and views all nonsectarians, who walk the path of evil, as outside the covenant, whether they be Jews or gentiles. The Pharisaic stance could not accept this approach wholesale, especially if we accept the sources which indicate the strong support for the Pharisees among the Judean population.[52] In this situation, the Pharisees avoided comparing their fellow Jews to gentiles, and therefore, two distinct statuses were created. While Jews commonly viewed gentiles as intrinsically impure (as we learn from the book of Acts), they only considered the actions of their fellow Jewish outsiders to be impure, as long as they chose not to join the circle of the pure.[53]

The Pharisaic Version of the Separation Tradition

Alongside laws that determine the degree of am ha-aretz impurity, there are also a few early laws incorporated in the rabbinic corpus that regulate social separation from them. On this matter, too, we can see that these directives are based on the same legal tradition that shaped the laws of separation from the gentiles in Jubilees as well as the prohibitions on contact with the men of injustice in the Community Rule. At the same time, as we have seen, the existence of a shared framework will emphasize the unique path chosen by Pharisaic law. This legal tradition replaced complete separation with intermediary practices, which were intended to ground the preferred status of the Pharisees and the associates without cutting them off from other Jews who were not stringent on matters of purity.

Mishnah Demai and Tosefta Demai list the forms of separation of the trustworthy "associate" from am ha-aretz. As we will see in chapter 6, each of these two sources assumes a different image of social relations between the stringent associates who observe purity and their surroundings. The difference between the two sources reflects a gradual decrease in social segregation during the second century and the rise of new forms of association. As we saw in the last section, in this case, too, the Tosefta represents a later halakhic discourse which was unfamiliar with the early social circumstances of purity observance. The regulations in Mishnah Demai 2:3, on the other hand, were known already to the Houses of Shammai and Hillel, and they fit in well with the tradition of separation found in Second Temple literature:

> If a person has taken upon himself to become an associate,
> he may not sell to an am ha-aretz either moist or dry [produce], nor may he buy from him moist [produce].
>
> He may not be the guest of an am ha-aretz, nor may he receive as guest an am ha-aretz who is wearing his own garments.

According to this fragment of early halakhah that was embedded in the Mishnah, an associate must not sell anything to an am ha-aretz, but may purchase from him dry food, which does not contract impurity; he must not be a guest in the home of an am ha-aretz but may host him as long as the am ha-aretz removes his clothes. These directives present a consistent approach to the am ha-aretz: one may enjoy the supply of am ha-aretz and draw him toward us, but one may not hand anything over to his possession or approach him. What is the meaning of this policy? How does it fit in with the general approach of the Pharisees regarding the impurity of am ha-aretz? To this set of prohibitions in Mishnah Demai, we must add a third one, on marrying the daughter of an am ha-aretz, which is formulated in similar language. The combination of these three prohibitions and their comparison to different versions of the laws of separation emanating from Ezra and Nehemiah reveal the Pharisaic reworking of this tradition. Tosefta Avodah Zarah 3:8–10 includes additional rulings regarding the permitted contact with am ha-aretz:

> <u>One may buy slaves from the 'am ha-aretz</u>—both mature and young, <u>and sell them slaves</u>—both mature and young.
>
> <u>One may take daughters from them</u>—young but not mature, the words of R. Meir. The rabbis say: even a mature girl, who accepts upon herself.
>
> <u>But he may not give them daughters</u>—neither mature nor young, the words of R. Meir. The rabbis say: he may give him a mature girl on condition that she not be required to prepare purities together with him. It happened that Rabban Gamaliel the Elder married his daughter to Shimon ben Netanel the priest and he stipulated with him that she would not be required to make purities together with him.[54]

According to the Tosefta, there is no limitation on the sale or buying of a slave to or from an am ha-aretz. Marriage between the groups, on the other hand, is a more complex issue. R. Meir and the rabbis dispute which of the daughters of ammei ha-aretz one may wed and whether the prohibition on marrying one's daughter to them is absolute. In both cases the issue troubling both sides is the observance of purity.[55] In the first dispute, the question arises of whether we can ascertain that the daughter of an am ha-aretz will change her behavior and begin observing the laws of purity, and in the second dispute, the question is how we will prevent a daughter of an associate from defiling pure foods in an am ha-aretz' home. The rabbis trust the woman's ability to maintain purity. The daughter of the am ha-aretz accepts the observance of purity-related practices on herself when marrying an associate, and the daughter of an associate who married an am ha-aretz does not have to deal with pure foods in the home of the am ha-aretz when there is a fear that they will be defiled. R. Meir, on the other hand, is more stringent and limits the possibility of intermarriage between associates and ammei ha-aretz. In his opinion, the daughters will not succeed in adjusting their behavior as necessary. The adult daughters of an am ha-aretz will not be able to accustom themselves to the new purity demands in the associate's house, and the am ha-aretz will expect the associate's daughter to prepare the pure foods in his house.

While the rabbis of the second century, R. Meir and the rabbis, dispute whether to include both young and adult daughters in each of the cases, both rely on a shared legal tradition: "One may take daughters from them, but he may not give them daughters." From the context of this dispute in Tosefta Avodah Zarah, we cannot know when this tradition was formulated, only that it precedes the activity of R. Meir and his colleagues (mid 2nd century CE). At the same time, when presented alongside those laws in Mishnah Demai regarding contact with the am ha-aretz, they reveal a consistent pattern. Although these three laws do not appear together, they are all phrased in a similar manner, in terms of both structure and content:

> He may not sell to an am ha-aretz either moist or dry [produce],
>> nor may he buy from him moist [produce].
>
> He may not be the guest of an am ha-aretz,
>> nor may he receive as guest an am ha-aretz who is wearing his own garment.
>
> <u>One may take daughters from them,</u>
>> <u>but he may not give them daughters</u>

The three rulings, the first two from m. Demai 2:3 and the last from t. Avodah Zarah 3:8, limit personal- and trade-related contact with am ha-aretz. Each of the rulings consists of two parallel units pertaining to the two sides of the relationship. Beyond the fixed phrasing, we can also identify a consistent asymmetrical approach: One may enjoy the services of am ha-aretz but may not hand him anything: he may not give him food, nor visit him, nor give him his daughter in marriage. As we can see, each of these three prohibitions is grounded in the early separationist tradition while at the same time reformulating it. Let us compare these laws to the obligation of separation in Jubilees and the prohibitions in the Community Rule that we have seen:

Jubilees 22	**4QS**
Separate yourself from the Gentiles,	to be separated from all the men of injustice …
and do not eat with them,	and he shall not eat with him in community.
and do not perform deeds like theirs.	Furthermore, no man of the men of the community shall give answer in accordance with their opinion relating to any Torah or judgment.
And do not become associates of theirs; …	Furthermore, he shall not be associated with him in possessions or in work, and no man of the men of holiness shall eat from their possessions nor take from their hand anything.
Be careful, my son Jacob, that you not take a wife from the seed of the daughters of Canaan.	

The concise instructions of Jubilees are described in detail in 4QS, apart from the marriage prohibition, which would not be relevant to the sectarian context. Members of the sect are prohibited from adopting the behavior of the men of injustice, niether fraternizing with them or joining them in business, and must not take anything from them, just as they may not take wives from among the Canaanites. The trio of tannaitic prohibitions that enforce separation from am-mei ha-aretz are parallel in content to the prohibitions that appear here: hosting ("do not become associates of theirs"), the taking of food ("and he shall not eat it with him in the community"), and marriage ("be careful that you not take a wife, etc."). Furthermore, Jubilees itself relies on Nehemiah 10:30–31, which places the separation from the peoples of the land at the center of the covenant to keep the law of Moses: "Join with their noble brothers, and take an oath with sanctions to follow the Teaching of God, given through Moses the servant of

God, and to observe carefully all the commandments of the Lord our Lord, His rules and laws. Namely: We will not give our daughters in marriage to the peoples of the land (ammei ha-aretz), or take their daughters for our sons." The essence of separation from the peoples of the land was therefore the commitment not to give them daughters in marriage or take their daughters in marriage.

The rabbinic law that forbids contact with am ha-aretz proffers a unique version of the marriage prohibition found in Nehemiah. The rabbinic law, of course, speaks of an am ha-aretz who is Jewish, unlike the peoples of the nations in Nehemiah, but the reliance of the rabbinic ruling ("One may take daughters from them, but he may not give them daughters") on the verses in Nehemiah is unmistakable. At the same time, during the process of adaptation of the Nehemiah proscription, and its transfer to an internal Jewish am ha-aretz, only half of the prohibition was preserved: as in Nehemiah, one may not give his daughter in marriage to an am ha-aretz, but he may marry his daughter. Subsequently, similarly to the partial revision of the marriage proscription, the additional features of separation—hosting and trade—were also adapted and reformulated in the same manner.

The result is a rich and complex picture of the development of the tradition of separation in Second Temple literature from the model suggested in Ezra and Nehemiah. The demands of separation from gentiles are detailed in Jubilees, and they were implemented during the Second Temple period toward other Jews as well, both in sectarian literature and in the Pharisaic tradition that is reflected in early tannaitic law. The book of Jubilees expanded the prohibition on marriage to gentiles in Nehemiah 10 to prohibitions on trade and social contact. This group of prohibitions served sectarian literature in determining the dimensions of separation from other Jews, whom they considered similar to gentiles. The textual comparison instructs us that the Pharisees were also partners in this exegetical and ideological tradition, and they, too, implemented the laws of separation, whose basis was the distancing from the impure nations of the land mentioned in Nehemiah, toward other Jews, whom they termed am ha-aretz. However, unlike the sectarian approach, which did not distinguish between gentiles and other Jews, the Pharisees established a nuanced gradation on this matter too, by implementing the separation laws only partially with regard to am ha-aretz. The Pharisaic policy revealed in the earliest layers of tannaitic literature established the realms of separation according to the same legal tradition, but at the same time it shifted the original intention of the text. Early rabbinic law replaced sweeping separation with unidirectional distancing, which allowed the Pharisees to establish a hierarchy of purity without demanding complete separation.

Conclusion

Palestinian Jews of the Second Temple period considered purity a privilege associated with group affiliation. Pure Jews were separate from impure gentiles, and the Qumran sectarians perceived all outsiders to be impure. The Pharisees also defined themselves in these terms while devising a relatively lenient form of separation for the achievement of purity. The various sources relating to am ha-aretz in tannaitic literature, against the background of their parallels in Second Temple literature, comprise a consistent picture, according to which early rabbinic law suggested a softened version of the separation tradition. This tradition stems from the notion of gentile impurity in Ezra and Nehemiah and continues with the book of Jubilees and sectarian law, which implemented this policy also toward fellow Jews. Early rabbinic traditions deal with the status of am ha-aretz within the same terminological framework, which may be termed "outsider impurity." At the same time, however, rabbinic sources systematically limited the severity of the prohibitions and offered interim legal categories, thereby limiting the severity of am ha-aretz impurity, as opposed to that of the gentile.[56]

The notion of outsider impurity received diverse interpretations by different groups, but all shared the notion that purification depended on recognized membership, as evident in Mishnah Hagigah 2:6–7. The difference between the sectarian approach and the Pharisaic approach related mainly to the level of impurity ascribed to those outsiders. Mishnah Demai 2:3, too, testifies to the correlation between social affiliation and purification. According to this mishnah, the associate who desired public recognition was required to limit his social and trade relations with ammei ha-aretz. At the same time, the reformulation of the instructions concerning hosting, eating, and marriage reveals the extent to which the separation tradition was reworked to establish an alternative relationship between the Pharisees and their impure surroundings.

Early rabbinic literature therefore preserves explicit expressions of the sectarian consciousness of the Pharisees, formulated through the prevalent language of outsider impurity. As opposed to attempts to describe the Pharisees as representing common practice, it is clear that purity served the Pharisees to delineate their social separateness. This consciousness did not prevent them from seeking to influence others or demanding that others observe certain purity practices, such as handwashing or separation from sources of impurity, but they did this from an elitist stance that was deeply rooted within a sectarian legal tradition and social worldview.

5

Inclusion and Marginalization

Introduction

Occasional contamination or contact with some impure person is practically unavoidable. Even the most diligent puritists are forced to contend with severe impurities that are part of the life cycle, such as contact with corpse impurity, experiencing genital discharges, or bleeding. Consequently, groups who sought to live a life of purity during the Second Temple period were compelled to create various mechanisms to enable routine day-to-day conduct and to provide standard solutions for contact with impurity in a variety of anticipated, ordinary situations. Thus, even the most stringent communities, such as the members of the community of Qumran, strove to contain impurity, to the extent possible, and to enable their members to avoid a state of constant tension or fear of contamination.

As we have seen in previous chapters, the Pharisees provided a complex set of solutions to maintain a pure sphere within impure surroundings. However, Qumran sectarians also had to address the inevitable presence of impurity in their midst. In fact, despite the added stringency of the Qumran sect and their puritist image, they too did not attempt to function within a sterile environment. Controlling the spread of impurity, alongside an acknowledgment of its unavoidable presence, stood at the heart of the halakhic discourse of the time, both among the Pharisees and the members of the Qumran Community.[1] Against the background of this shared challenge, I would like to reevaluate the differences between Qumran law and Pharisaic purity policies as reflected in the teachings of the early rabbis. I shall show that the two legal systems have in common a shared halakhic discourse and principles but that each group implemented them according to its own worldview. While the Pharisees allowed a flexible and simple transition from impurity to purity, Qumran law created a strict system of gradual purification that required constant awareness of purity at all times. By uncovering the shared halakhic infrastructure, we may come to appreciate another facet of the inclusive social policy of the Pharisees.

Graded Purification

Scholars dispute whether Qumran law, like the rabbis, acknowledged the intermediate status of the tevul yom, that is to say, one who has performed ritual immersion but has not completed the course of purification.[2] In this section, I argue that although Qumran law dismissed the role of immersion on the last day of the purification procedure, it too shared the concept of gradual purification, which it incorporated in a different form. This halakhic dispute had far-reaching implications on the organization and management of communal relations.

Scripture prescribes different protocols of purification, but the relationship between these procedures is unclear.[3] With respect to short, one-day impurities, such as one who touches the bed of the zava, the Torah rules that he "wash his clothes, bathe in water and remain unclean until the evening."[4] In contrast, in cases of a full week of impurity, such as in the case of the zav or zava themselves, the Torah only mentions the period of impurity, but does not refer to the completion of the process in the evening. This is most evident with respect to the zav: "When one with a discharge becomes clean of his discharge, he shall count off seven days for his cleansing, wash his clothes, and bathe his body in fresh water, then he shall be clean."[5] Presumably, bathing on the seventh day is enough to complete the purification process. It is possible to resolve this discrepancy in two opposing ways, each of which was adopted by one of the halakhic systems of the Second Temple period. One homogenizing possibility is to assume that in both one-day and seven-day purifications the process is completed only at evening.[6] Another possibility is to distinguish between two levels of purification, before and after sunset.[7] While the latter position appears explicitly in rabbinic sources and seems to reflect earlier Pharisaic positions, Qumran sources reflect the former option. As we shall see, this exegetical decision had wider implications for their respective policies.

According to the rabbinic stance, those who immerse cease to defile others and are permitted to partake of ordinary food, but they still defile the terumah (heave offering) or sacrificial foods. Thus, for instance, a zav who had counted seven "clean" days following the cessation of discharge, could partake of unconsecrated pure food after immersion on the seventh day of his purification process.[8] Similarly, one who had experienced a seminal emission, whose impurity lasts only one day, could immerse immediately and be pure for the consumption of unconsecrated food. But a priest who had immersed was still required to wait until nightfall before partaking of the terumah (m. Ber. 1:1). This exegetical approach follows the purification process of the woman who has given birth (Lev. 12:1–5). After her initial period of impurity, one week if she has given birth to a male and two if she has birthed a female, she immerses and enters a period during which she is basically pure but is still forbidden to come in contact with holy foods.[9] In this situation, although the woman is not pure with regard to hallowed things, she may return to regular activity in the domestic sphere. Similarly, one who has immersed on the seventh day of his purification but has not yet completed the process by waiting for evening is a tevul yom, who is permitted to partake of unconsecrated food, but defiles holy foodstuff

The rabbinic category of tevul yom was arguably already known in the Temple period and was a topic of dispute among the Pharisees and the Sadducees. The Mishnah says that a tevul yom priest prepared the red heifer, in opposition to the Sadducean stance. The Tosefta illustrates this with a story about R. Yohanan b. Zakkai, who defiled the Sadducee high priest through touch and then demanded of him that he immerse and burn the heifer immediately, ensuring that he would be only a tevul yom while burning the heifer.[10] In contrast, 4QMMT emphasizes that with regard to the red heifer: "all these (who deal with the red heifer) ought to be pure at sun[se]t, so that a pure man sprinkles the impure."[11] In accordance with their halakhic stance, the sectarians required "a man who was pure of any impurity,"[12] arguing that one was rendered pure only after sunset and that immersion was insufficient. Considering the polemical nature of the 4QMMT, it seems clear that they were rejecting a more lenient position, such as was held by the Pharisees.[13] The question remains, however, whether the Qumran sectarians acknowledged the purity status of the tevul yom but required a higher degree of purification, or they simply did not consider the tevul yom to be pure at all?[14]

The wording of 4QMMT seems to point toward the latter option. Furthermore, additional sources imply that Qumran law did not admit to the intermediary status of the tevul yom. These sources emphasize the fact that purity is always dependent on completing the period of purification by waiting for sunset. In general, as Martha Himmelfarb has observed, these sources follow the language of the Torah on these points. However, some of the reformulations indicate that the full procedure is necessary for any form of purity, as may be inferred from the Temple Scroll (11QT 49:20–21), according to which sunset following the seventh-day ablution is a prerequisite for contact with *any* type of pure object. On the other hand, there is no positive indication that immersion itself on the last day could provide access to any sort of purity.[15]

Upon first glance, then, there appears to be a fundamental dispute concerning the possibility of gradual purification. A closer look, however, reveals a high degree of resemblance between the approaches of the different communities. Qumran law, too, acknowledged the existence of a graded process of purification which began with immersion. In fact, both groups adopted parallel mechanisms that enabled the inclusion of impure persons in the community to some degree even before the completion of their purification process. The difference between the two was in the ways that they implemented this mechanism, so as to reflect their distinct approaches toward purity observance. As in the previous chapter, while the Pharisees shared some basic principles with sectarian law, they adjusted this infrastructure to a more inclusive policy.

In a series of articles, Jacob Milgrom pointed out that Qumran law added an immersion immediately following contact with a source of impurity.[16] Regarding corpse impurity, the Temple Scroll tells us: "and everyone who come to the house shall bathe in water and wash his clothes the first day" (49:16–17). And regarding one who has had a seminal emission: "And the m[an] who has had a nocturnal emission shall not enter the whole Temple until three days have [pa]ssed. He shall wash his clothes and shall bathe on the first day, and on the th[i]rd day he shall wash his clothes and bathe; and after the sun has set he shall enter the Temple" (45:7–10). According to Milgrom, the third-day ablution was intended only for Jerusalem, and therefore, the addition of the first-day ablution provided the minimal level of purity required for daily conduct. He surmises that similar to the leper who returns to the camp after washing (Lev. 14:8), the removal of this initial degree of impurity immediately upon contracting it was sufficient to enable one to return home.

Particularly significant for the reconstruction of the purification process in Qumran is 4Q514 I 1 7–9, concerning the zav, to which Milgrom dedicated a few discussions: "(7) No one may eat who is yet in his primary uncleanness, who has not begun to be clean from his seminal flow. (8) Indeed, no one who is yet in his primary uncleanness may eat. All of those who are [un]clean of days, on the day of (9) their pu[rification] they shall bathe and wash in water and they shall be clean. Afterwards they may eat their bread according to the or[dinance]."[17]

Anyone with an abnormal flow from his genitals is required to immerse immediately after the discharge ends ("on their day of purification," see Lev.

15:13) and only then is permitted to eat. The text does not mention pure foods, and it therefore seems, as Milgrom concludes, that he must abstain from any kind of food until he bathes.[18] At this stage, he is still required to count seven days until he completes his purification on the last evening, but the first-day ablution allows him to eat again. This reminds us of Philo, who says that partners must distance themselves from contact with anything after they have had sexual relations until they purify themselves.[19] In this situation, eating is also forbidden until after the bathing has taken place.

We see, then, how Qumran law created some form of a gradual procedure. But how similar, in fact, are the Pharisaic tevul yom status and the "first-day ablution" of Qumran law? Notably, each approach promoted a different immersion, and these advance the process in different ways.[20] In Qumran, one must immerse immediately following detachment from the source of impurity. According to the Pharisees, on the other hand, one does not immerse immediately after the discharge ends (although it may have been a popular practice), but only on the final day of the waiting period. We can see, therefore, that the two groups do not dispute the possibility of partial purification. Each group utilizes the mechanism of initial purification. At the same time, the subtle differences between the two mechanisms, which at first glance appear to be purely technical, are indicators of the ideological gap between the two groups. The different position of this immersion alters the nature of the purification process.

As opposed to the status of tevul yom in the Pharisaic tradition, the first-day ablution in sectarian law does not purify the person. While the impure person has removed the source of impurity, and subsequently ceases to defile his surroundings, he is not pure at this stage and is still forbidden to approach any type of pure food until the culmination of the period of purification. The prohibition on eating before the first-day ablution is not intended to protect the food from the impurity of the purifier—who is still forbidden to consume pure foods even after immersion—but is a type of sanction that forces the purifier to distance himself from the source of impurity. Presumably, the purifier would be compelled to eat defiled food at this stage and would only partake of pure foods after the purification process was completed, with the sunset of the final day.[21]

According to the Pharisees, on the other hand, immersion takes place only as one approaches complete purification on the final day. Accordingly, not only does one cease to defile his surroundings following immersion, this immersion even enables him to be completely pure for certain matters. Only the Pharisees view immersion before the completion of the purification period as sufficient for one to be considered pure and eat unconsecrated food in purity.

From a different perspective, the Qumran "first-day ablution" creates an intermediate status. According to the Pharisees, the "final day ablution" distinguishes between a long period of complete impurity and a new status of purity with regard to unconsecrated foods. Thus, the Pharisees enable a person to remain impure and transform his status only toward the end of the process. Consequently, during this entire period one can act without fear of contracting impurity. It is only when one decides to immerse in preparation for the end of the purification period that he must be careful with regard to impurity. The transition is complete and, ultimately, depends solely on one's choice.

Qumran law on the other hand demands a gradual process of reintegration. During the intermediate period one must be careful of direct contact with impurity while at the same time also distance oneself from pure persons whom he might defile. This approach reflects the assumption that even one who is not yet pure is subject to strict purity regulations until his purification process is completed (see the following section). This policy created an extended process of social reintegration, as opposed to the Pharisaic stance, which enabled one to remain impure and to choose the moment at which he wished to exit this state.

The Levels of Impurity: Structural Parallels and Differences in Details

As we saw, the differences between the Pharisaic tevul yom and the sectarian "first-day ablution" indicate different perceptions of the purification process: Is there an obligation to be purified, and subsequently what is the social status of one who is still undergoing purification? A close comparison between the two systems will reveal additional tendencies and fundamental disputes between the two purity doctrines.

According to the tannaitic system, the process of purification is accomplished in three stages, each of which elevates one to a higher level of purity:

(1) following immersion on the last day, one is considered pure for the consumption of unconsecrated food (tevul yom);
(2) at the end of the day, one is considered pure for the consumption of the terumah;[22]
(3) in bodily impurities, such a zav or zava the bringing of sacrifices on the following day is a condition for partaking of consecrated food.[23]

This system, to which already the early rabbis allude, is perplexing.[24] The Torah provides no basis for this tripartite division and for the distinction between the level of purity required for the consumption of the terumah and of consecrated foods. The biblical system presents only two levels of purity and periods of purification: one for consumption of ḥullin, unconsecrated foods, and the other for consumption of consecrated foods (Lev. 12:1–5). Second Temple sources as well as archaeological findings maintain the biblical division of two levels of purity.[25] In this vein, Qumran literature distinguishes only between "ordinary purity" and "purity for hallowed things."[26]

Upon first glance, it appears that there is an unbridgeable gap between the binary system of the Bible and Qumran law, on the one hand, and the three levels of purity described in tannaitic literature, on the other: purity for unconsecrated food, purity for the terumah, and purity for hallowed things. One gets the impression that the rabbis appended an additional level of purity and created artificial distinctions between different types of food. However, a closer look reveals that the tannaitic system in fact reflects the same structural framework as in Qumran law. The correspondence is evident in the following table:

	Tannaitic Law	**Qumran Law**
First Immersion[27]	Pure for the consumption of unconsecrated meat and tithes[28]	Permitted to eat
Sunset on the Final Day of Purification	Pure for the consumption of the terumah	Ordinary purity
Sacrifices on the Eighth Day	Pure for hallowed things	Pure for hallowed things

One can see from this table that the two halakhic approaches reflect a shared structure. In rabbinic law, however, the details are consistently implemented in a more lenient manner for both the consumers of unconsecrated foods and of the terumah. On one level, the leniency regarding the terumah serves a practical need. A priest who experiences a period of zov, or the wife of a priest who has given birth and is interested in eating with her husband, will always be able to partake of the terumah, even if they are far from Jerusalem. Full function in purity, including the purity of terumah consumption, is not dependent on proximity to the Temple or on sacrifices. Even priests can live a full life of purity without visiting the Temple in Jerusalem. Only those coming to Jerusalem in any case and are interested in consuming sacrificial meat (which is anyhow only consumed in Jerusalem) must bring the purifying sacrifices. In other words, unlike the biblical scheme, where the people of Israel live around the Tabernacle and therefore must strictly observe the laws of purity, this ruling enables management of purity while distant from the Temple, and even partaking of the daily priestly food independently of the Temple.[29]

On another level, this parallel structure discloses the differences of approach toward the nature of purity observance beyond the holy realm. As we have seen, according to rabbinic exegesis, the full process of purification, including sunset of the seventh day, relates specifically to the consumption of the terumah, and not to those who partake of unconsecrated foods, as it is understood in sectarian literature. Vered Noam has already noted this rabbinic tendency: while promoting the purity of unconsecrated food, they associated the biblical instructions of purification particularly with the holy realm.[30] Qumran law, on the other hand, required the full purification process for any kind of pure food. This distinction has an additional, but no less significant aspect, regarding the purpose of eating daily food in a state of purity in each of the legal systems. According to Qumran exegesis, the obligation to eat ordinary foods in purity is part of the general concern for the holiness of the camp. In accordance with the biblical model of the Israelite camp, anyone residing around the Tabernacle is required to observe purity to secure the hallowed realm in their midst. They are all part of the same ecological system of holiness and purity. The daily foods in Qumran, even if not consecrated, are close to being considered as such.[31]

The Pharisaic approach is based on a different understanding of purity, as we have seen in the previous chapters. The Pharisees' desire to distance impurity from their own foods was not based on its association with the holy realm. Rather, it expressed an independent motivation to maintain the inner purity of their selves. According to this approach, it is sufficient to remove impurity from the body by immersion to eat unconsecrated foods. Admittedly, this procedure is hardly enough to allow one to approach the Temple, but it is sufficient to consider oneself pure. This purity of the self has a standing of its own, outside the holy realm. This Pharisaic system reshaped the legal tradition to create an independent form of mundane purification.

The Double Challenge of the Purification Process

Qumran law requires one to immerse immediately upon cleansing oneself from the source of the impurity. Following this immersion, one is still not permitted to come into contact with pure food and therefore unable to participate in sectarian meals. But at the same time this person is not allowed to come in contact with impure things. Due to this complex situation, much of the legal instructions in Qumran literature is dedicated to providing guidance for those in this intermediate period. The status of both impure people and those who completed their process of purification was straightforward. Those who suffered impurity were isolated and those who were already pure were admitted back into the community. By contrast, the intermediate period required a dual effort. It is not surprising, therefore, that a significant portion of sectarian laws of purity is devoted to defining the restrictions imposed during the period of purification, as well as the process of reintegration from the margins back into the community. In what follows, I examine two texts. The first (4Q274 1 i) relates to the management of social contacts during this stage, and the other from the Temple Scroll concerns contact with foods and vessels (11QT 49:2–11).

Against the background of the numerous laws on this topic in Qumran literature, the complete disregard for this intermediate stage in the Pharisaic tradition and in rabbinic law is striking. In this tradition, which dismisses the demand for immediate immersion, one remains completely impure until the end of the purification process, and the purifier is released from observing any form of purity during this period. Furthermore, even the available parallels between the legal systems indicate their distinct tendencies. Both Qumran law and the teachings of the Houses of Shammai and Hillel deal with the possibility of incorporating those with minor impurities in agricultural activity, and they even discuss similar cases, which betray their shared legal discourse. At the same time, this comparison, to which we will turn in the latter part of this chapter, highlights the flexibility and leniency of Pharisaic law, which substituted the rigid social marginality of the impure with minimal gestures of intermediate impurity that could be easily and immediately removed. Thus, early rabbinic law maintained the principle of early purity laws, while ensuring that minor impurity did not affect the person's status or his social integration.

Contact between Impure Persons

The intermediate level of purity is discussed in detail in 4QTohorot^a (4Q274 1 i).[32] This fragment, which deals with the contact between different categories of impure persons—the leper, the zav, and the menstruant—has garnered much attention from scholars, who have identified in it a unique image of purity. But, as I now show, it primarily reveals the practical mechanisms through which the members of the sect sought to contain the presence of those who had not completed their process of purification.

> (4) And the woman discharging blood for seven days shall not touch the man discharging or any utensil [t]hat the man discharging has touched or lain (5) on or that he has sat on. And if she touched, she shall launder her clothes and bathe, and afterwards she may eat. And with all her strength she shall not mingle during her seven (6) days in order n[o]t to defile the ca[m]ps of sanctities of Israel, and also, she shall not touch any woman [discharg]ing blood for man[y] days.

(7) And the one who counts, whether male or female, shall not tou[ch the man discharging his dischar]ge (or) the menstruant in her bleeding unless she is pure from her bleeding, for behold, (8) the bleeding blood is considered like a discharge [to] the one touching it.

And [anyo]ne who touches a person from all (9) these unclean ones during the seven days of [his] puri[fication] shall [no]t eat, as if he were defiled by [a human cor]pse, [and he shall b]athe and wash (his clothes) and afterwar[d] (Col ii 1 1) he shall e[at.]

The section begins with reference to the menstruant, who is forbidden to touch a zav and "any woman [with a discharge] of blood of seve[ral] days." Next, the "one who counts," that is, he who is counting seven days from the cessation of his discharge until his purification (Lev. 15:13), is forbidden to come into contact with other impure persons.

Upon first glance, these rulings suggest a surprising approach. While the rabbis attributed equal defiling power to the zav and the menstruant and do not forbid contact between them,[33] here they are distanced from one another. In general, the prohibition against contact between impure persons is absent from Talmudic literature, and this would appear to reflect different conceptions of impurity. According to Milgrom, the laws in this passage from Qumran derive from their dynamic, and even demonic, understanding of impurity. Each impure person is controlled by a separate demonic power. Therefore, the menstruant must distance herself from the impurity of the zav, even if she is already impure. According to the rabbis, however, impurity is a legal status that is unthreatened by autonomous forces.[34] In my view, while Qumran law is clearly distinct from the rabbis' approach, it is not the result of some ontological difference. As we will see, the policy of Qumran law derives directly from the creation of an intermediate status during the period of purification. While Pharisaic law canceled this stage, according to Qumran law one is subject during this time period to a complex system of distancing from both the impure and the pure.

The details of the passage illuminate the complex observance of purity during the period of purification. According to lines 7–8, although those "who count" have not yet completed their process of purification, they are forbidden to come into contact with the source of the impurity itself—the genital discharge, the menstruant's blood, and the seminal emission. When those who count, having already undergone the initial purification, touch these impurities, their condition worsens, and they are again forbidden to eat until he has immersed.[35] The discharges that emit from the menstruant's or the zav's body contaminates the person who has begun the purification process and has already removed the source of impurity.

The Complex Status of the Menstruant

The distinction between one who still carries the impure substance and one who has removed the source of impurity and must keep away from it also aids us in clarifying the distinction between a menstruant and a zava, who is "discharging blood for many days." How can we explain the fact that the menstruant is forbidden to come into contact with the zav or his vessels (line 4), as well as with the zava (line 6)? Why is the impurity of the menstruant lighter than that of the zav and zava? As we saw, the level of impurity is dependent on the actual presence of an impure substance on the person. This also explains why the menstruant's impurity is lighter than that of the zav, although—as line 8 implies—the impurity of the discharged substance itself (blood, semen, and irregular discharge) is the same.[36] The physical situation of the menstruant distinguishes her from the zava and places her in an intermediate status. Although she is considered impure for seven days from the beginning of her bleeding, during a significant portion of this time she is not actively bleeding and does not carry the source of her impurity.[37] In some sense, then, during the first part of the week the menstruant is similar to a person who is suffering genital discharge, whereas during the latter part of the week she is similar to one who has cleansed himself of the source of impurity. Although no survey of menstrual law has survived from Qumran literature, from this passage it appears that the menstruant is somewhere in between a bleeding zava and one who counts to her purification.

Other legal traditions divide the menstrual period into two periods as well. Samaritan halakhah distinguished between two levels of basic impurity: the *niddah*, whose impurity is severe and who is distanced, and the *dawah*, whose impurity is light.[38] The niddah condition is caused by the initial bleeding, the source of the severe impurity, which defiles anything the woman comes into contact with for seven days. Therefore, the first obligation of the woman is to cleanse herself of the initial blood, thus preventing continued defilement. After removing this blood, the woman is in a status of minor impurity, dawah. Samaritan halakhah teaches that even if the menstruant continues bleeding throughout that week, she only transmits a minor impurity to people and vessels, which is removable through washing or wiping. According to the Samaritan stance, the distinction between the two types of bleeding explains the fact that the woman completes her purification within one week. The initial blood imparts a week of impurity, and it is the source of impurity, but after it is removed, the impurity of the blood she experiences on following days is less severe; therefore, even if a woman bleeds for seven days, she may immerse on the evening of the seventh day.[39] This is also the approach of Karaite halakhah, which distinguishes between "first blood" and "second blood." The seven-day impurity derives from the first blood. The vessels on which a menstruant sat during her initial bleeding are defiled with seven-day impurity, and a man who has relations with a menstruant is impure for seven days if he lay with her during this initial period. The woman must cleanse herself of this blood, and then the impurity she imparts lasts only until nightfall.[40]

In light of these approaches, we can better appreciate the complex status of the menstruant according to Qumran law. On the one hand, the menstruant is required to distance herself from the rest of the community, for fear she will transmit impurity to her surroundings. On the other hand, the passage warns the menstruant to refrain from contact with a zava, who is continuously discharging blood. The menstruant is apparently allowed to mingle with other people, but she must take care not to defile her surroundings. In addition, those who are counting seven days toward their purity are forbidden to come in to contact with the menstruant. In contrast, people who are experiencing unusual discharges are not warned to refrain from contact with others, as they are anyhow distanced from the city.

These laws reflect a reality in which both those who count and the menstruants are allowed into the community. In this situation, particularly because their level of impurity is low, there is fear that they might come into contact with each other. At the same time, the menstruant might be outside the camp alongside *zavim* and is perhaps even encouraged to be there, to limit the fear that she "defile the ca[m]ps of sanctities of Israel" (line 6). She is, however, warned to avoid contact with the zavim, for she will not be able to complete her days of purification if she is not careful to distance herself from the source of impurity. The menstruant might be found in both places and must be careful to abstain from physical contact with both the inside and the outside group.

This fragment from Qumran delineates ways for maintaining purity while at the same time associating with others who are still undergoing purification. The governing principle is that impure people defile their surroundings only when carrying the impure substance. Thus, even people who have not completed their purification process must refrain from direct contact with this source of impurity and its carriers. We are thus faced with a complex situation, in which the pure individual, the person who is counting toward purity, and the menstruant all operate in the same sphere but are limited in terms of contact.

The intermediate stage of purification thus poses challenges, which require sophisticated mechanisms of distancing and social control.

Distancing the Menstruant in Nonsectarian Sources

Sectarian literature is consistent in its strict demand to separate the menstruant. As in 4Q274, the Temple Scroll also locates the menstruant alongside the zav outside the cities: "And in every city you shall make places for those contaminated with leprosy, and with sores and with scabies, so that they do not enter your cities and defile them; and also for those who have a flux and for women when they are in their menstrual impurity and after giving birth, so that they do not defile in their midst with their menstrual impurity" (11QT 48:14–17). This source accords with the assumption that the menstruant was distanced out of the city together with the zavim for at least part of the week.

Nonsectarian sources, on the other hand, are content with a more modest form of separation within the city. Thus, Josephus writes: "He [Moses] expelled from the city both those whose bodies were attacked by leprosy and those with spermatorrhoea. He segregated until the seventh-day women whose secretion occurs for them in accordance with nature, after which he permitted them, as already pure, to associate with the community."[41] As opposed to the zav, the menstruant is not banned from the city but only distanced from the shared domicile until the seventh day. Josephus also does not distinguish between different stages of menstrual impurity, as in Qumran law, and the menstruant lives in some form of separation in the house for all seven days. A similar testimony as to the common form of distancing during the Second Temple period is implied from tannaitic literature as well. With respect to a dispute between the Houses of Hillel and Shammai concerning table fellowship, R. Shimon b. Eleazar, who lives at the beginning of third century, comments: "Come and see how purity spreads!.... The previous generations would not eat with menstruating women."[42] Unlike the norm during the late tannaitic period, the early observance of eating in purity included distancing the menstruant from eating with others. Similarly, there is evidence that special beds were given to menstruants so that they would not defile the regular furniture in the house.[43] Evidently, then, the menstruants were not sent outside the city or outside their homes[44] but rather had a place within the regular order of the house, with separation enforced for eating and sleeping.

In this situation, was there any point in distinguishing between different stages of menstrual impurity and easing contact following the first few days? It is not coincidental that Pharisaic tradition, which was lenient regarding menstrual impurity to begin with, did not care to develop a distinction between the stages of menstrual impurity. This accords well also with the absence of "first-day ablution" in Pharisaic tradition. According to m. Zavim 5:10, unlike the extended process the leper undergoes, in the case of the zav there is no difference between the days of discharge and the seven days following. The same is true for the zava and for the menstruant, where we find no reference to an intermediate stage of impurity during the period of purification.[45] This is the spirit in which we should understand R. Akiva's determination, "'And she who is in menstrual infirmity': She shall remain in her menstruation until she immerses in water."[46] In other words, the same level of impurity applies for all days of menstrual impurity until the final immersion.

It appears, therefore, that the fact that rabbinic law did not develop a distinction between the different stages of menstrual impurity, as opposed to other halakhic approaches, which demanded a graded process of purification, reflects an ideological stance. According to this approach, the woman's impure status was tolerable and could be maintained until she chose to immerse, and she was released from the severe restrictions tied to the gradual purification procedure. In contrast to Qumran law, this Pharisaic-rabbinic tradition did not take advantage of the exegetical possibility of distinguishing between the actual presence of the impure substance and the process of cleansing and purification, with regard to both the zav and the menstruant.[47] Rabbinic law did not demand the distancing of impure persons from the city or the community at any point. At the same time, delaying the immersion to the final day, or even later, canceled the role of the purification process as a period of living on the margins of the community, as structured by the sectarian policy.

Liquids and the Spread of Corpse Impurity

The creation of an intermediate stage in Qumran law, unfamiliar in Pharisaic tradition, entailed a dual obligation. The members undergoing purification from various bodily discharges were not allowed to touch pure members, but at the same time, they were required to maintain a basic level of purity and distance themselves from sources of impurity. Qumran law developed the same mechanism also with respect to corpse impurity. According to the Temple Scroll (11Q49:5–12),[48] whoever is exposed to corpse impurity must immerse immediately (the "first-day ablution"), upon which they cease to defile their surroundings. This immersion, like the cessation of bodily discharge, allows the impure person to eat and prevents the further spread of impurity. At the same time, however, in the case of corpse impurity, unlike the menstruant and the zav, this intermediate stage, which extends until the priest sprinkles the lustration waters mixed with the ashes of the red heifer, can last a long time. From the Temple Scroll it appears that people would regularly remain in this intermediate stage, and therefore, special guidance is required regarding proper behavior during this extended period. As we see, a central characteristic of purity observance during this intermediate stage is distancing from liquids, which can awake the dormant impurity of this situation.

Here is the full unit concerning corpse impurity:

> (5) If a person dies in your cities, the whole house in which the deceased dies shall be unclean (6) for seven days; everything there is in the house and everything which goes into the house shall be unclean (7) for seven days; and all food over which wa[t]er is spilt shall be unclean; every drink (8) shall be unclean; and the clay vessels shall be unclean and everything there is in them shall be unclean for every pure person; (9) and the open (vessels) shall be unclean for every person of Israel, all the drink (10) that is in them. *vacat*
>
> (11) And the day on which they remove the dead person from it, they shall cleanse the house of every (12) stain of oil, and wine, and dampness from water; they shall rub its floor, and its walls and its doors; (13) with water they shall wash its hinges, and its jambs, and its thresholds and its lintels. The day on which (14) the dead person is brought out from it, they shall cleanse the house and all its utensils, the mills, and the mortar, (15) and all the utensils of wood, iron and bronze, and all the utensils for which there is purity. (16) And they shall wash the clothes, the sacks and the skins. And the person: everyone who was in the house (17) and everyone who come to the house shall bathe in water and wash his clothes the first day. (18) And on the third day they shall sprinkle over them the waters of purification, and they shall bathe and wash their clothes (19) and the utensils which are in the house. *vacat*
>
> And on the seventh day (20) they shall sprinkle a second time, and they shall bathe and wash their clothes and their utensils. And they shall be clean by the evening (21) from the dead person, so that they can approach all their pure things. And the person who were not contaminated by [the dead].

Commentators have debated the exact meaning of the difficult rulings in lines 7–10. These lines distinguish between two groups of people. The text refers both to vessels that serve "every pure person" and to vessel impurity "for every person of Israel." For a pure person, the contents of the vessels are contaminated even if the vessels are sealed, whereas only open vessels are defiled for all of Israel. This raises two questions: First, what is the basis for extra stringency regarding the content of closed vessels, while the Torah explicitly deems sealed vessels to be pure (Num. 19:15)? And second, who are the two groups mentioned in the Temple Scroll?

According to Yigael Yadin, the Temple Scroll here distinguishes between those who are stringent regarding purity and those who are not, similar to the rabbinic distinction between the associate and am ha-aretz.[49] Alongside the instructions directed at the pure, the scroll adds a system of purity laws directed at those who are lax with respect to purity observance. Noam, on the other hand, has suggested that certain groups accepted on themselves extra stringencies, and according to them, even foods found in sealed vessels contracted corpse impurity.[50] The few who adopted this stringent practice are those termed "every pure person" in the Temple Scroll. Noam does not provide a clear source for this practice, but she surmises that it is based on an ancient pietist tradition lacking a biblical foundation. Both approaches, however, assume that the Temple Scroll is relating to nonscriptural practices that are uncharacteristic of Qumran legal policy.[51]

Unlike Yadin and Noam, I suggest interpreting these laws and the reference to two levels of purity directly on the basis of the biblical verses themselves, as these were interpreted by the authors of the Temple Scroll. The dual ruling in the Temple Scroll, I believe, responds to an exegetical tension found already in scripture regarding the way in which clay vessels are defiled. The two levels of impurity, according to the reading of the author of the Temple Scroll, correspond to the different modes of contamination that appear in the Torah. There is no extra stringency, as Noam posits, or testimony to lack of observance of purity law, as Yadin suggests,[52] but rather two levels that are an inherent feature of any purification process: during purification and after its completion. People in both stages are required to distance themselves from impurity, but to differing degrees.

First, we must note that it is unclear how clay vessels are defiled according to the biblical sources. According to Leviticus 11:33, in the case of a creeping thing, the clay vessel is defiled from within; similarly, in the case of corpse impurity (Num. 19:15), a closed vessel does not contract impurity. According to Leviticus 15:15, however, the clay vessel contracts impurity also externally, and not only from within, and this mode of contamination is also mentioned regarding an oven in Leviticus 11:35. Rabbinic law distinguishes between clay vessels and other vessels. Clay vessels do not contract impurity from outside contact, but only from their inside. The presence of a creeping thing in the vessel, even if there has been no direct contact, defiles the vessel and its contents. Other vessels, on the other hand, are defiled only by direct contact, whether internal or external.[53] According to this approach, the creeping thing defiles a clay oven, as well as the food and drink inside it, only from within (as opposed to the plain meaning of the verse!). The Temple Scroll, on the other hand, suggests a different solution to the tension between the verses, predicated on the existence of different levels of purity. Here again are the relevant rulings:

1. and the clay vessels shall be unclean
2. and everything there is in them shall be unclean **for every pure person**;
3. and the open (vessels) shall be unclean **for every person of Israel**, all the drink that is in them.

For a pure person, the vessels and their content are rendered impure even if they are sealed (line 2). For any other person of Israel, on the other hand, only open vessels and their contents are defiled (line 3). Note that, according to line 2, where the vessel contracts impurity through external touch, its entire contents are rendered impure. When the vessel contracts impurity through its opening (line 3), on the other hand, impurity passes only to liquids. How can this distinction be justified? It appears that the explanation lies in the difference between the two routes offered in the verses. On the one hand, a clay vessel may (in some cases) contract impurity through touch (following Leviticus 11:35) and is then completely defiled. On the other hand, the case in line 3 follows Leviticus 11:33: "as to any liquid that may be drunk, it shall become unclean if it was inside any vessel." Therefore, any open vessel is defiled if it has a liquid in it. To clarify the difference between the two routes, the author of the Temple Scroll distinguishes between two levels of purity: the vessels of the most pure are more sensitive to impurity and are defiled even when closed. The vessels of all of Israel, on the other hand, contract impurity only through direct contact with liquid carriers.

Who are these two groups, and from where does the author of the scroll derive the distinction between them? The solution for these questions can be found in the following lines. The end of this column mentions: (1) "the people who were not contaminated by [the dead]," alongside (2) the person who was contaminated by the dead and is in the process of purification. These two groups arguably correspond to the other pair mentioned a few lines earlier: "the pure person" and "every person of Israel." It appears that the author of the Temple Scroll distinguishes between two situations: the pure person is someone who "has not been contaminated by the dead," whereas one who has removed the corpse impurity through the first-day ablution is associated with "every person of Israel," who have not been sprinkled and have not yet completed their purification process.

The people who "have not been contaminated by the dead," are considered completely pure and must therefore avoid even indirect contact with corpse impurity. They cannot partake of food found even in a sealed vessel, which was only indirectly defiled by the corpse. "Every person of Israel," on the other hand, including those who have not yet completed their process of purification, must distance themselves only from that which was *directly defiled by the corpse*, such as open vessels with liquids that have absorbed the corpse impurity. A person who was in the house together with the corpse must remove the impure substance through the first-day ablution. Subsequently, he will refrain from partaking of anything that has come into direct contact with the corpse and has absorbed its impurity. Foods that were in closed vessels in the home in which the corpse was located, and were therefore not directly contaminated, however, are appropriate for his consumption.

We learn of the power of liquids to "absorb" corpse impurity from the subsequent lines. Concerning the purification of the house, it reads: "They shall cleanse the house of every / stain of oil, and wine, and dampness from water; they shall rub its floor, and its walls and its doors" (49:11–12). These liquids, which absorbed the impurity of the corpse, have soaked into the house, and one must remove and scrape them from all parts of the house, even those that do not themselves contract impurity, such as the floor and the walls.[54] The process of purification cannot begin before the corpse is removed and all traces of its impurity, remaining in liquids throughout the house, are removed. We learn more of the role of impure liquids from the parallel instructions in the Damascus Document (12:15–17): "And all the wood and the stones and the dust which are defiled by a person's impurity, while with stains of oil in them, in accordance with their uncleanness will make whoever touches them impure." This law appears to address a similar situation to the one we saw in the Temple Scroll. Therefore, anything that is in the house and has oil on it, even wood, stone, and dust, is contaminated.[55] Furthermore, according to the Damascus Document, "in accordance with their uncleanness will make whoever touches them impure." Due to their absorbing nature, liquids preserve the same degree of impurity, such that one who touches them will contract the same level of impurity, thus continuing to carry the source of impurity.[56]

If the walls have absorbed the impurity through its liquid carriers, the food found in the house in open vessels has likewise soaked up impurity. Dry foods contaminated with corpse impurity are forbidden for one who is completely pure. But those who are only careful not to touch the source of impurity would clearly not touch the liquids found in open eating vessels. Therefore, the following is true also of those who have not completed their purification process: "and the open (vessels) shall be unclean for every person of Israel, all the drink that is in them." Liquids are a major carrier of impurity and are therefore avoided by those who have immersed and removed the initial source of impurity but have not yet completed the process of purification.

Here we reach the second matter. The author of the Temple Scroll managed to utilize the difficulty regarding the ways in which clay vessels are contaminated to create two different behavioral directives that correspond to the two levels of purity. And here his basic working assumption is also revealed: Since one must maintain a basic level of purity even before completing the process of purification, the Torah itself already determines what foods he may consume. Those who were in a house with a dead corpse are obviously not allowed to consume pure foods until they complete their process of purification, but in the meantime, they must be careful not to consume foods that have absorbed the impurity of the corpse. At the same time, those who are completely pure and partake only of pure food, will avoid even indirect contact with impurity and will abstain even from foods that were kept in a sealed vessel within the home of a dead person.

Qumran literature therefore presents a consistent legal system, which encompasses both corpse impurity and bodily impurities. Just as one who counts to his purity from zov refrains from direct contact with the discharge, thus one who has contracted corpse impurity and has removed the initial impurity through a "first-day ablution" will refrain from touching the remnants of the corpse impurity, such as those that were absorbed in moist foods. Notably, however, unlike the impurities of genital discharges, those who are partially purified from corpse impurity are not termed "counters," who are destined to be purified within a few days, but rather "every person of Israel." Presumably, this term reflects the regularity with which this situation occurred, whereby after performing their first-day ablution, most people could not complete their purification process. While awaiting the future sprinkling of lustration water, they still observed a basic purity regimen and refrained from direct contact with corpses and the liquids that carry their impurity.

Against the background of this developed purity regimen during the period of purification, the silence of rabbinic law on the matter is striking. As in the case of the zav and the menstruant, the level of impurity of one who has contracted corpse impurity remains the same until he has been sprinkled with the waters of lustration on the third and seventh days. There is no requirement of initial immersion to remove the impure substance.[57] We do not find any demand that one begin the process of purification immediately upon contamination, and he may undertake the two sprinklings later as well. Anyone desirous of purification can purify themselves and their vessels with lustration water at any point, so long as they have waited at least three days since contracting the impurity.[58] The continuing period of impurity absolves the worry of being contaminated by impure objects and people until one chooses to purify oneself and transform his own status.

Integrating Impure Persons in Agricultural Activity

As we have seen, Qumran law distinguishes between three situations: impurity, purification, and complete purity. Completely pure people refrain from eating dry foods that were contaminated, whereas those undergoing purification only refrained from consuming liquids and moist foods that had absorbed the impurity. The intermediate status occupied Qumran law in other contexts as well, as we learn from additional fragments regarding the harvest of fruit. These pieces reveal how the Qumran sect implemented the principles we surveyed in its daily conduct. These groups of laws and their parallels in the teachings of the Houses of Hillel and Shammai provide a close-up look at the social workings of the sect, and the differences between it and the Pharisaic mode of operation. As we saw in previous chapters, the teachings of the Houses exhibit a shared legal discourse with Qumran literature, which highlights the contrasting ideologies of the different groups.

In Qumran Law

Fragment 4Q274 3 regulates purity observance during harvesting and reveals that members of differing levels of purity were involved in this activity. Surprisingly, even in Qumran one was not expected to be completely pure to partake in the harvest. However, this required a careful and precise division of labor. The main portion of the fragment deals with the power of liquids to spread impurity to the fruit and vegetables in the field. The fragment opens with a warning regarding the impurity of soft fruits, whose liquids have exuded and were then touched by an impure person. Later on, the fragment addresses vegetables moistened by dew or placed in water, which an impure person may not touch (following Lev. 11:38). Beyond these general determinations, it is possible to reconstruct a few more specific laws from between the fragmented lines, which correspond to the same principles we have seen: "And every (fruit) which has a seal [... will contaminate] *for a more pure person.*" Apparently, as far as the "more pure person" is concerned, the fruit is contaminated, despite the fact that it is "sealed" with a stalk and no liquid has issued from it.[59] In contrast, those counting their days of purification (lit. "impure for days") mentioned in the previous line, must beware not to touch fruits that exude liquids. Therefore, while soft and wet fruit are impure for all, "the more pure" are careful not to eat even sealed fruits that have contracted impurity.

This fragment reveals the role of liquids in spreading impurity through different intermediaries. One who is undergoing a process of purification threatens the foods of "the more pure" when his touch is accompanied by liquid. On the other hand, even one who is not completely pure, but who distances himself only from direct contact with sources of impurity, must distance himself from impure liquids. The completely pure person, however, will not consume even dry foods, such as a sealed fruit, which an impure person touched. These fragments reveal how people of varying levels of purity could manage alongside one another, dividing the work among themselves with respect to the stages of harvest and the species of fruits.

Another fragment on harvesting, 4Q284a (4QHarvesting), reveals that these principles were implemented in Qumran literature also with regard to the particular structure of the sect. Within the social structure of the sect, there were many individuals at the intermediate level of impurity. Aside from those who were undergoing purification after experiencing zov or those purifying from corpse impurity following the first-day ablution, this group included also (and perhaps primarily) candidates to the sect or members who were temporarily punished.[60] This fragment reads as follows:[61]

1. [...]
2. [but] they shall [no]t glean them [any impure person and any person ...]
3. [who] does not touch the liquids of the Many, for these [...]
4. [they may gle]an it,[62] and the figs {and the *bachaʿim*(?)}[63] [he shall not eat if]
5. their [jui]ce comes out wh[en one] presses them. They all shall glean [...]
6. [anyone] who has not been brou[ght into the cov]enant. And if they are crushed [with a vessel[64]]
7. [in the fiel]d he may not defile them with all his might <by opening them> before he pours [them]
8. [they shall gle]an[65] in purity and [finish] their work and [shall bring to his house ...]

In this fragment we learn how in practice those who "do not touch the liquids of the Many" were able to integrate in the agricultural activity of the community. From the fragment, it appears that different groups were in charge of harvesting different types of fruit. In the first lines (2–4), those who do not touch the liquids of the Many are forbidden from harvesting crushable fruit (grapes?)

that are inevitably moist already when gathered. The fragment then moves on to discuss figs (lines 4–6), but the instruction regarding them is unclear. It appears that, as opposed to the previous category of fruit, "all" (line 5) may glean fruits that do not produce liquid.

Lines 6–8 move on to address a different situation, in which fruits have been "pressed" and produce liquid. It is unclear whether we are still addressing the figs, and the pressing is undesirable, or different fruit, such as olives, which are intended to be pressed, as Joseph Baumgarten suggests. According to Baumgarten, the impure person is permitted to deal with olives from the time of harvesting until the olive is cracked, in preparation for the pressing of the oil out of the olive. However, from the moment the oil exudes from the olive, the impure person is distanced from the production process. The partial fragment does not allow us to determine whether we are speaking of olives in particular, or of an intentional pressing process more generally. However, it does warn that those who do not touch the drink of the Many must make every effort not to squeeze the fruit they touch.

The intermediate status of those who "do not touch the liquids of the Many" is pertinent to the organizational structure of the sect. As we learn from the Community Rule, this social status refers either to the period of initiation into the sect or when returning from a long period of banishment. The place of the member within the organization of the sect was embodied in his ritual status, and the position of the marginalized was modeled after those undergoing a period of purification, singled out by their removal from liquids.[66] Thus, liquid impurity plays a substantial role in facilitating the creation of complex social structures, as it served to segregate those with lesser impurity on the margins of communal activity, before allowing them to join in.

The Houses of Hillel and Shammai

The laws of harvesting provide an opportunity for a close comparison between the approach reflected in Qumran law and the early tannaitic approach regarding the integration of people of lesser impurity into agricultural activity in particular, and into the community in general. The Mishnah preserves a few fragments of teachings of the Houses of Hillel and Shammai that address similar situations and use similar terminology to that found in the Qumran fragments. This is yet another example of the overlap between the teachings of the Houses of Hillel and Shammai and the legal discourse of the Second Temple period. Like Qumran law, early rabbinic law also limited some impure people from harvesting and barred others from handling moist fruits. But having eliminated the purification process, the Houses of Hillel and Shammai made sure to maintain a similar legal structure without distancing community members to the social margins.

The Battle over Grapes and Olives

According to Qumran law, anyone who imparts impurity to liquids must refrain from harvesting crushable fruit, lest their liquids be secreted, but must also be careful at a later stage of the process regarding the pressing of other fruit, such as olives. This basic distinction between the two types of fruit is known also from the Talmud in the name of Hillel and Shammai, according to whom "one must vintage [grapes] in purity, yet not gather [olives] in purity." To assess the similarity to Qumran law, we must carefully trace the roots of a particularly dramatic tradition that made its way into the Babylonian Talmud (b. Šabb. 17a):

> When one vintages [grapes] for the winepress, Shammai maintains: It is made fit [to become unclean]; while Hillel ruled, it is not made fit. Said Hillel to Shammai: Why must one vintage [grapes] in purity, yet not gather [olives] in purity? If you provoke me, he replied, I will decree uncleanness in the case of olive gathering too. A sword was planted in the Bet Midrash and it was proclaimed, "He who would enter, let him enter, but he who would depart, let him not depart!" And on that day Hillel sat submissive before Shammai, like one of the disciples, and it was as grievous to Israel as the day when the [golden] calf was made.

From this Babylonian tradition, it appears that Hillel and Shammai disagreed regarding whether grapes that were intended for pressing are fit for impurity already from the moment of harvesting. This dispute was so bitter that it led to a violent struggle, which ended with Shammai's forcible determination that "one must vintage [grapes] in purity, yet not gather [olives] in purity." With regard to olive gathering, there was no issue with impure persons participating, since the olives were not yet made susceptible to impurity. But why did this halakhic topic become the arena of such bitter strife?

The similarity to Qumran law would appear to provide an explanation for the tension between Hillel and Shammai. Shammai's stance is similar to that of the Qumran sect, which holds that "crushable" fruit are fit to receive impurity from the moment of gathering. According to this approach, any moistening of the fruit, whether intentional or not, makes it fit to receive impurity.[67] Hillel, on the other hand, believes that the owner's intention is the determining factor, and there is thus no real difference between grapes and olives. In both cases the owner is not interested in the liquids exuding from the fruits until they have been brought to the wine- or the olive press for pressing, and it is only at this stage that they are fit to receive impurity. According to this interpretation, the two Houses represent such opposing approaches regarding the role of intention in the contamination process, that the final decision could be made only by force. The very similarity of Shammai's approach to Qumran law might justify the polemical tone of his dispute with Hillel.[68]

This explanation is sound, but it is based only on the Babylonian tradition. A look at the parallel Palestinian tradition demonstrates that there is no reason to assume that the early rabbis were divided on the question of making fruit susceptible to impurity. Both parties shared the notion, common to Qumran law as well, that purity must be maintained once liquids have issued from the fruit, even if this happened unintentionally.

In the Palestinian Talmud (y. Šabb. 1:7 [3c]), there is a similar list of disputes between the Houses of Hillel and Shammai. However, in place of a general dispute regarding harvesting for the winepress, as in the Babylonian Talmud, there is a more specific debate regarding the question of "how to gather grapes of *beth peras*," that is, an area suspected of including graves. All rabbis agree that one must harvest the grapes in purity, since their moistness makes them susceptible to impurity. In this particular situation, however, since the vineyard is situated in an impure field, the two houses suggest different methods for maintaining the purity of the fruit:

> How can the grapes of a *beth peras* be gathered? The men and the vessels must be sprinkled [once] and then a second time. Thereupon they gather the grapes and take them out of the beth peras. Others then receive [the grapes] and take them to the winepress. If the latter set [of persons] came into contact with the former, they become unclean. This is according to the House of Hillel. The House of Shammai say: [The gatherer] must hold the sickle in palm fiber, or cut off the grapes with a sharp flint, letting [the grapes fall] into an olive-basket, and then he takes [them] to the winepress. (m.'Ohal. 18:1)

The House of Shammai suggests a course of action that prevents the dissemination of impurity from the beth peras to the grapes, by using implements that are immune to impurity. The House of Hillel, on the other hand, enacts a type of ceremony that inoculates the harvesters and their vessels from the impurity of the beth peras, but in fact, immediately following the harvest, they are deemed to be impure and are distanced from the workers who take the grapes to the winepress. While disputing the solutions in this unique case, the basic assumptions are shared by both houses, and all agree that grapes must be harvested in state of purity.

It is thus doubtful that the ancient tannaitic tradition included a stance that actually permitted harvesting in a state of impurity. It was agreed that one must harvest in purity, since the grapes inevitably exuded liquid, which made them susceptible to contamination. Only in the Babylonian Talmud was it assumed that the susceptibility of fruit to impurity was wholly dependent on the owner's intention, and this view of Hillel was rejected only due to Shammai's violent behavior.[69]

The early tannaitic sources therefore maintain the distinction, shared with Qumran law, between harvesting grapes and olives. This distinction underlies the detailed instructions on the pure manufacturing of oil and wine in the two final chapters of tractate Teharot. These chapters consist of a substantial foundation of early rabbinic teachings, thereby offering a comprehensive view of the way this topic was conceived in the teachings of the Houses of Hillel and Shammai. Here we learn not only of the role of liquids in the spread of impurity but the identity of those who could threaten the pure liquids.

When Do Olives Become Susceptible to Impurity?

The rulings attributed to the Houses of Hillel and Shammai in chapter 9 of tractate Teharot address several different routes of processing olives for pressing. Since it is impossible to press all the olives immediately after the harvest, different mechanisms were created to make the procedure most efficient and productive. In this respect the rabbinic laws of purity resonate with Roman agricultural writing, instructing how to ensure the highest quality of produce. The Mishnah opens (9:1) with the case of olives that are transferred to the vat before they are taken to be pressed. This is apparently the regular process, certainly in a rural farm in which the owner of the olives is not the one who operates the olive press, and must wait his turn.[70] During this period the olives soften and fill with liquid.[71] This aids the pressing process significantly, and there were those who even believed that the quantity of oil was increased by this process.[72] The Houses of Hillel and Shammai dispute the precise point in time at which the olives were considered ready for pressing:

> Since when are olives susceptible to impurity?
> After they sweat in the vat, but not in the (harvesting) basket. Such are the words of the House of Shammai. R. Simeon says: the period of sweat is three days. The House of Hillel says: After three olives connect together.
> Rabban Gamaliel says: After their preparation is completed, and the Rabbis accept his view.

In addition to storage in the vat, the Mishnah mentions two other processes. Mishnah 9:5 addresses the case of olives left in a damping basket, and two options are included therein:

> One who leaves the olives in a damping basket:
> If in order to moisten them, so they are easily pressed—
>   the olives become susceptible to impurity;
> If in order to moisten them, so they may be salted—
>   the House of Shammai say: The olives have been rendered susceptible
>   and the House of Hillel say: They have not yet been rendered susceptible.
>   One who crushes olives with impure hands renders them impure.

Both the softening and the salting aid the production of oil from the olives.[73] The Roman author Columella describes a speedy process of choosing olives in which the quality of the oil is preserved through an initial processing of the olives: crushing, softening of the olives, and salting.[74] In this case, too, the House of Hillel waits for the end of the process, after softening and salting, when the olives are crushed in preparation for their pressing.

At times the olives are spread on a roof to be dried. In this case they are transferred to the olive press without preparation and softening, and their susceptibility to impurity is delayed (9:6). When they are brought to the olive press they are covered with leaves, and this is the final stage before they are placed in the press. The Houses of Hillel and Shammai dispute this case as well (9:7):

> If one decides to carry to the press only one or two portions of olives—
>   The House of Shammai say: He may chop the olives out in a state of
>   impurity, but he must cover them in purity.
>   The House of Hillel say: He may also cover in a state of impurity.
>   R. Yosi says: He may even dig with metal hatchets and bring the olives to
>   the press in a state of impurity.

There are several possible channels for transferring the olives to the olive press: placing the olives in a vat as they wait to be pressed; placing them in a damping basket to make them easier to press; or bringing them to be crushed. In each of these routes, the Houses of Hillel and Shammai dispute the precise stage at which the olives are ready for pressing and thus susceptible to impurity.

Who Threatens the Olives?

The majority of the cases that deal with the preparation of olives for pressing address the question of when olives become susceptible to impurity (m. Tehar.

9:1–3 and 5–7). As we learn from 9:2, before the olives become susceptible to impurity, even those with bodily impurity, such as zavim and zavot, do not threaten the olives. Following that stage, however, impure people cannot touch the produce. At one point, however, the Mishnah deviates from this straightforward distinction and seems to reflect a more complex system of distancing. As we saw previously, with respect to olives in the damping basket, the Mishnah rules: "One who crushes olives with impure hands renders them impure" (9:5). Why does the Mishnah deviate from the general discussion on handling the olives in purity to address the specific case of impure hands? Is this only an example for an impure person who touches olives that are fit to receive impurity? Is there a real difference between the beginning of the mishnah, where the language is that of susceptibility, and its end, where the mishnah chooses to mention impure hands in particular?

As we learn from the beginning of the mishnah, olives found in the damping basket were basically susceptible to impurity. However, in order for a person of lesser impurity to defile the olives there is need for an additional condition—the olives must really be wet. Therefore, the hands defile only if the olives are crushed open: "If someone crushed olives with unwashed hands, he causes them to be unclean." The olives, then, are susceptible to impurity already from the time they are softened, but the transfer of hand impurity, which is a lesser impurity, is dependent on the actual presence of liquids. On this point the comparison to Qumran law is illuminating.

As we saw in fragment 4Q284a, those forbidden to touch liquids are explicitly warned not to crack the fruit and touch its liquids ("he may not defile them with all his might <by opening them>"), just as the Mishnah enjoins one with hand impurity not to crush the olives. When dealing with the olive press, the Houses of Hillel and Shammai relate specifically to the threat of imparting a lesser impurity through contact with liquids. Like the members of the Qumran sect who "do not touch the liquids of the Many," rabbinic law forbids a person with impure hands from participating in the advanced stages of oil preparation that involve liquids. The status of the person with impure hands in early rabbinic law is similar to those who count the days toward purification in Qumran literature and are distanced from the "liquids of the Many."

Producing Pure Wine

A similar picture arises from the discussions regarding purity during the process of wine production in the last chapter of Teharot. There, too, the Mishnah focuses on the fear of impure hands, which might spread impurity through contact with liquid (10:4):

> One who is placing grapes [into the treading basin]:
> If they are taken from the baskets or from the soil surface—
> The House of Shammai says: He must place them with pure hands, and if he placed them with impure hands, he has defiled them. The House of Hillel say: He may place with impure hands, but he must separate the *terumah* in the state of purity.
> If they are taken from the grape-basket or from the leaf surface—
> all agree that he must place them with pure hands, and if he placed them with impure hands, he has defiled them.

The mishnah states that the moment of bringing the grapes into the treading basin is the determining stage with regard to the observance of hand impurity, in accordance with the type of surface on which it was laid: a regular or designated grape basket; ground or leaves.[75] But this mishnah is troubling, since, as we have seen, one must ostensibly treat the grapes with purity from the moment of harvesting. Commentators grappled with this issue and posit that the mishnah deals with an irregular case of grapes that were initially harvested for eating, and then transferred to the winepress. Therefore, they were only made fit for receiving impurity at the winepress.

However, unlike the accepted interpretation, this mishnah is, in fact, not concerned with the grapes' susceptibility to impurity. The terminology of "susceptible to impurity," which appears with regard to olives (9:1, 3, 5, 6), is not mentioned here. This mishnah is concerned specifically with hand impurity. As we have seen, the Houses of Hillel and Shammai agree that "one must harvest grapes in purity," and they dispute only whether one can touch those same grapes with impure hands, which can convey their impurity only through liquids. If the grapes are in a grape basket or lying on a surface of leaves, the liquids do not soak into them and continue to moisten the grapes; therefore, all agree that they impart impurity from the hands to the grapes. On the other hand, when the grapes have been resting on a surface that can soak up their liquids, the two Houses debate whether there is enough moisture remaining to transfer hand impurity to the grapes.

According to the House of Hillel, "He may place with impure hands, but he must separate the terumah in the state of purity" (10:4). This formulation adds another aspect to our understanding of the role of liquids. The House of Hillel permits touching these dry grapes with impure hands, but if the person wishes to separate the terumah at this stage, it is necessary to keep the hands pure. In other words, while hands do not defile unconsecrated foods without liquids, this lesser impurity directly defiles the holy terumah (m. Zabim 5:12).[76]

The early mishnah is therefore based on the following principles: (1) One who is completely impure is distanced from the grapes already from the harvest, even if they are dry; (2) the lesser hand impurity does not defile the grapes without the mediation of liquid; and (3) even this lesser impurity defiles the terumah directly.[77] And again, the comparison to Qumran is illuminating. From the beginning of fragment 4Q284a, it appears that one who "may not touch the liquids of the Many" may not harvest soft fruit for fear that the fruit will exude its liquids. At the same time, from fragment 4Q274 3, we learn that contact with a fruit with a seal is considered impure only with respect to those who are completely pure: "And every (fruit) which has a seal [... will contaminate] for a more pure person." Remarkably, this statement exhibits linguistic similarity to m. Tehar. 10.5, which also describes the treatment of sealed grapes as distinguishing people of different levels of impurity.

We see then that the two systems share common principles and distanced members who were not yet completely pure from pure liquids. Both, then, clearly belong to the same legal tradition. At the same time, this similarity highlights Pharisaic revisionism. The Pharisees transformed the marginalized status of the person undergoing purification, who according to Qumran law was distanced from "the liquids of the Many" for a prolonged period, into the inconsequential hand impurity.[78] Indeed, those suffering lesser hand impurity could not participate in the agricultural activity so as to not defile the liquids, but they could easily join the group by simply washing their hands.

Conclusion

Gradual purification was a common feature of the legal systems of the Second Temple period. At the same time, each group shaped a different system of social relations around it. The presence of the impure person was unavoidable even in a community that was stringent on matters of purity, but the status of the impure and those undergoing purification, and the ways in which they were integrated back into the communal activity, shaped the community's structure and signaled its values. While Qumran law integrated this principle into the structural foundations of the sect organization, Pharisaic law, as reflected in the early teachings of the Houses of Hillel and Shammai, radically limited the social implications of partial purification.

In Qumran law, everyone was always under a strict regimen of separation from impurity, including those who have not yet fully purified themselves from previous occurrences. The condition of the person who has distanced himself from the source of impurity but has not yet completed the process of purification is the most difficult one. Consequently, the greatest share of legal energy is devoted to those who are at this stage, and the most constraints are placed on their conduct. They are not allowed to eat contaminated food but, at the same time, cannot join in the pure food of the many. Qumran law forces purification by forbidding anyone who has not immersed to eat, but the person undergoing purification remains on the margins of the community until the process is completed. Thus, alongside the pure community, there always exists a marginalized group, which included not only those who awaited the completion of their purification process but also a variety of members of a lower status, candidates and transgressors. They participated partially in agricultural activity but could not share in the sect's meals and were required to distance themselves from fruits that exude liquid, which might spread their impurity further.

This sociolegal system clearly embodied the "expansionist approach," to use Gedalyahu Alon's terminology, which was based on the extension of the holiness of the Temple to the daily realm. Following the biblical model, the Israelite camp was considered an inseparable part of the holy realm, and separation practices were shaped accordingly.

Pharisaic law used the same legal building blocks but arrived at an alternative system of social relations based on the Pharisees' distinctive approach to purity observance. From their point of view, eating daily foods in a state of purity served to secure the integrity of their own purity within their mundane domain and was therefore made possible by immersion alone. Having immersed, the tevul yom was therefore considered to be completely pure, even if he could not yet consume sacrifices or the terumah. Although it adopted a graded model of purification, the Pharisaic system in fact eliminated the burden of a prolonged procedure. Here lies the fundamental difference between Qumran law and Pharisaic tradition, which did not demand immediate removal of impurity, and allowed immediate reintegration at one's own will into the association of the pure, without waiting on the margins.

The Houses of Hillel and Shammai shifted the extensive occupation with the status of the partially impure to the limited realm of hand impurity. The rabbis maintained the distinction, within the community, between partial and complete purification, which determined the access to pure liquids and moist foods. In this system, however, a simple action of handwashing was sufficient to transform one's condition and complete the process. The Pharisees preserved the legal structure but avoided applying it for the sake of stratifying social status within the community.

PART III

TRADITION AND INVENTION

6

Changing Social Contexts

Purity after 70 CE

Thus the rabbis taught:

> from the day that the Temple was destroyed there is no purity or impurity.[1]

According to this statement of Rav Natronai Gaon, the destruction of the Temple brought about the eradication of purity observance, and this observation is presumably supported by archaeological findings. Ronny Reich argues that there is a substantial decline in the number of immersion pools (miqva'ot) constructed after 70 CE, and he attributes this to the destruction of the Temple and the cessation of priestly gifts brought to Jerusalem. According to Reich, the Temple and the priestly gifts were the central motives behind purity observance; with their demise, the need for purity diminished, and the observance of purity survived only among a small number of pious individuals.[2] A similar picture emerges from Itzhak Magen's research on the production of stone vessels, which, according to rabbinic law, are considered to be insusceptible to impurity and, therefore, serve the needs of those who eat in the state of purity. Magen claims that the destruction of the Temple resulted in the demise of the stone vessel industry as well.[3] Against this background, the rabbis' comprehensive occupation with purity matters in the following period has been commonly viewed as primarily intellectual, serving as a replacement for actual purity observance.[4]

However, the assumption that widespread purity observance dissolved following 70 CE (apart from the prohibition on sexual relations with a menstruant) has recently been called into question. Both textual and archaeological evidence point to a graded and complex process. As opposed to the field of sacrifice law, which became theoretical immediately with the destruction of the Temple, major aspects of purity law were maintained until the late stages of the Talmudic era. Rabbinic literature and archaeological findings exhibit a striking correspondence, reflecting the changing reality to which the rabbis were compelled to respond, and there is no sign of a sudden termination of purity practices similar to that of Temple worship. The question is not whether purity was observed after the destruction but rather what its extent and nature were and which factors affected it.

Thus, for example, rabbinic sources document the continuous usage of the ashes of the red heifer, which was preserved for many years after the destruction of the Temple. During the second century, rabbis were approached multiple times to determine actual cases concerning lustration water (the water prepared with these ashes), and the use of this form of purification is attested even during the fourth century.[5] A survey of cases brought before the rabbis also indicates that a substantial share of questions brought before the tannaim related to purity matters and that purity observance declined significantly only toward the third century.[6] Either way, questions regarding various impurities, primarily corpse and menstrual impurity, were brought before the rabbis throughout the entire period, and a concern over vessel and food purity is evidenced not only among the rabbis and the priests.[7]

As Yonatan Adler has recently demonstrated, the archaeological findings also testify to continued purity observance beyond 70 CE. While Jerusalem was no longer inhabited following the destruction, Jews in the rural Judean environs continued to use and construct miqva'ot. Jewish settlement in these areas continued until the Bar Kokhba revolt and with it the proliferation of local miqva'ot. These were found even in places settled only after 70 CE. At the same time, the findings from the period following the Bar Kokhba revolt are scarcer. Multiple miqva'ot were found in Sepphoris, Beth She'arim, and Susya, but only a few in other settlements. The findings of stone vessels paint a similar picture. Stone vessels continued to serve the inhabitants of Judea following the destruction of the Temple, and while their usage declined during the second half of the second century, it did not disappear.[8] These findings clearly point to a change in the scope and nature of purity observance, although its cultural and religious ramifications are open to interpretation. For if purity is indeed independent of the Temple, what are the factors that shaped its scope and meaning in the following generations, and how should we characterize the purity observances that remained after 70 CE?

On one level, even after the destruction of the Temple the priests continued to receive heave offering (terumah), and they were expected to consume it in purity. However, this does not cover the whole picture and scholars sought additional explanations for the prolonged concern for purity in the following decades. Jodi Magness interprets these findings as an indication of the continued activity of various separatist sects.[9] Stuart Miller, on the other hand, suggests that the domestic context of the miqva'ot in Sepphoris reflects a new household form of purity observance, which replaced the former purity of the Temple.[10] This orientation arguably finds support in sources that testify to the popular observance of purification following sexual relations, even against rabbinic guidance.[11] On this point, Miller joins others who opine that purity spread throughout wide social circles particularly during the period following the destruction of the Second Temple, due to a desire to substitute the cultic experience provided by the Temple with an accessible experience of holiness through daily purity practices.[12]

Evidently, then, the archaeological findings are open to a wide range of interpretations, and the question remains: What shape did the concern for purity take after 70 CE, and what kind of religious ideals and experiences did it cultivate? Admittedly, we lack the tools to determine the scope of purity observance during this period, particularly given the complexity and variability of the phenomenon, but we can trace its changing character through its textual expressions. As we saw in the first chapter, immersion following sexual intercourse or contact with a corpse was familiar and prevalent among Second Temple Jews since it was perceived as a biblical obligation. We should, therefore, not be surprised if this norm persisted in later times as well. But to what extent did purity observance continue to order daily life and organize people's surroundings? Considering the fundamental role of social support in the observance of purity, were the social affiliations that enabled the safe observance of purity maintained, or were they replaced by alternative forms of social relations?

As we see in this and the following chapter, a comparative textual analysis of tannaitic material provides us with answers for many of these questions. Admittedly, tannaitic law does not provide a direct and transparent image of the prevalent norms within Jewish society of the time. However, I would argue that it does offer a vivid reflection of some fundamental social changes, which refashioned purity observance. Arguably, while formulating their legal policy and transmitting the legal traditions of Second Temple Jerusalem, the rabbis were compelled to adapt to these changing circumstances. Unlike the Second Temple period, which provides multiple comparative sources for the study of Pharisaic purity ideology, with respect to the later tannaitic period, we lack nonrabbinic sources against which we could precisely interpret the legal tendencies of the rabbis. At the same time, a close textual analysis of the rabbinic compositions will enable us to trace the changing realities that determined rabbinic iterpretations and innvations in this field.

The History of Purity Associations

As we saw in chapter 4, according to early legal traditions—in both Qumran and early rabbinic sources—the right of purification was granted only to those who were publicly associated with a recognized group and adopted their form of purity observance. Tannaitic literature includes, in fact, two distinct procedures for becoming an associate (ḥaver), who is deemed to be trustworthy with regard to matters of purity, and these are detailed in Mishnah and Tosefta Demai. The two procedures are not only distinct in their details, but each of them also reflects a different social setting. As I argue in this chapter, the deep changes that took place in the social structures in Jewish Palestine and the changing forms of ritual practice during the second century led to a rephrasing of the laws regarding the relationship between those who observed purity laws and the ammei ha-aretz. While purity observance determined group membership and played a public role in shaping intersectarian relationships during the Second Temple period, these structures collapsed with the decline of purity observance and new forms of association were created to support those holding on to these traditional practices.

We begin with comparing the requirements for becoming an associate in both sources:

Mishnah Demai 2:2-3
If one has taken upon himself to become an associate,
He may not sell to an am ha-aretz either moist or dry [produce], nor may he buy from him moist [produce].
He may not be the guest of an am ha-aretz, nor may he receive as guest an am ha-aretz who is wearing his own garment.[13]

Tosefta Demai 2:2
If one has taken upon himself four[14] matters, he is accepted as an associate: [he must accept upon himself] not to give terumah and tithes to an am ha-aretz, and that he will not prepare pure foods for an am ha-aretz, and that he will eat unconsecrated foods in a state of purity.

What is the relationship between the two sets of instructions?[15] While previous scholars attempted to merge the Mishnah and the Tosefta into one long procedure, I argue that they represent two distinct phases in the history of purity observance. Separating the two allows us to uncover the close affinity of the mishnaic instructions to Second Temple separatist traditions, while at the same time highlighting the social settings assumed in the later stages of tannaitic law.

In his commentary on the Tosefta, Saul Lieberman attempts to reconstruct a graduated and complex process from these two sources.[16] According to his suggestion, the requirements mentioned in the Tosefta, such as taking on oneself the obligation of eating unconsecrated foods in purity and refraining from giving terumah to an am ha-aretz, serve as mere prerequisites for becoming an associate. Only later on, once one has completed the process of acceptance into the association, was he required to also accept the more stringent commitments detailed in the Mishnah and to distance himself from am ha-aretz. In addition, this lengthy process includes more stages that are mentioned in a set of laws from the Tosefta, intended to gradually develop the candidate's proficiency at purity observance.[17]

If we follow the sequence of laws in the Tosefta, according to Lieberman's reconstruction, following the initial commitment previously quoted to eat in a state of purity, the candidate was expected to act as an associate outside of the association: "If one approaches to take upon himself (the matters of the associate)—if he already practices it in private, we accept him and then teach him; otherwise, we teach him and then accept him" (t. Demai 2:10). Next, the candidate was accepted with respect to "wings," which Lieberman interprets as hand purity, and following this for "purities," that is, particular stringencies of those who eat unconsecrated foods in purity. The Tosefta stresses that one must take on himself the observance of "wings" to be considered trustworthy also with respect to "purities" (2:11). Finally, even after being accepted into the association, according to this reconstruction, one becomes an associate with regard to liquids after thirty days and a complete associate, including with respect to clothing, only after twelve months. Such is the view of the House of Shammai, while the House of Hillel is more lenient and prescribes a period of thirty days for these two final matters (2:12). Then, finally, as we have mentioned, come the commitments prescribed in the Mishnah.

Scholars have suggested ways to somewhat reduce the numerous stages of this long, cumbersome process, as suggested by Lieberman,[18] but these suggestions cannot eliminate the basic problem with any such ungainly procedure, that does not feature even in the most strict and graded initiation process into the Qumran sect.[19] Beyond the unlikelihood of such a complicated procedure, a close analysis of the Tosefta itself reveals that it actually incorporates two incongruent processes that were juxtaposed in sections 11–12. One process (2:11) speaks of acceptance to "wings" and "purities," and another process (2:12), in the name of the Houses of Hillel and Shammai, discusses "liquids" and "clothing." These are actually parallel terms, and they reflect two different approaches to the institution of association, pertaining to distinct historical stages. Once we unveil the difference between the two, we can zoom out to the general difference between the Mishnah and the Tosefta.

Although it appears in the Tosefta, section 2:12 is, in fact, a fragment of an early legal tradition attributed to the Houses, which is bound to the Mishnah and should not be interpreted within the sequence of the Tosefta. In their discussion, the Houses refer to three key terms: *acceptance*, *liquids*, and *clothing*. Notably, the only additional source that deals with liquids and clothing within the framework of the commitments of the associates is our Mishnah, Demai 2:3, and the Houses, in the Tosefta, appear to be deliberating the details of the mishnaic instructions:

Mishnah Demai 2:3	**Tosefta Demai 2:12**
If one **accepts upon himself** to become an associate,	Until When does one **accept**?
He may not sell to an *am ha-aretz* either **moist** or dry [produce], nor may he buy from him **moist** [produce].	The House of Shammai say: for **liquids** thirty days;
He may not be the guest of an *am ha-aretz*, nor may he receive as a guest an *am ha-aretz* who is **wearing his own garment.**	for **garments** twelve months. The School of Hillel say, for either thirty days.

According to the Mishnah, one who seeks to become an associate must refrain from two forms of contacts with an am ha-aretz—namely, food trade and hosting. The question that arises from this Mishnah is what period of probation is necessary to be considered a trustworthy associate. This is the matter on which the Houses of Hillel and Shammai disagree. Their respective answers correspond to the order of the details in the Mishnah: liquids (as well as moist foods) first and then clothing. According to the House of Shammai, there is a difference between trade and hosting. Refraining for a month from trading with ammei ha-aretz is a substantial challenge and is therefore sufficient to prove one has reordered his trade relations. Hosting, on the other hand, requires a longer period of inspection. At the end of this process, the candidate who has been able to separate himself from the impurity of ammei ha-aretz in both realms is recognized as an associate.

The previous section in the Tosefta (2:11) offers an alternative criterion for becoming an associate, and it focuses on the process of attaining the required proficiency in purity observance. First, the candidate learns to observe "wing" purity, that is, the purity of his clothes (and not hand purity as Lieberman suggested),[20] followed by training to handle pure food, "purities." The impurity of clothing is a severe form of impurity, and one must therefore learn to prevent his clothes from becoming impure before he can start handling pure foods, which are easily defiled. The process of training to become an associate, first clothes and then foods, is similar to that of a child growing into a purity-observing family and developing his own skills: "When a child starts to go around independently, his garments are considered pure, but we may not prepare pure foods near his body.... Once he knows how to control [lit. guard] his body, we may eat pure foods that touched his body. When he learns to control his hands, we may eat pure foods that his hands touched."[21] Here too, one first trains to keep his clothes pure before learning how to observe food purity.

There is thus a marked difference between the two procedures: while section 11 lays out the stages for developing the required proficiency and control over one's own environs, the Mishnah, which was further discussed by the Houses of Hillel and Shammai in section 12 of the Tosefta, is concerned with establishing firm boundaries between the associate and am ha-aretz. The associate is required to abstain from the drinks and moist foods of an am ha-aretz and to distance himself from his clothing. Unlike section 11, which presents a gradual process of training (comparable to a child's education), section 12, together with the Mishnah, views the separation from the am ha-aretz's company as the hallmark of the associate's identity.[22] In this context, it appears that the skill of purity observance is taken for granted, and one is examined through his ability to distance himself from one who does not observe purity.

The Laws of the Ḥaver: From Sect to Voluntary Association

Having observed this difference between the two procedures, we can now return to the fundamental difference between the two lists of requirements for becoming an associate (ḥaver) in the Mishnah and the Tosefta. These do not represent two stages in one long process, but two distinct models of association. The essence of association in the Mishnah, which, as we have seen, was already familiar to the Houses of Shammai and Hillel, is the social separation from am ha-aretz, which was rooted in the sectarian discourse of Second Temple Judaism. While scholars have pointed out the affinity between the procedure of admittance into the rabbinic association and sectarian practices,[23] closer scrutiny reveals that it is only the early mishnaic traditions and the related teachings of the Houses of Hillel and Shammai that reflect sectarian modes of initiation.

First, the early rabbinic rulings share with Qumran law the demand for a period of probation. In the initiation process into the Qumran Community, the candidate is required to undergo several stages of testing and examination.[24] Following a one-year probationary period, the candidate may then partake of the pure foods of the sect, after which, after yet another period of examination, he can also share in the liquids of the sect. Similarly, of all the laws of association in tannaitic literature, it is only in the teachings of the Houses of Hillel and Shammai where we find a distinct period of candidacy and testing lasting a month or a year. In contrast, as we have seen, the adjacent laws in the Tosefta describe a process of training but do not include any aspect of testing or feature a specific period of time allotted to this process. The training takes as long as it takes.

An additional point of similarity between Qumran and the early layer of rabbinic law relates to the candidate's access to dry and moist foods during the process of initiation. As we saw in the previous chapter, contact with pure liquids requires a higher level of purity, and therefore only full members were permitted to touch "the drink of the Many." A corollary distinction between dry and moist foods appears in Mishnah Demai 2:3, and in the teachings of the Houses of Hillel and Shammai. One is permitted to accept dry food from an am ha-aretz, since it is unsusceptible to impurity, as opposed to moist foods and liquids, which were surely contaminated by am ha-aretz. The observance of liquid purity distinguishes the associate from his surroundings, similar to the full members of the Qumran Community. And finally, the exclusive occupation with social separation as the quintessential obligation of the associate is characteristic of the sectarian context of the early legal traditions. As we saw in chapter 4, according to the Community Rule, one who joined the Community accepts a series of commitments, all of which aim to separate the member from all men of injustice.[25] This is also the essence of the associate's obligations according to Mishnah Demai 2:3—namely, the separation from the impure am ha-aretz.

Against the sectarian background of these laws within the world of Second Temple Judaism, we can revisit the role of the "association" within the Pharisaic social fabric. Scholarship on the Pharisees has been puzzled by the dual terminology denoting those who are strict in the matters of purity: associate (ḥaver) and Pharisee (*parush*). These terms appear concurrently in the early tannaitic layer. What is the relationship between the Pharisees and the associates?[26] Now that we have isolated the early fragments of association laws in tannaitic literature, we may surmise a suggested relationship between these two groups.

In early rabbinic sources, both the associate and the Pharisee are contrasted to the impure am ha-aretz, though they are mentioned in different contexts. The Pharisee is careful to distance himself from am ha-aretz on specific occasions, for fear of defiling his own clothes and foods (m. Ḥag. 2:7; t. Šabb. 1:15). Thus, the Pharisee is primarily concerned with his own purity and the purity of those around him. The associate, unlike the Pharisee, adopts far-reaching social-distancing practices, which include an extreme limiting of any social or commercial contact with am ha-aretz. It is this severe social separation that publicly marks him as trustworthy.

It therefore appears that personal observance of purity characterized the Pharisees and distinguished them from other, less devout Jews. At the same time, the social boundaries between these different groups were understandably broad and blurry, and they included a wide range of practices of separation from their impure surroundings. Therefore, one who sought to be considered fully trustworthy in these matters was not required to take on oneself purity observance, which was already a familiar part of his routine, but rather to ensure his ultimate social separation from am ha-aretz.[27] One can view the Pharisaic association as a select group of Pharisees renowned for their trustworthiness in matters of purity. In any event, the association was not intended to ensure purity observance, which was a firmly established component of the Pharisaic way of life. Therefore, the Mishnah does not include eating in the state of purity among the obligations of the associate, as this was already assumed within Pharisaic circles.

The Tosefta reflects a different model of association, which is not based on social isolation. As we have seen, the obligations in the Tosefta do not include any components of separation, and only a degree of personal expertise in matters of purity. To characterize the social role of the association in the later tannaitic period, we turn to examine an alternative model for purity observance that is reflected in the teachings of later tannaim and does not entail social separation. As I argue, this model corresponds to the private voluntary association familiar from the Greco-Roman world.

Am ha-aretz in Tractate Teharot: Purity without Social Separation

The most comprehensive unit in the Mishnah to systematically regulate the contact of the associate with am ha-aretz appears in m. Teharot 7:1–8:5.[28] This pericope primarily represents the teachings of R. Akiva's Galilean disciples,[29] and it maps the domestic spaces that are impacted by the presence of am ha-aretz. First, the am ha-aretz appears in the associate's realm and defiles the space by his presence, unless carefully supervised. Then the Mishnah turns to cases in which the am ha-aretz defiles the associate's vessels on his own property. See, for instance, the following cases:

> 7.3 One who leaves artisans inside his house—the house is impure. The words of R. Meir, and the Rabbis say: Only the places that they can reach out and touch are impure.

7.4 The wife of an associate who left the wife of an am ha-aretz to grind inside her house: If the millstone stopped—only the places that she can reach out and touch are impure.

If there were two of them—the house is impure anyway. The words of R. Meir, and the Rabbis say: only the places that they can reach out and touch are impure.

7.5 One who leaves an am ha-aretz in his house to supervise it: If he can see the people entering and exiting—foods, liquids and open earthenware are impure, but beddings, seatings and sealed earthenware are pure.

If he cannot see neither the people entering nor the people exiting, even if he is carried and bound hand and foot—all is impure.

8.1 One who lives with an am ha-aretz in the courtyard, and forgot artifacts in the courtyard, even sealed jars or a sealed oven—they are rendered impure. R. Judah deems the oven pure, as long as it is sealed. R. Yosi says: Even the oven is impure, unless he builds a ten handbreadth-tall partition.

8.4 One who leaves his house open and finds it locked, locked and finds it locked, open and finds it locked—it is pure; locked and finds it open— R. Meir deems it impure, and the Rabbis deem it pure, since [we maintain that] burglars came, changed their mind and left.

8.5 The wife of an am ha-aretz who entered the house of an associate to take his son or animal—the house is pure, since she entered without permission.

These mishnahs instruct that the degree of am ha-aretz's control over space, alongside the associate's ability to supervise him, are the central criteria for determining the severity of impurity. The issue of supervising an am ha-aretz who does not know how to abstain from contact with impurity is the focus of the discussions of the same rabbis in 10:1–3 concerning the observance of purity during oil and wine production. While the surrounding instructions regarding the maintenance of purity during these procedures that are attributed to earlier rabbis are not concerned with the involvement of am ha-aretz in this process,[30] this issue surfaces in the discussions of rabbis of the later tannaitic period. Thus, for instance, we read in the following discussion: "10.3 Olive press workers and grape harvesters—It is enough to bring them into the cave. The words of R. Meir. R. Yosi says: he must oversee their immersion. R. Simeon says: If they consider themselves to be pure, he must oversee their immersion, and if they consider themselves impure, he need not oversee their immersion." These groups of laws in tractate Teharot take for granted that an am ha-aretz may regularly be found in an associate's house. The wife of an am ha-aretz grinds corn in the associate's home together with his wife (7:4). The associate leaves vessels with the am ha-aretz for safekeeping, and they even enter each other's homes without permission. The am ha-aretz works at the associate's home or in his olive press or winepress. The parallel Tosefta even describes a situation in which the associate sleeps in the house of an am ha-aretz.[31] It appears then that there are no restrictions on the associate's contact with am ha-aretz. At the same time, since am ha-aretz does not know how to beware of impurity, he requires constant supervision. Even when he attempts to observe purity, his efforts are fruitless, and therefore, objects in his possession may even impart the severe corpse impurity, even if he believes that he is able to manage this situation.

Evidently, then, these laws do not limit relationships between the associate and the am ha-aretz; however, the associate must be aware of their implications. These social relationships with am ha-aretz are considered a tolerated reality that does not impede purity observance. This tolerant policy stands in opposition to Mishnah Demai 2:3, which, as we saw, limits contact with am ha-aretz. The more lenient standards of Tosefta Demai, on the other hand, are in line with Mishnah Teharot and its social policy of nonseparation from the am ha-aretz.

While Mishnah Demai forbids the associate from giving any type of food to am ha-aretz, "he may not sell to him either moist or dry [produce]," and limits economic ties with him, the prohibition in the Tosefta is limited to giving the am ha-aretz tithes or terumah, in fear that he will defile the sacred foodstuff. Conversely, the obligation to observe the purity of unconsecrated foods is limited to the associate's food alone, as he learns to maintain the purity of his own foods. The associate is not responsible for the purity standards of his neighboring am ha-aretz. Furthermore, the instructions for the associate in Tosefta Demai do not include any restrictions on hosting, and the associate is not required to distance himself from am ha-aretz, socially or commercially, apart from the concern for the purity of the priestly gifts. Evidently, then, the obligations of the associate in Tosefta Demai reflect a social setting that lacks any form of distancing. This, as we have seen is also the case in tractate Teharot, there we find the associate and the am ha-aretz hosting each other in their homes. In addition to marriage ties between the associate and the am ha-aretz, we even hear of a son or slave of an associate who studies with an am ha-aretz and is nonetheless still considered as an associate.[32] In this respect, Tosefta Demai coincides with Mishnah Teharot, as they both reflect the teachings of later tannaim.

The contrast between Mishnah Demai, on the one hand, and Tosefta Demai and Mishnah Teharot, on the other, is best explained in light of the differences between the world of the Second Temple Pharisees and the social and ideological reality of the late Galilean tannaim. In contrast to the sectarian nature of the laws of association in the early Mishnah, which rely on the separatist tradition of the Second Temple period, the laws of association shaped in the Galilee at the end of the tannaitic period are an attempt to adapt the legal traditions to a new social order. If the term *associate* in the early Mishnah serves as an appellation signifying the faith bestowed on those of the Pharisees who have proven their sectarian-like separation from their impure surroundings, in the Mishnah of the second-century rabbis it had come to designate anyone who observed the laws of purity. In other words, the very fact of purity observance was enough to garner this sobriquet. To achieve this title, one must accept on oneself a demanding and peculiar way of life, and learn how to preserve the purity of his clothing and food and to function alongside ammei ha-aretz in his vicinity. The associate, therefore, continues to function alongside ammei ha-aretz, including his family members and friends, and does not alter his social identity; rather, to facilitate his personal purity skills, he voluntarily chooses to join an association, a sort of club for those who eat in purity.[33]

In addition to offering support for those who sought to adopt a demanding way of life, joining the association served another professional purpose, comparable to the function of the Greco-Roman voluntary associations.[34] As opposed to the sectarian organizations familiar to us from Second Temple times, the relationship between the members of these associations was intended for limited purposes.[35] The association met occasionally, performing shared ritual activities and providing the needs of its members. At the same time, it was supported by powerful patrons and garnered public influence through inscriptions and civic activity.[36] Membership in these voluntary associations was not meant to substitute one's social affiliations. It appears that, on this matter, the associations described in the Mishnah of the Galilean rabbis followed the model of these voluntary associations rather than the sectarian model of the Qumran Yaḥad or the Pharisaic association.

We know very little regarding the organization of these purity associations, their size, whether they held routine meetings and who led them, apart from the existence of a training process and the possibility of being rejected from the association (t. Demai 3:4). A comparison to the voluntary associations, however, illuminates one facet of its professional role. This association, whose members were perhaps called "persons of the synagogue" (m. Zabim 3:2),[37] served the purity needs of the public. Since the associates have gained expertise in matters of purity, they could provide professional assistance in separating terumah and tithes in a state of purity. After, all, even those who were not regularly observant in these matters were in need of such knowledge when separating the priestly share form their own produce. Therefore, the associates were responsible to aid these occasional purity needs, and they offered their professional services for hire.[38] This pattern aligns with that of contemporary Greco-Roman voluntary association. While supporting their members in their own ritual needs, the members of the voluntary associations provided services to the public, who, in return, was expected to support them.

To conclude, the survey of the laws of association indicates a fundamental change in the social setting of purity observance. In this process, purity ceased to function as an identifying marker of an ideological movement and became a matter of personal and professional choice, within a society characterized by a variety of purity norms and blurred boundaries between differing levels of observance. This reality, however, posed new challenges and entailed the construction of new forms of social relations. The associate had to constantly take into consideration the presence of the impure am ha-aretz whom he considered to be completely ignorant and incompetent in purity matters. Inevitably, this situation affected the reliability of the am ha-aretz, who, despite his goodwill, could not be trusted and required constant supervision. As we see in the next section, textual adaptations in the Mishnah bear witness to the rise of this new suspicious approach toward the incompetent am ha-aretz.

The End of Trust: Between Two Tractates

Among other cases of am ha-aretz who defiles the associate's home, Mishnah Teharot 7:6 includes tax collectors and burglars. The Mishnah discusses whether tax collectors can be trusted when saying that they did not touch anything in the house. Notably, although the am ha-aretz is given the chance to describe what has occurred, his testimony is, in fact, almost worthless. Thus, we read in this Mishnah according to its major textual witnesses: "Tax collectors who entered a house: the house is defiled. If there was a gentile with them—they are trusted in saying: 'We entered but we did not touch.'"[39] Apparently—and the Tosefta (8:5) confirms this interpretation—tax collectors are only trusted if they are the sole source of the information that they entered the house. Otherwise, they are not believed when they say they have not touched anything. Therefore, only if a gentile—that is, their supervisor—was present, can we really believe that they acted carefully, "for the fear of the gentile is upon them." The presence of their supervisor counteracts the suspicion that they unlawfully ransacked the house.

The reliability of the tax collector is discussed again in Mishnah Hagigah 3:6, but there we find an opposing stance: "Tax collectors who entered a house—and similarly burglars who restored [stolen] vessels—are trusted in saying: We did not touch [anything]." The Tosefta and the Babylonian Talmud offer a few solutions for this apparent contradiction.[40] However, in light of the previous analysis, I would argue that in this case, too, one can identify a fundamental shift between the early and late Mishnah, and between the world of the rabbis of first century Judea and that of the Galilean rabbis of the second century. With this initial legal difference as our starting point, we can further compare the distinct settings reflected in each of the tractates.

As a first step, we should note the relative complexity of Mishnah Teharot in comparison to the parallel ruling in Mishnah Hagigah:

Hagigah 3:6	**Teharot 7:6**
Tax collectors who entered a house—	Tax collectors who entered a house—the house is defiled.
	If there was a gentile with them—
they are trusted in saying:	they are trusted in saying:
"We did not touch"	"We entered but we did not touch"

When considering the relationship between the two parallels, the most plausible reconstruction is that Mishnah Teharot is based on the shorter formulation in Mishnah Hagigah, but limits it to a particular case. According to Mishnah Teharot, therefore, the tax collectors are to be believed only if a gentile supervisor is present, thus canceling out the sweeping trustworthiness attributed to them in the early law, as it appears in Hagigah. There is therefore reason to believe that the law was reworked in tractate Teharot, but what could be the reason for the different estimation of the tax collector in each tractate?

Multiple sources testify to the disdain toward tax collectors, who were perceived as the embodiment of untrustworthiness and the worst type of criminals, involved in theft and cheating. In the Gospels, Jesus is reproved for dining with tax collectors and sinners,[41] and in other traditions, he himself marks them as the worst kind of sinners.[42] The condemnation of the tax collectors alongside the gentiles, the prostitutes, and other sinners appears to be a matter of general consensus. But this profession was despised outside of Judea as well. For example, Lucian states that, at times, people descend to the lowest point to survive and are willing to betray the trust placed in them by embezzling, stealing, or becomes tax collectors. While at times a person reaches these lows out of distress, he cannot expect others to share their meal with him. Furthermore, even in Hades, all those who occupied themselves in shuffling and confusion are tied together: adulterers and pimps, tax collectors, sycophants, and libelers.[43]

We should, therefore, not be surprised that tax collectors were treated as the archetype of untrustworthy people in rabbinic literature as well. Beyond the fact that the money that they collected is considered stolen and they are compared to thieves and robbers, they are unfit to serve as witnesses,[44] and they are the only ones that are prevented from joining the association by dint of their profession: "At first they would say that an associate who became a tax collector, is banished from the association; later they decreed that as long as he serves as a tax collector he is not trustworthy, but once he resigns he is considered trustworthy." This is also the background for the contrast that appears in the following story: "There was a case of a woman who married an associate and tied his phylacteries on his hand for him. Then she married a tax collector and she tied his receipts to his hand."[45] Against this background, we can fully understand the policy of Mishnah Teharot, which refuses to trust the tax collector who ransacked the house. How, then, can we explain the more lenient ruling of Mishnah Hagigah? How can these despicable people be trusted?

To answer this question, we must examine the wider context of these two mishnahs. The ruling regarding the tax collector in tractate Hagigah reflects a general policy of cooperation with those who are considered unclean. An overview of the literary unit in Hagigah indicates that even those who were not themselves scrupulous in their purity observance understood the importance of the matter and, if needed, would know how to prevent the spreading of impurity. The suspicious approach toward the tax collector in Mishnah Teharot, on the other hand, is in line with the general approach expressed in this unit toward ammei ha-aretz, who cannot be trusted in matters of purity since they lack the relevant skill and knowledge. The difference between the two tractates, therefore, does not stem from a specific change regarding the tax collector but rather from the fact that each of the sources represents a social policy shaped in a different sociohistorical context.

The Spheres of Trust in Judea

The trust bestowed on tax collectors and burglars in Mishnah Hagigah 3:6 is part of a wider system of trust detailed in that chapter (3:4–6):

Greater stringency applies to *terumah* [in comparison to hallowed things]:

[1] **In Judea** all are trusted regarding the purity of wine and oil throughout the year; and only at the season of the winepresses and olive vats regarding terumah.

[…]

Regarding jugs of wine and of oil of terumah,[46]

all are trusted during the season of the winepresses and the olive vats and prior to [the season] of winepresses seventy days in regard to jugs of wine and jugs of oil.

[2] **From Modi'im inwards** [the potters] are trusted in regard to earthenware vessels; from Modi'im outwards they are not trusted.

[…]

Tax collectors who entered a house—and similarly if burglars restored [stolen] vessels—they are trusted in saying: We have not touched [anything].

[3] **And in Jerusalem** they are trusted in regard to hallowed things, and during a festival also in regard to terumah.

This group of laws is organized according to three geographical circles: (1) the region of Judea, (2) the area between Modi'im and Jerusalem, and (3) Jerusalem. This implies that the level of trustworthiness increases as we approach Jerusalem. From its position within this unit, we learn that the law regarding the reliability of the tax collectors and the burglars, which is mentioned in the second part, is limited to a specific area: "inward from Modi'im." The difference between Mishnah Teharot and Mishnah Hagigah, therefore, may stem from their geographical context. Mishnah Teharot, which is etched with the seal of the Galilean rabbis, does not believe the tax collectors. In the vicinity of Jerusalem during the Second Temple period, on the other hand, the rabbis assumed a high level of trustworthiness, even with respect to tax collectors.[47]

Another law in this unit contradicts m. Teharot and provides an additional indication for the differences between the locations. According to the first law in this unit, all are trustworthy regarding the purity of terumah during the season of wine and oil production. According to Mishnah Teharot, on the other hand, those who prepare the oil and the wine and seek to separate terumah or tithes from them require supervision: "One who completes the preparation of his olives in the vat, and leaves one basket-full, must hand it to the priest. The words of R. Meir. R. Judah says: He must bring him the key immediately. R. Simeon says: By the next day" (9:4). This law teaches that one must hand over basketfuls of olives to a priest immediately, before they are made susceptible to impurity, to avoid any fear of the terumah being contaminated. The priest must be responsible for the olives before they are prepared for pressing, and the owner of the olives is not trusted to say that he prepared pure oil from them. According to the disciples of R. Akiva participating in this discussion, only that portion of olives that is separated from the regular process of production is kept pure and under supervision of a skilled priest. Already the Talmud pointed out that this practice contradicts the determination of Mishnah Hagigah, which trusts all on the matter of terumah purity during the period of wine and oil production.[48]

Other laws in Mishnah Teharot concerning the maintenance of purity in the winepresses and the olive vats, attributed to those same Galilean rabbis, also raise similar difficulties. Mishnah Teharot 10:1–3 requires the owner to continuously supervise the workers even when they immerse. The workers are forbidden to leave sight of the owner, for fear they will become impure without him noticing. How can we line up these laws, which require constant supervision of ammei ha-aretz workers, with the general trustworthiness granted during the olive and oil pressing, according to Mishnah Hagigah? The amoraim offer several solutions to this incoherence.[49] Among other suggestions, Rav Yosef highlights the distinction between Judea, discussed in Mishnah Hagigah, and the situation in the Galilee, addressed by the rabbis in Mishnah Teharot.

It does indeed appear that according to the late Galilean rabbis, there is no possibility to trust an am ha-aretz on matters of purity, since he lacks the minimal proficiency necessary for its maintenance. Consequently, supervision is suggested as the only possible solution to this problem. Once the am ha-aretz disappears from the associate's eyesight, we must assume that despite his best intentions, he has defiled his surroundings. Arguably, then, the early Mishnah regarding the tax collectors in Hagigah was reworked to align with the attitude toward the am ha-aretz unit in Teharot, which is clearly of a later Galilean provenance.

But here the question I presented specifically with regard to the tax collectors presents itself again, more broadly: Why does Mishnah Hagigah assume that everyone can be trusted, including those who are not strict observers of purity laws? Seemingly, the policy laid out in Mishnah Teharot is more understandable: One who does not stringently observe purity should presumably be inspected and supervised. The question becomes even stronger when we take into account the sectarian nature of purity observance during the Second Temple period. How does the widespread policy of strict separation from impure outsiders, discussed in chapter 4, line up with the sweeping trust granted in Mishnah Hagigah to those who are not themselves pure?[50] How can we describe the seemingly paradoxical practice of the Judean Pharisees, who separated themselves from am ha-aretz yet at the same time were ready to trust even the worst among them?

The Market Forces of Purity

An analysis of the literary unit in Mishnah Hagigah reveals that the trust placed in the tax collectors promoted a general economic policy.[51] Mishnah Hagigah outlines the domains within which one can safely trade without fear of impurity.[52] These directives reflect the needs of the market and the shared interests of all involved parties. Within the commercial setting that arises from the Mishnah, even people who did not personally observe purity, and even the despised tax collectors, share in the public interest that purity be maintained throughout Judea.

The laws in this unit indicate the sweeping trust granted wherever the commercial value of purity is publicly acknowledged. The Mishnah does not distinguish exclusively between trustworthiness for sacrifices and trustworthiness for terumah, as the title of the unit would imply, but rather between the realm of personal observance versus the public sphere. Thus, despite the obvious variations of personal observance, public and commercial interests dictated a basically uniform purity practice for all. Mishnah Hagigah suggests that, in Judea, all were willing to partake in the observance of purity, to one degree or another, and this shared ethos thus crossed social distinctions. Even those who were not observant of purity laws in their private conduct, the am ha-aretz, were capable of, and expected to, adjust their behavior to the commercial interests of purity observance in the vicinity of Jerusalem.

The unit opens with the following rule: "In Judea all are trusted with respect to the purity of wine and oil throughout the year; and with respect to terumah only at the season of the winepresses and olive vats." Ostensibly, this rule is not limited to a particular kind of wine and oil.[53] Presumably, although people are not usually trusted with respect to the produce they hand over to the priest, wine and oil traders are believed when stating that their merchandise is pure. In other words, one may be trusted concerning the quality of what he sells rather than what he gives for free. Apparently, the Mishnah is talking of regular unconsecrated wine and oil that is sold in the marketplace, and the merchants are trusted regarding their wine and oil due to their financial interest in supplying the general commercial needs of the Temple city.[54] Indeed, the designation of wine produced in Judea for libations is alluded to in the Tosefta and stated explicitly in the Talmuds, but this is certainly not the exclusive designation of wine sold in Judea.[55] How, therefore, should we imagine that such a market, which is expected to provide a range of consumer needs, both for the Temple and for daily use, operates?

Elsewhere, the rabbis distinguish between the level of purity required for sacrifices themselves and the purity required for those things intended for future consecration or for the foods consumed together with the sacrificial meat. For instance, Tosefta Teharot 1:5–6 distinguishes between the level of purity required for sacrifices, "the holy consecrated things of the Temple," and the level of purity required for that which has not yet been consecrated, such as grain offerings that have not yet been placed in Temple vessels. In these cases, the level of purity required is equal to that of unconsecrated food. Similarly, unconsecrated foods that were intended to supplement the sacrificial meals in Jerusalem were not considered hallowed and therefore required a lower level of purity (m. Tehar. 2:8).[56] All produce sold in Jerusalem could therefore have been kept at a relatively low level of purity until it was sanctified or consumed with sacrificial meat. These sources reveal a reality in which pure oil and wine were sold in the marketplaces of Judea, and these products were intended for personal consumption in purity, for those who observed it, or to be brought to Jerusalem and consumed together with sacrificial meat.[57] This reality dictated the widespread trustworthiness granted to the general public regarding the purity of oil and wine.

On the other hand, terumah was not sold in the marketplace but rather handed to the priests, and therefore, the public had less interest to maintain its purity. The separation of terumah is a troublesome duty that demands observance of purity only to hand it over to the priest; this obligation is a nuisance, and the owner of the fruit receives no recompense for it. The priest is supposed to receive his share immediately with the production of the oil and wine, and the homeowner is therefore trusted regarding the purity of terumah only during the period of production of the wine and oil. Beyond this, any postponement of the terumah defiles it, and the priest must question the likelihood that the person was actually careful to maintain the purity of the oil or wine for a long period of time before it was given to him. Even the vessels intended for terumah were preserved only for a brief period of time. According to the Mishnah here, these jugs were prepared especially in advance, and during this period, one could buy them, knowing they were pure for terumah.

Another occasion for giving terumah was the pilgrimage to Jerusalem. The purity of terumah was publicly maintained during these periods. Jerusalem's marketplaces supplied goods to facilitate the needs of those coming to the Temple to sacrifice year-round, and the merchants could be trusted to say that their products were fittingly pure. However, as we learn from Mishnah

Hagigah 3:6, as well as from the final chapter of Mishnah Sheqalim, pilgrims brought their terumah with them to Jerusalem particularly during the three festivals. Although the practice of bringing terumah to Jerusalem is not mentioned in other tannaitic sources, since, according to rabbinic law, the priest may receive the produce anywhere, we learn from other Second Temple sources that this was in fact a familiar practice. Already in Nehemiah, it says: "We will bring to the storerooms of the House of our God the first part of our dough, and our gifts [of grain], and of the fruit of every tree, wine and oil for the priests" (10:38; see also 12:44; 13:5). We hear similarly that Tobit (1:6) brought the first fruits to Jerusalem together with all the priestly gifts. Also according to the book of Judith (11:13), the terumah of grain and the tithes of wine and oil were kept in Jerusalem for the priests. In the middle of the first century CE, Philo explained why all the priestly gifts were brought to Jerusalem before they were distributed to the priests (*Laws* 1:152).[58] In contrast to the rabbis who distinguished between the heave offerings (terumah), which were handed over to the priests, and first fruits, which were brought to Jerusalem, both Josephus and Qumran law imply that the priests received their share in Jerusalem from the first fruits.[59] Furthermore, Qumran law presumably also mandated an annual priestly gift from the dough, which was brought to Jerusalem together with the other gifts.[60]

We see then that the brief law in Mishnah Hagigah ("And in Jerusalem they are trusted in regard to hallowed things, and during a festival also in regard to terumah") fits into the picture that arises from the early nonrabbinic sources and testifies to the practice of bringing the priestly gifts to Jerusalem during the festivals. Due to this practice, it was determined that all pilgrims are trustworthy with respect to the purity of the terumah they brought with them. This Mishnah reflects the practice of Second Temple Jews, who were careful to maintain purity in specific public contexts, and particularly in preparation for the pilgrimage to Jerusalem.[61]

To conclude, the basic principle that underlies the policy of Mishnah Hagigah is the lack of distinction between different groups when a shared public interest was involved. In this context, rather than appointing supervisors (as in the modern model of the kashruth *mashgiach*) to ensure the appropriate conduct of all those involved in distributing the produce in the market, the Mishnah assumes that everyone acknowledged the need to maintain purity in particular shared spaces, where purity dictated the market needs. Therefore, according to my interpretation, Mishnah Hagigah does not limit the reliability of the general public to Temple matters. Even the tax collectors and the burglars are not trusted exclusively with regard to holy foodstuff; rather, it is assumed that within the vicinity of Jerusalem they were aware of their obligation to maintain purity in their contact with others and were capable of so doing.[62] The purity norms practiced in the marketplaces of Judea were sufficient to enable consumption of foods together with sacrifices and also for anyone desiring to regularly eat in the state of purity. According to Mishnah Hagigah, the observance of purity is woven into social norms on two complementary levels. On the one hand, the observance of purity delineates the contours of society, and it classifies people into groups in accordance with their level of purity. At the same time, within the markets of Judea, purity played a major economic role, and therefore, everybody valued it equally, shared a concern for it and had the capacity to ensure its maintenance in their interactions with others.

Conclusion: From Judea to the Galilee

In this chapter, I have argued that Mishnah Teharot reflects the reality of the late second-century rabbis of the Galilee. At this stage, it was not possible anymore to believe am ha-aretz on matters of purity, since the most basic conditions required for this trust were lacking. The am ha-aretz lacked both personal awareness and some form of public support for the observance of purity. In this reality, the only option open to someone who strove to maintain personal purity was to join a voluntary association and, as we learn from Mishnah Teharot, personally supervise those places he feared would be contaminated by others. Mishnah Hagigah, in contrast, is directed at the general public and is phrased as a public policy. The latter assumes that purity awareness is shared by all, even those who are not personally stringent on matters of purity. In the world of this Mishnah, observance of purity is considered a public matter serving commercial interests, and it is therefore shared by all. Within this framework, purity separates different groups, but everyone—including am ha-aretz—is perceived as taking place in this public value, and special mechanisms for protection against am ha-aretz are therefore unnecessary.

The changing of mechanisms from general reliability to personal supervision reflects, according to the interpretation I have offered, not only the eroding trust in am ha-aretz but also the change in the public value of purity observance in the eyes of the rabbis. While tannaitic literature naturally does not record the changes that took place in the extent of purity observance, it inevitably compelled them to reformulate and reinterpret earlier traditions. A close textual analysis reveals how specific laws were reformulated to fit later circumstances. In addition, they uncover the changing audiences of the rabbinic rulings. The early legal traditions, as reflected in Mishnah Hagigah, are formulated from a public standpoint and present themselves as reflecting widespread social norms. The Mishnah of the later Galilean rabbis, on the other hand, is limited to the perspective of the private individual who finds himself in an unsupportive environment and is consequently devising new social institutions to protect his personal realm from defilement.

7

The End of Purity

Introduction

In the previous chapter we saw that the renewed framing of the laws of am ha-aretz reflect wider social and religious processes, as well as the marginalization of purity within Jewish society. Although legal literature cannot directly reflect complex social conditions, I have nonetheless claimed that changes in rabbinic legal discourse may inform us of the rabbis' attempts to adapt the law to changing circumstances. The study of the social history of Palestinian Jews therefore stands to benefit from a study of the history of rabbinic law. In this case, archaeological findings are also in line with halakhic trends, as these are reflected in different layers of rabbinic literature and in the gap between the legal system of the early rabbis and that of the later tannaim, who operated in the Galilee during the latter half of the second century.

Rabbinic legal sources reveal a further decrease in the observance of purity that continued in the following period as well. Strict purity observance became extremely rare, and even among the rabbis there were those who contented themselves with minimal gestures toward purity, or with the observance of purity during certain days of the year. Evidence of these developments may be gathered from sporadic statements within the latest strata of tannaitic literature and they become even more apparent in later Talmudic sources. Unlike the textual analysis in the previous chapter, which revealed a systematic reworking of substantial earlier materials by the Galilean disciples of R. Akiva, who represent the peak of tannaitic activity, the testimonies to the following stages toward the end of the period are more sporadic and coincidental. The testimonies for the general neglect of purity are generally characteristic of the

Tosefta, which was redacted later than the Mishnah, and they continue into the Talmuds and later sources. In this chapter, we shall trace these clues, which do not amount to a reshaping of the halakhic system, but are rather scattered in exegetical comments, which are appended to earlier traditions, and they point out how foreign these purity practices have become in the eyes of their later transmitters.

Changing the Meaning of "Pure Foods"

In his book *The Galilean Am ha-Aretz*, Adolf Büchler sought to limit the significance of purity observance among the Pharisees and the rabbis and to prove that the majority of purity laws in tannaitic literature were directed solely at the priests, for the sake of the terumah they received, and had limited impact on the social behavior of other groups.[1] The apologetic and tendentious tone employed by Büchler, who was clearly attempting to defend the Pharisees and their rabbinic followers against accusations of separatism, is unmistakable. At the same time, one cannot deny that a significant portion of the tannaitic sources do indeed assume, whether explicitly or implicitly, that purity observance was necessary only for the consumption of terumah. See, for instance, the following source concerning the stages of child education: "Once he [the minor] knows how to control [lit. guard] his body, we may eat pure foods [teharot] that touched his body. When he learns to control his hands, we may eat pure foods touched by his hands. And how is he examined? They immerse him and hand him unconsecrated food as if was terumah. If he is capable of controlling his body, we may eat pure foods that touched his body. If he is capable of controlling his hands, we may eat pure foods that his hands touched."[2] From this source it appears that "pure foods" (teharot) relates to the holy terumah in particular, and it is with regard to this that the child is tested. In light of sources such as these, Büchler and others deduced that pure foods (teharot) in tannaitic literature regularly signify terumah even when not mentioned explicitly.[3] This approach is characteristic of later halakhic literature as well, which abandoned the notion of eating unconsecrated foods in purity and focused on the obligation to maintain the purity of the priestly gifts.[4] However, in spite of the attempt to paint all tannaitic literature uniformly, I will claim that the identification of the term *teharot* with *terumah*, in particular, is characteristic of the later layers of tannaitic material, due to the decrease in purity observance in the third century. Through these sporadic comments the rabbis abandoned the all-encompassing ideology of purity and returned to the limited biblical notion of observing purity within the holy sphere alone.

Early traditions seem to indicate that the term *teharot* was not limited to priestly foods and included any pure foods in general. For instance, the Mishnah testifies that despite their disputes, the Houses of Hillel and Shammai did not abstain from preparing pure foods together.[5] In light of their own separation from am ha-aretz, this declaration emphasizes the continuing cooperation between the two academies. In this case the term *pure foods* represents the regular foods of these groups. In addition, early laws of menstrual impurity discuss the possibility that a woman will defile pure foods (teharot) during her period. Thus, for example, the opening law in tractate Niddah, attributed to the Houses of Hillel and Shammai, addresses the fear that pure foods handled by a woman will be rendered impure retroactively (m. Nid. 1:1–2). It therefore appears that the fear of defiling pure foods shaped the day-to-day behavior of these rabbis and touched on wider circles beyond the priests who partook of terumah.[6]

On the other hand, in three different cases we can discern a textual emendation intended to limit the term *teharot* to *terumah*. The first case is the Tosefta quoted previously, regarding a child who is learning to observe purity. The Tosefta here addresses the stages of development of the child with regard to pure foods, and the basic principle it suggests is this: if the child knows how to take care of his body, one may consume pure foods he has touched. To this basic level the Tosefta added a comment on how to test the child. The child is led to believe that he is holding terumah, and we observe his behavior. Although this comment presents itself as an interpretation of the basic instruction, there is a marked difference between the two textual stages. Basically, the child is considered faithful with regard to pure foods once we learn from his ability to control himself. In the additional comment, however, we find a more stringent requirement. To protect the purity of the terumah, we must test the child. Considering the danger of desecrating the holy foodstuff, the stakes are too high, and we cannot risk their purity without examining the child first. At this stage, one is required to exhibit a real proficiency to protect the terumah. This, however, was not necessarily the original meaning of this instruction, which allowed for a gradual adjustment to higher standards for treating pure, unconsecrated foods.

Two additional sources concerning the "preparation of pure foods (*teharot*)" for others also testify to the addition of the holy terumah only in later exegetical comments. A ruling from Tosefta Demai addresses the extent of the prohibition to prepare pure foods for an am ha-aretz: "R. Yosi ben Hamshulam testified in the name of R. Nathan, who said in the name of R. Eleazar Hisma, that one may not prepare pure foods (teharot) for an am ha-aretz." Following this testimony, the baraita adds a reservation: "He may not knead his terumah dough in a state of purity, but he may knead his unconsecrated dough in a state of purity."[7] It is only from the added comment that we learn that the prohibition relates specifically to terumah. According to this explanation, an associate must not prepare the terumah for a priest who is an am ha-aretz and is not careful in matters of purity, for fear that the priest will defile the holy terumah. On the other hand, an associate may help an am ha-aretz set aside terumah from his produce so that he may later give pure terumah to the (associate) priest. In the eyes of the transmitter of the earlier tradition, there is therefore a necessary linkage between "preparing pure foods" and the setting aside of terumah.

Another source reveals that the rabbis themselves disputed whether the early tradition regarding the preparation of teharot for others relates particularly to the setting aside of terumah in purity:

> R. Judah says: a deaf-mute person who separated the terumah, his action is valid. R. Judah said: The story tells of the sons of R. Yoḥanan ben Gudgeda, who were deaf-mute, and all the pure foods [teharot] in Jerusalem were prepared by them.
> The rabbis replied: Is that a proof? Pure foods do not require thought, and are therefore prepared by a deaf, a mentally disabled person and a minor. Separating *terumah* and tithes, on the other hand, requires thought.[8]

In its original Second Temple context, the story about the involvement of R. Yoḥanan ben Gudgeda's deaf children in the preparation of *all* the pure foods in Jerusalem had a clear polemical intention. The purity of disabled persons was a contested issue, as we learn from the sectarian letter 4QMMT. Among its complaints against the lenient approach to purity adopted by the authorities in Jerusalem, the letter includes the following argument: "And concerning the deaf, who have not heard the laws and the judgments and the purity regulations, and have not heard the ordinances of Israel, since he who has not seen or heard does not know how to obey (the law): nevertheless, they have access to the sacred food" (B 52–54). Rabbinic tradition, however, transferred the story to another question: who is fit to separate the holy terumah? From their perspective, the issue here is not purity but rather mental capacity.

R. Judah learns from the case of the sons of R. Yoḥanan b. Gudgeda that a deaf person, who is considered mentally disabled, may set aside terumah. He understands that their involvement in preparing pure foods proves that they also would set aside terumah and tithes. Evidently, however, the rabbis who dispute him denied this inference.[9] According to rabbinic tradition, Yoḥanan b. Gudgeda would regularly maintain a high degree of purity observance, as if he was eating sacrificial meat (see following section). Due to his strict observance, his sons were also trusted to prepare all the "pure foods" of Jerusalem. It is only in a later reality, when many people were aided by experts in setting aside terumah in purity, that their story was reinterpreted as though they had handled terumah in particular.

We see that traditions regarding "pure foods" were later interpreted as relating to terumah. One may surmise that the decrease in the daily observance of purity led to the creation of a dual system. On the one hand, the public continued to maintain the purity of terumah and was aided by purity experts to handle their terumah in the state of purity.[10] On the other hand, only a select few maintained the purity of unconsecrated foods. Consequently, laws that had originally related to the purity of unconsecrated foods were now applied to terumah. At the same time, the consumption of ordinary food in purity was perceived as a marginal phenomenon, as we will see in the following section.

The Pure Few

Several posttannaitic sources present the practice of eating unconsecrated foods in purity as an unusual and marginal phenomenon, maintained by only few pietists. Thus, for instance, we read in the fifth-century midrash Pesiqta de-Rav Kahana regarding King Saul, who was anointed and ruled immediately: "For what merit? For the good deeds he possessed, and the fact that he was humble and modest and would eat unconsecrated foods in purity."[11] A similar statement appears in the Babylonian Talmud regarding Abraham, who refrained from bringing the bread made by Sarah to the angels: "Ephraim Maksha'ah, a disciple of R. Meir, said in his teacher's name: Our Patriarch Abraham ate ḥullin only in the state of purity, and that day our mother Sarah had her menstrual period."[12] The Talmud assumes that, had Abraham not been particularly stringent on eating unconsecrated foods in purity, he would have eaten Sarah's foods. This example itself, however, proves that the tradition regarding Abraham was reformulated after purity observance had faded. In the earlier, Palestinian parallel in *Genesis Rabbah*, a different version of R. Ephraim Maksha'ah's words appears: "Sarah had her menstrual period and consequently defiled the dough."[13] The distancing of the impure menstruant from the dough was taken for granted by the Palestinian transmitter as a standard practice; however, in Babylonia, impure women were not distanced from food, and therefore, the Talmud adds the comment that Abraham was unusually meticulous in this respect.[14]

Textual processes such as these feature already in the Tosefta, in the final layers of the redaction of tannaitic literature. Here, too, we can distinguish between the earlier tradition, which assumes that eating in purity is a prevalent norm, and the later reworking of the tradition, which views this practice as an unusual one, shared by only a singular few. In tannaitic literature, we find two sages who ate unconsecrated foods in purity: Yoḥanan ben ha-Ḥoranit and Rabban Gamaliel. Ostensibly, the very fact that the sources note this piece of data testifies to the rarity of this practice. But in these cases, too, a close examination of these traditions reveals the ways in which a familiar, widespread custom of eating in purity was later identified as an exceptional practice.

Let us begin with the source regarding Yoḥanan ben ha-Ḥoranit. In Mishnah Eduyot 4:6, the Houses of Hillel and Shammai discuss how to prevent olives from being contaminated. For this purpose, the olives must be kept away from their own liquids lest they become susceptible to impurity: "The House of Shammai say: One need not perforate a barrel of pickled olives, and the House of Hillel say: One must perforate it. But they agree that if it was perforated and the lees stopped it up, it is not susceptible to impurity." The House of Hillel demands that the barrel be perforated so that its liquids will drain out, whereas the House of Shammai believe that the sap that is secreted from the pickled olives is not considered a liquid that renders the olives fit to receive impurity. From the following story from the Tosefta, it appears that early rabbis attempted to act in accordance with these directives:

> Said Rabbi Eliezer ben Rabbi Zadok: When I was studying Torah with Rabbi Yoḥanan ben ha-Ḥoranit, I observed him eating his bread dry, for those were years of scarcity. I went and told my father, who said to me: Bring him some olives. So I brought him some. He examined them; but when he saw that they were moist he said to me, I do not eat olives. So I went and told my father, who said to me, go and tell him that the olive jar was perforated according to the position of the school of Hillel, but the lees have stopped it up.
>
> This shows that he was careful to eat unconsecrated food in the state of purity.
>
> Though he was a disciple of the House of Shammai he was guided by the opinions of the House of Hillel.[15]

R. Yoḥanan ben ha-Ḥoranit followed the stringent opinion of the House of Hillel. When he saw that the olives he received from R. Zadok were moist, he assumed that they had been rendered susceptible to impurity in a nonperforated barrel. Out of fear of impurity, he refused to accept them from R. Zadok.[16] The Tosefta comments on this behavior of Yoḥanan ben ha-Ḥoranit: "This shows that he was careful to eat unconsecrated food in the state of purity."

This sentence creates the impression that eating in a state of purity was an unfamiliar phenomenon in Yoḥanan's surroundings and that the narrator was compelled to explain his unusual behavior by noting that it derived from his unique practice of eating in a state of purity. In fact, however, this sentence is clearly a secondary insertion into the primary tradition. This sentence interferes the sequence between R. Yoḥanan's behavior and the explanation in the final sentence that he acted according to the position of the House of Hillel. Indeed, in a parallel in the Babylonian Talmud (b. Yebam. 15b), the entire story appears word for word, aside from the clarifying insertion, "This shows that he was careful to eat unconsecrated food in the state of purity."

Once we are aware of the textual revision, we may reconstruct adequately the original historical situation. According to the original source, R. Yoḥanan ben ha-Ḥoranit followed the standard practice of consuming unconsecrated foods in purity, and therefore all the foods they sent to each other were pure. However, at a later stage, when this practice had diminished, the transmitter of the tradition in the Tosefta marked this as an unusual practice, thereby adding R. Yoḥanan to the select few who maintained it.

The second rabbi who is described in tannaitic literature as eating unconsecrated foods in purity is Rabban Gamaliel. But in this case, too, the authenticity of this tradition, which implies that this was a rare practice, should be questioned. Arguably, the current version of the tradition appears to reflect a later redaction, from a period when eating in purity was no longer familiar. As we have seen in chapter 4, Mishnah Hagigah 2:6–7 lays out a range of purity levels, from the impure am ha-aretz to the highest purity required for those involved in sprinkling purification waters. In this framework, both the Mishnah and the Tosefta offer examples of people who maintained a high level of purity. There is, however, a fundamental difference between the two parallel sources:

Mishnah Hagigah 2:8	Tosefta Hagigah 3:3
The garments of am ha-aretz possess midras impurity for the Pharisees. The garments of Pharisees possess midras impurity for those who eat terumah. The garments of those who eat terumah possess midras impurity for [those who eat] hallowed things. The garments of [those who eat] hallowed things possess midras impurity for [those who occupy themselves with the waters of] purification.	

Yose b. Yo'ezer was the most pious in the priesthood, yet his napkin was [considered to possess] midras impurity for [those who ate] hallowed things.	Rabban Gamaliel would eat in accordance with the purity required for unconsecrated food all his life, yet his napkin was [considered to possess] midras impurity for [those who ate] hallowed things.
Yohanan b. Gudgeda used all his life to eat [unconsecrated food] in accordance with the purity required for hallowed things, yet his napkin was [considered to possess] midras uncleanness for [those who occupied themselves with the water of] purification.	Onqelos the proselyte used all his life to eat [unconsecrated food] in accordance with the purity required for hallowed things, yet his napkin was [considered to possess] midras uncleanness for [those who occupied themselves with the water of] purification.

Following the list of the levels of purity of different groups—namely, (i) am ha-aretz, (ii) Pharisees (who eat unconsecrated foods in purity), (iii) priests eating terumah and partakers of hallowed things (such as sacrificial meat), and (iv) those involved in the sprinkling of purification waters—the Mishnah demonstrates these differences through familiar examples. Notably, the Mishnah does not think it is necessary to provide an example for one who eats unconsecrated foods in purity, such as the Pharisees. After all, in the world of this Mishnah, this was a well-known and widespread phenomenon. Cases of higher levels of purity observance, on the other hand, were indeed worthy of comment. Yose b. Yo'ezer was a pious priest who was supposedly careful to maintain the purity of all his foods as though they were terumah. Nevertheless, he was impure for hollowed things. Yohanan b. Gudgeda, the Mishnah emphasizes, ate all his meals in the level of purity required for the Temple and for sacrifices his entire life.

Unlike the Mishnah, the Tosefta notes Rabban Gamaliel's unique practice of eating unconsecrated foods in purity.[17] This source seems to indicate that during the Yavneh period, immediately after the destruction of the Temple, the practice of eating unconsecrated foods in purity faded, and therefore Rabban Gamaliel's conduct deserved special mention.[18] A closer look at the language of the Tosefta, however, throws this conclusion into question. The statement in the Tosefta that Rabban Gamaliel would eat "in accordance with the purity required for unconsecrated food," and that his napkin possessed midras impurity (i.e., a garment that conveys severe impurity even through indirect shifting) for those who ate hallowed things, is bewildering for two reasons. According to the principles that arise from the Mishnah itself, the clothing of those who eat unconsecrated foods in purity, the Pharisees, possess midras impurity for those who eat terumah. Why does the Tosefta skip a stage and determine that Rabban Gamaliel's napkin possessed midras impurity for those who ate hallowed things rather than for terumah? In addition, the phrase "in accordance with the purity required for unconsecrated food" is awkward and does not appear elsewhere in Talmudic literature. One may eat unconsecrated foods in purity, and one may eat unconsecrated foods in accordance with the purity required for a higher level of sanctity, such as terumah or hallowed things; but eating unconsecrated food "in accordance with the purity required for unconsecrated food" is a convoluted expression for a fairly simple situation.

It therefore appears that the description of Rabban Gamaliel has somehow been confused or revised, and we cannot derive any conclusions regarding the extent of the practice of eating unconsecrated foods in purity during his time. It is more probable that the original tradition stated, "Rabban Gamaliel used all his life to eat unconsecrated food in accordance with the purity required for terumah, but his napkin possessed midras uncleanness for those who ate hallowed things." According to this reconstructed formulation, the Tosefta provides an exact parallel to the Mishnah, the difference between them being that the Mishnah relates to figures that were active during the time of the Temple, and the Tosefta refers to those after its destruction.[19] Both sources share the assumption that eating unconsecrated foods in purity is a prevalent practice, which requires no examples, unlike the higher levels of purity observance. With time, the Tosefta was corrected from "with the purity required for *terumah*" to "the purity required for unconsecrated foods,"[20] and following this, this later rabbi became the prototype of one who eats unconsecrated foods in purity.[21]

Arguably, then, the description of Rabban Gamaliel as one who ate unconsecrated foods in purity his whole life is more congruent with his figure in the eyes of third-century rabbis than it is with the actual period in which he lived, during the beginning of the second century, and reflects the ideal of purity as they perceived it. This portrayal resonates with the instruction Rav Ḥiyya the Great gives to Rav, from the beginning of the amoraic period: "If you can eat unconsecrated foods in purity all year round, very well! And if not, eat [unconsecrated foods in purity] seven days a year."[22] Evidently, then, at the beginning of the third century, the rabbis acknowledged the difference among those few who ate in purity, between those who managed to maintain this practice all the time and those who ate in purity for only a limited time span. Against this background, Rabban Gamaliel is presented in the current version of the Tosefta as a unique example for one who steadily maintained the purity of unconsecrated foods ("all his days").

Rethinking Handwashing

The restriction of purity concerns to the realm of terumah and its diminishing relevance to the daily practice of nonpriests is reflected in the renewed interpretation of the ancient practice of handwashing. Here, too, the transformation of the legal traditions reveals the changing nature of this observance. Initially, when eating in a state of purity was an accessible norm, handwashing could naturally fit within this framework. Thus, for instance, as we saw in the third chapter, the confrontation between Jesus and the Pharisees concerning handwashing reflected their opposing perceptions of purity. A century and a half later, on the other hand, when the pure consumption of unconsecrated foods was a rare sight, the widespread custom of handwashing, too, acquired new meaning beyond the realm of purity.[23] The clearest expression of this tendency appears in a post-Talmudic source, but we will see that the attempt to base handwashing on priestly rites of sanctification, rather than on purity laws, which had become inaccessible and foreign, appears already in tannaitic sources from the beginning of the third century.

The late midrash Tanna debe Eliyyahu seeks to justify handwashing before a meal based on the priestly obligation to wash hands and feet at the entrance to the Tabernacle:

> A friend [of the questioner in the previous chapter] who also knew Scripture but not Mishnah came and sat near him. [Then asked me whence came the precept of washing the hands]. I replied: "My son, washing the hands is prescribed by Torah." "But, my master," my questioner [said], "It was not prescribed to us at Mount Sinai." Thereupon I said: . . . "Likewise, we infer the precept of washing the hands from the Torah, for it was first said to Moses and to Aaron and to his sons as well, 'Thou shall make a lever of brass' [Ex. 30:18], which Moses, Aaron and his sons were to use for washing, as it said 'when they go into the Tent of Meeting.' But with regard to Israelites, where does Scripture command washing the hands? In the verse 'sanctify yourselves and be holy' [Lev. 11:44]. On the basis of this verse, Rabban Gamaliel would eat unconsecrated food in a state of purity. He was wont to say that holiness was not given to the priests alone, but to the priests and Levites and all Israel, as Scripture tells us 'Speak to all the congregation of the people of Israel and say to them: You shall be holy, for I the Lord your God am holy' [Lev 19.2]. Hence it is said, when a man belittles the washing of hands, it is an omen of ill fortune for him."[24]

As in Jesus's dispute with the Pharisees regarding handwashing, in this source, too, handwashing represents the obligation to heed oral tradition. The questioner acknowledges only the written law, and in response, the author seeks to anchor this obligation scripturally. According to his approach, not only priests but all Jews are commanded to be holy and therefore obligated to ritually sanctify themselves through handwashing. As we saw in the third chapter, according to Jacob Neusner,[25] the Pharisees adopted a priestly lifestyle, viewing the domestic table as an altar and every person as a priest. In this vein, Neusner suggested that handwashing before a meal embodied the adoption of the priestly act of sanctification before the Temple service. Surely, however, we cannot rely on this late post-Talmudic source for the understanding of the world of the Pharisees and their conception of purity and holiness. In fact, this source should be viewed as a later attempt to reinterpret handwashing, in a world in which purity has ceased to function as a meaningful religious category.

This tendency, however, did not begin only in the post-Talmudic period. The following sources reveal that the view that handwashing was required only for terumah and that it was an extension of the sanctification of the hands and feet before the priests' entrance to the Temple service, developed already toward the end of the tannaitic period. Thus we read in the Sifre on Numbers:

> [1] "As a service of gift have I given your priesthood (to you)" (Nu. 18:7): This equates the eating of holy foodstuff in the provinces [i.e., terumah, etc.] with the service of the Temple in the Temple. Just as with the service of the Temple in the Temple, he first washes his hands and then serves, so, with the eating of the holy foodstuff in the provinces—he first washes his hands and then eats.
>
> [2] And it once happened that R. Tarfon was late in coming to the house of study, whereupon R. Gamaliel asked him: Why are you late? And he responded: I was serving (as a priest). [Said] R. Gamaliel: All of your words are a puzzle. Is there (Temple) service now (that the Temple has been destroyed)? [Said] R. Tarfon: It is written "As a service of gift have I given your priesthood (to you)." This equates the eating of holy foodstuff in the provinces with the service of the Temple in the Temple.
>
> [3] Rabbi [Judah the Patriarch] says: "This equates the eating of holy foodstuff in the provinces with the service of the Temple in the Temple"—Just as with the service of the Temple in the Temple, he first washes his hands and then serves, so, with the eating of holy foodstuff in the provinces—he first washes his hands and then eats.
>
> But perhaps just as there, he washes both his hands and his feet, so, here!
>
> Would you say that? In a place (the Temple) where he must wash his hands and his feet (for the Temple service), he does so; but in a place where he needs to wash only his hands, that is what he does.
>
> We hereby learn the washing of the hands to be scripturally prescribed.[26]

The homily concludes that the sanctification of hands and feet in the Temple is the source for the practice of handwashing before eating. A closer look at the homily even allows us to trace the creation of this perception back to a statement of R. Judah the Patriarch dating to the end of the tannaitic period. In a story that appears in section [2], R. Tarfon, who lived at the end of the first century, compares the consumption of terumah to Temple worship in general, to emphasize the importance of terumah consumption even after the destruction of the Temple. Just as Temple worship is greater than Torah study, so too the status of terumah consumption, and by implication R. Tarfon's tardiness to the study hall, was justified.

This comparison, offered by R. Tarfon, sets the backdrop for the statement uttered by Rabbi Judah the Patriarch three generations later. Just as the priests must wash their hands and feet, sanctifying them before commencing Temple service, the same must be done before the consumption of terumah, which is itself a form of holy worship. R. Judah the Patriarch's statement offers a double innovation: first, he limits the obligation of handwashing to the consumption of terumah; second, he links this obligation to scripture. Following in his footsteps, the redactor duplicates this innovation in the opening section of the midrashic unit.[27]

Another attempt to establish the custom of handwashing on biblical verses appears already in earlier midrashic sources. But there is an illuminating difference between the two cases. With respect to the zav, who suffers abnormal genital discharge, the Torah prescribes: "If one with a discharge, without having rinsed his hands in water, touches another person, that person shall wash his clothes, bathe in water, and remain unclean until evening" (Lev. 15:11). The midrash on this verse includes the following statement by R. Eleazar b. Arakh: "From here they supported hand purity with the words of the Torah."[28] It is noteworthy that R. Eleazar b. Arakh, who lived at the end of the first century CE, did not claim that handwashing was actually derived from scripture, since it was admittedly a rabbinic ordinance. Rather, in response to those who "doubted hand purity," such as Jesus and Eleazar ben Hanoch (m. Edu. 5:6), he sought to somehow provide scriptural supporting for this custom. To this end, he chose a verse that could demonstrate the role of unwashed hands in the spread of contamination. This choice clearly indicates that at this stage, the rabbis associated handwashing with the fear of spreading contamination, similar to the discourse we identified in the gospel traditions in chapter 3. A century later, on the other hand, Rabbi Judah the Patriarch ignored the purifying role of handwashing and the power of hands to defile foods and derived the obligation of handwashing from the sanctification in the Temple.[29]

Another aspect of the transformation from purification to sanctification is the reframing of several details of the laws of handwashing. In this respect, a comparison between Mishnah and Tosefta Yadayim is revealing. The first two chapters of Mishnah Yadayim shape handwashing as a clear purification rite. In the Mishnah, the laws prescribing what vessel to use for handwashing and how precisely to pour the water facilitate a graded process of removal of impurity. Within this framework, the remarkable similarities between handwashing and the laws of purification waters (for removal of corpse impurity) are particularly striking. Thus, for instance, the laws relating to the vessel for washing hands are equivalent to those concerning the vessel for preparing purification waters:

Mishnah Yadayim 1:2	**Mishnah Parah 5:5**
Water may be poured over the hands out of any kind of vessels, even out of vessels made of cattle dung, of stone or of clay.	Purification water may be prepared in all kinds of vessels, even in vessels made of cattle dung, of stone or of clay. The mixture may also be prepared in a ship.
Water may not be poured from the sides of vessels or from the bottom of a ladle or from the bung of a barrel, or in one's cupped hands, for one may not draw, nor sanctify, nor sprinkle the water of purification, **nor pour water over the hands** except in a vessel.	It may not be prepared in the sides of vessels, or in the bottom of the ladle, or in the bung of a barrel, or in one's cupped hands, for one may not draw, nor sanctify, nor sprinkle the water of purification, except in a vessel.

The comparison between these parallel sources clearly shows that the Mishnah in tractate Yadayim is a reworking of the Mishnah in Parah. Handwashing is substituted in Mishnah Yadayim for purification waters, and thus, the reference to handwashing is inserted in the last sentence into the procedure of purification from corpse impurity. Since, unlike immersion in a miqveh, the water for handwashing is applied from a vessel, the analogy to purification waters sprinkled from the vessel is only to be expected.

And yet, unlike the exclusive framework of purity law in which the laws of handwashing were shaped in Mishnah Yadayim, Tosefta Yadayim adds a new frame of reference. The Tosefta repeatedly compares the laws of handwashing to the priestly Temple service.[30] Thus, for instance, it reads: "The priests sanctify in the Temple only with a vessel, and the suspected women drink the waters from a vessel and the lepers are purified with a vessel" (t. Yad. 1:7).

Whereas the Mishnah compares the purification of hands to purification from corpse impurity, the list in the Tosefta enumerates priestly rites undertaken particularly in the Temple.

Against the background of our earlier findings, it appears that the Tosefta here serves as yet another testimony to the attempt to place the laws of handwashing within the context of Temple practices, similar to the midrash that compared handwashing before eating terumah to the sanctification of feet and hands before Temple work. As part of this shift, these sources testify, albeit indirectly, to the diminishing care for purity and the reinterpretation of handwashing as a nonpurifying act.

New Popular Forms of Purity Observance

According to the rabbinic teachings, purity observance, on all levels, derives from a uniform system of principles concerning the dissemination of impurity. All foodstuff, whether it is ordinary food or terumah, is defiled in the tent of a corpse, and indirect contact with those with severe impurity, such as a vessel shifted by a menstruant, defiles its contents—even if it is unconsecrated food. There are indeed particular demands relating to hallowed foods (m. Hag. 3:1–3), but as far as terumah and ordinary foods go, the same distancing measures from impurity are required. Tannaitic literature assumes that the laws of defilement apply to ordinary food as well and that impurity operates in the same manner with respect to all foods, apart from the fact that terumah is invalidated at the third level of impurity and ordinary food only at the second. From the rabbinic perspective this is a minor difference within a shared system of principles. One who seeks to observe the purity of unconsecrated foods is therefore required to be acquainted with the complex rules governing the spread of impurity, including indirect impurity and the power of liquid impurity.[31] Evidently, this form of observance requires professional knowledge and a support network.

We would have no need to note this familiar feature were it not for the fundamental change that occurred in the nature of purity observance in the post-tannaitic period. In the Palestinian Talmud and in later Palestinian halakhic literature, we see the rise of a new form of purity observance, which is incongruent with the set principles of the spread of impurity familiar to us from the earlier sources. At this point in time, the desire to live a life of purity and distance oneself from impurity was refashioned in a manner that had very little in common with the systemic schema of rabbinic purity laws. Two different styles of purity observance were thus created: one was directed at maintaining the purity of terumah, which was based on a detailed acquaintance with the complex channels of impurity dissemination; the other was related to daily foods, which was popular in nature and focused on distancing from direct contact with sources of impurity. The first required professional knowledge, while the second, more intuitive form of observance provided a consciousness of purity within everyday life without committing itself completely and systemically to tracing the threat of impurity. This latter purity is, to a great extent, an am-ha-aretz-style purity, which was later backed up by halakhic literature. In what follows, we will point out several indications of the consolidation of this purity style alongside the waning of systemic observance of purity.

The development of the laws of am ha-aretz in the Palestinian Talmud provides an apt expression for the creation of this alternative form of purity observance. At this stage, am ha-aretz ceased to be viewed as a threat to ḥullin (unconsecrated foods), and even in the eyes of the rabbis themselves, he remained a threat only to terumah. Palestinian amoraim were compelled to reinterpreted Mishnah Hagigah 2:7, to the effect that the impurity of am ha-aretz was practically annulled with regard to ḥullin. As we saw in chapter 4, the structure of the Mishnah indicates that each of the groups imparts equal impurity on the groups that are on a higher level of purity. For instance, am ha-aretz defiles the Pharisees to the same extent that a Pharisee defiles one who eats terumah. This structure, however, completely dissolves in the Palestinian Talmud.

After a complex discussion of the meaning of Mishnah Hagigah 2:7, the Palestinian Talmud reaches the following conclusions:[32] with respect to the purity of terumah, the Talmud interprets the Mishnah according to its plain meaning. The body of the Pharisee and anyone who does not eat terumah in purity carries only a light impurity and defiles the terumah only through direct contact. On the other hand, people with severe impurity, such as the gentile and the menstruant, defile terumah vessels even through indirect contact. Regarding ḥullin, however, the Palestinian Talmud paints a fundamentally different picture, which is incongruent with the plain meaning of the Mishnah. In this context, not only does am ha-aretz not defile through indirect contact, he does not defile at all. Furthermore, the conclusion of the following discussion is that even the zav himself (like the gentile and the menstruant) can defile ḥullin only through direct contact, in opposition to the principles of both the biblical and the tannaitic purity systems. Regarding the question of why, according to the Mishnah, there is a fear that the clothes of an am ha-aretz might defile, R. Yassa answers: "since the wife of the am ha-aretz [might have] sat on it naked." R. Yassa emphasizes that the impure woman sat on the clothes while naked, meaning that she transmits her impurity only through direct contact, unlike the familiar paths of defilement of the menstruant.[33]

All these statements are directed at one goal: to sever the observance of ḥullin purity from the familiar principles of impurity transmission, which are henceforth applied only with regard to terumah, and to suggest, in its place, a minimal system of distancing within daily conduct. It must be emphasized that the Palestinian Talmud does not completely disprove the value of maintaining the purity of ḥullin; it rather creates a new standard for this endeavor. One who seeks to prevent his daily food from being contaminated, as a sort of popular form of observance, is only required to distance himself from direct contact with severe impurity. Within this framework, even the am ha-aretz himself can partake in this practice and is no longer considered impure. Thus, a new style of observance evolved, which included limited forms of distancing from the menstruant within the realm of everyday food consumption.

Palestinian halakhic literature from the amoraic period and later provides further testimony to this style of observance. Thus, for instance, we are already familiar with the custom, prevalent from the time of the Second Temple, to immerse in a miqveh after engaging in sexual relations. The prevalence of this immersion emerges also from the discussion in the Palestinian Talmud, which portrays a bizarre reality whereby people care more about immersing after sexual relations than prohibited sexual relations (such as with a menstruant or a married woman). The tension recorded in the Palestinian Talmud on this matter reveals that some rabbis objected to this immersion, which they viewed as a distorted expression of muddled piety.[34]

Another expression of the differing standards of purity observance and the existence of a popular style of purity observance can be found regarding distancing from the menstruant. At the beginning of the third century, R. Shimon b. Eleazar testified that the practice in his circles was to eat with menstruants.[35] Resh Lakish, too, would eat with menstruants, as is evidenced in the following story: "R. Shimon b. Lakish entered the place of R. Yannai. The women saw him and escaped from him. He replied to them: You should beware of me, since I am an am ha-aretz with respect to pure foods."[36] The women in R. Yannai's home distanced themselves from Resh Lakish so as to not defile him, but he warned them that they must beware *his* own defilement, as he was not consistently strict on matters of purity.

Later sources reveal that in Palestine, in contrast to the Babylonian custom, Jews continued to be wary of the contaminating force of menstruants well into the post-Talmudic period.[37] Therefore, menstruants were prevented from preparing food, touching furniture, and even, to some degree, from nursing their children. At the same time, according to one testimony, the menstruant was only distanced from moist food.[38] This observance of purity law reflects the new standard, which is not based on the biblical or tannaitic principles of impurity transmission. From a strict legal perspective, the menstruant defiles even dry foodstuff, but in practice, there was no effort made to control her touch. Therefore, only contact with moist food, which could intuitively be imagined to spread her defilement, was considered as contaminating.[39]

Following the weakening of the early legal principles and the adoption of alternative standards, we witness a parallel phenomenon: the blurring of the distinction between the laws of purity and impurity and the realm of food prohibitions. A detailed expression of this tendency can be found in the following ruling, which is included in the *Ma'asim* literature from Byzantine Palestine:[40]

> If a mouse or a swarming thing fell into the liquor or other liquids, one must weigh the liquids. If the weight is a thousand times that of the mouse it is permitted, less than that, it is prohibited. If one of eight swarming things falls into a clay vessel full with liquids, you shall assess if the ratio is one to a thousand. If so, the liquid is permitted and the vessel is pure. Less than that, the liquid is prohibited, and it is prohibited to use it for light in the synagogue, but in his house it is permitted.[41]

Later rabbinic authorities found this ruling perplexing, as it seems to confuse different considerations. The impurity of a swarming thing is not, after all, canceled out by a mixture and is not similar to a forbidden food item, which is annulled if its relative size is outweighed. This consideration is irrelevant in the field of purity. In a different version of this ruling we even find that one may purify a clay vessel by drying it in the sun, an action that lacks any precedence in Talmudic purity laws. According to classical rabbinic law, a defiled clay vessel cannot be purified in any way other than by being broken.[42] Despite the dearth of textual evidence concerning these practices, we can identify two characteristic tendencies here. The first is taking care to avoid only direct contact with impurity and ignoring the paths of the spread of impurity. Therefore, even a clay vessel is defiled only when wet. Second, since the early laws of purity are no longer familiar, this halakhic ruling adopts alternative halakhic principles from other more familiar and accessible fields.

Conclusion

In light of the general tendencies described in this chapter, we may further explain the purity practices that appear in the Palestinian halakhic literature of late antiquity. As opposed to those who sought to view the type of rulings mentioned in the Ma'asim literature as a kind of "pietistic doctrine,"[43] Hillel

Newman correctly claims that these purity laws are not esoteric or elitist in nature, and they coincide with similar tendencies within other communities in Palestine during late antiquity in Palestine, such as the Samaritans. At the same time, Newman tends to attribute this occupation to priestly tendencies.[44] Thus, for instance, the distinction between the level of purity required for a synagogue and that required at home is supposedly tied to the evolution of the synagogue in Byzantine Palestine into a "Lesser Sanctuary."[45] Therefore, Newman carefully suggests that the application of Temple law to the synagogue might express the growing influence of the priests during this time period. However, in light of general tendencies uncovered in this chapter, the explanation seems to lie elsewhere. Purity observance at the end of the Talmudic period in Palestine was characterized by its sporadic, popular nature, and was primarily based on an intuitive recoiling from sources of contamination held in wide social circles. The aspiration to maintain purity ceased to order daily interactions but was redirected to the synagogue, as an expression of its Temple-like sanctity. These gestures of purity and sporadic attempts to avoid contact with defiling substances continued to exist even after the complete breakdown of the systematic lifestyle of Pharisaic purity, transmitted through the teachings of the early rabbis. The principles of organized purity were abandoned, but its memory and the value of purity were maintained.

Epilogue

The Rabbinic Movement within Shifting Religious Cultures

Although the roots of rabbinic purity discourse are embedded in the social and religious world of Second Temple Judaism, the changing circumstances of Palestinian Judaism in the following centuries also left their imprint on this key concept. There are no signs within early rabbinic literature of a revolution in the rabbinic worldview following the destruction of the Temple. Yet it is fairly clear that the final generation of the rabbis of the Mishnah, in the early third century, not only recognized a gap in the level of purity observance between themselves and the early rabbis but were also compelled to develop an alternative perception of this ancient practice. In the last two chapters, we tracked a wide range of textual and exegetical strategies used to amend and adjust early traditions to the social, cultural, and scholarly contexts in which the later rabbis operated. The reshaping of rabbinic purity laws thus provides a window into the profound changes in the religious and social world of the Jews of Palestine in the first centuries of the Common Era.

One of the challenges with which this book has dealt is the fact that the primary sources do not provide us with sufficient tools for a comprehensive history of purity observance during this period. Indeed, the rabbis barely refer to specific historical events or turning points, let alone provide substantial descriptions of popular practices. Exacerbating these limitations is the lack of external nonrabbinic testimonies of Jewish ritual practices during the first two centuries after the destruction of the Temple. In the end, all we have are two general facts that provide a framework for reconstructing the history of a major facet of Jewish religious culture: the fall of the Jerusalem Temple and the ensuing collapse of social structures and institutions and the destruction of Judea following the Bar Kokhba revolt and the rabbinic move to the Galilee.

While archaeological findings point to a general decrease in purity observance, the analysis of the history of rabbinic law serves to uncover an array of particular trends that were tied to this historical process. While early rabbinic literature does not provide a transparent image of society in general, the laws of purity by their very nature were embedded into this reality and suggested mechanisms for operating within it. A careful reading of this legally oriented literature enables us, therefore, to reveal the changing social contexts in which these laws were shaped. In this book, I sought to demonstrate how the frameworks of traditional ritual activity were constantly refashioned within shifting circumstances.

Early rabbinic sources do not testify to an immediate reassessment of purity observance following the destruction of the Temple. Unlike the famous ordinances of Rabban Yohanan b. Zakkai, who provided non-Temple alternatives to some festival rituals, no new institutions were created in the realm of purity, and some of its major facets could be maintained in this new reality. The development of rabbinic purity discourse is only indirectly indebted to the failing of the two revolts. The disappearance of intersectarian discourse, and the redrawing of the contours of Jewish society during the tannaitic period, seem to have had a greater impact on the reshaping of purity laws. As we have seen, the legal activity of the Pharisees was characterized by systematic, even defiant, leniencies, in opposition to Qumran law. Although they shared with the Qumran authors a common heritage of sectarian legal traditions and basic conceptions of purity, the Pharisees' declared intent was to manipulate these traditions so as to allow more access to purity practices, as well as to limit their discriminating force. Purity provided the language through which the Pharisees promoted their particular social identity and their unique religious ideology. To this end, they created new forms of purity knowledge and promoted peculiar practices. These allowed some level of control over one's surrounding and enabled the maintenance of the purity of the self despite the risk and uncertainty of one's social interactions.

Unlike their Pharisaic predecessors, the rabbis of the early second century were concerned mainly with organizing purity traditions into a coherent system. Consequently, purity discourse was shifted from the public sphere, as a means for promoting a peculiar form of social identity, into the study hall and into the rabbis' exegetical and scholarly world. The most conspicuous result of this tendency is the creation of a complex system of degrees of impurity (e.g., m. Tehar., chap. 2). The teachings of the Galilean rabbis following the Bar Kokhba revolt, however, point to a fundamental transformation of the very purpose of purity observance. At this point, purity was transformed from a marker of group identity to a form of personal religious distinction. As indicated in chapter 4, this transition is most apparent in the revolutionary interpretation given to Mishnah Hagigah 2:6, according to which, "if one bathed without being held [to be fit] it is as though he has not bathed." In its original meaning, within the sectarian discourse of Second Temple Judaism, this ruling stipulated that it was impossible to gain purification unless one was a declared member of a pure group. Ultimately, however, this ruling lost its public meaning, the verb *to hold* (*huhzak*) was reinterpreted, and it was consequently assumed that intention alone determined the efficacy of the procedure. In the eyes of the exegetes of this early ruling, personal choice was sufficient to ensure purity, and public recognition lost its value. Since the responsibility for this way of life was placed, toward the end of the tannaitic period, on the shoulders of the individual, and he could not rely on a social support network, the decision to be pure was at his sole discretion.

This paradigmatic shift entailed legal and conceptual changes on multiple fronts. Thus, a great deal of effort was devoted to adjusting the early attitude toward am ha-aretz, using several exegetical strategies. The early approach in Judea was based on the public value of purity. In this reality, even those who were not committed to maintaining purity within their own homes knew how to preserve it in the public domain and in their contact with others who required pure products for their use. The markets, therefore, operated at a sufficient level of purity, and even questionable characters such as the tax collectors were considered trustworthy within this domain. The existence of a clear social distinction between groups, which corresponded to their level of purity observance, exalted the public status of purity even in the eyes of ammei ha-aretz. The practice of the Galilean Jews of the second half of the second century, on the other hand, was characterized by a complete alienation toward this way of life, and they lacked both the knowledge and the means to cooperate in the maintaining of purity. Even if they would have held the pure pietists in high esteem, they lacked the means for systematically including it in their communal life. It is difficult to trace the roots of the normative difference between Judea and the Galilee. However, the transfer of the rabbinic movement to the Galilee following the Bar Kokhba revolt demanded that they reformulate their own Judean legal traditions to fit new social realities.

As is evident from the redaction of Mishnah Teharot, in a reality in which social awareness and support were lacking, supervision and control became the central principles in the attempt to protect oneself from am ha-aretz impurity. The requirement that someone who observes purity should be aware of his surroundings was now directed specifically toward the declared representative of nonobservance within the social world of the Galilean rabbis—namely, the am ha-aretz. This type of person, who was incapable of controlling his movements with regard to impurity, was viewed as similar to a child or an animal, requiring constant supervision. This view of am ha-aretz is so antithetical to the view familiar to us from earlier Second Temple traditions that the rabbis were compelled to reformulate the early ruling regarding tax collectors and burglars who entered a house. Unlike Mishnah Hagigah, according to Mishnah Teharot these persons must not be believed if they claim they have not touched vessels, and the Galilean rabbis, therefore, proceed to detail the level of supervision required over them, in attempt to control the invisible reach of the hand of the am ha-aretz.

The changes in the laws of am ha-aretz testify to the changing social frameworks for the activity of the religious elite and its channels of interaction with other groups. Early legal traditions, characteristic of the sectarian worldview of the Second Temple era, reflect a clearly stratified society, divided according to the degree of purity observance. Within this framework, the Pharisees could promote their ideology by creating a detailed alternative to some movements, as well as collaborating with others within specific public spheres. In the teachings of the Galilean rabbis, on the other hand, we encounter a mixed multitude, lacking clear social boundaries. The normative difference between the associate and the am ha-aretz does not correlate to any familiar social distinctions, and aside from their respective levels of legal knowledge, they both belong to the same social circles. With the absence of set boundaries that would enable a clearly demarcated operating space, tensions and suspicions grew. At the same time, within this amorphous social system, the standing of some highly proficient individuals stood out. They could aid others in setting aside the priestly share in a state of purity, and while they might choose to form an association that supported their own purity observance, it did not define their social affiliation. Thus, the knowledge of these individuals served the community in its entirety. This new setting for diverse standards of practice within Jewish society set the stage for the creation of new forms of religious distinction. These circumstances, in turn, illuminate the nature and character of the emerging rabbinic movement during the latter part of the second century.

The social status of the rabbis and the relationship between the emerging "rabbinic Judaism" and the customs and identities of other Jews is one of the central issues that occupies scholars of this period. With the absence of relevant historical sources outside rabbinic literature, our acquaintance with Jewish society of this time is largely dictated by the perspective and interests of this learned elite. We do not have a simple way of measuring the extent to which the halakhic activity of the rabbis represents wider societal and legal norms or whether it existed only in the margins of Jewish society in Palestine, serving the needs of a small circle of followers. We can assume, however, that the status of the rabbis did not remain stable during this tumultuous period, and it seems likely that it was tied to structural changes within Jewish society. These include the institutional disintegration of the early rabbinic movement with the transfer from Judea to the Galilee, alongside the growing influence of the Patriarch in the third century and his supportive role of the rabbinic elite. Arguably, the change of legal discourse from public policy to private piety provides an indication for the transformation of rabbinic status within Jewish society.

This book provides a history of purity as a major body of Jewish legal traditions and one of the main pillars of religious culture within ancient Judaism. At the same time, it has sought to advance our understanding of the social backdrop of rabbinic legal activity and to bring rabbinic literature and law making to the forefront of the study of Jewish society in Palestine. Against this background I have argued that the changes in the laws of purity in general, and the laws of am ha-aretz in particular, signal to a great extent the nature of rabbinic activity during the two first centuries. Initially, the Pharisaic movement of the Second Temple period, functioned as an organized elite with a distinct social identity. In contrast, toward the end of the tannaitic period, the rabbinic movement lacked an organized institutional framework and the rabbis operated as individuals within a network of diverse religious standards. In this limited capacity the rabbis sought to offer tools for individual observance of the law within an unsupportive surrounding. Ultimately, however, as the lines between the rabbis and their surroundings blurred, giving rise to new communal institutions, other ritual practices filled in for the role of purity within ancient Judaism.

NOTES

Introduction

1. Compare also his following lamentation: "The (loss of) purity has removed the taste and aroma (of the fruits), the tithes (that were not separated) have removed the fat of the grain" (m. Sot. 15:2; t. Sot. 15:2; t. Maʿas. Š. 5:30).

2. Yonatan Adler (2014) points out the correspondence between R. Shimon b. Eleazar's comment and the changes in archaeological findings between the two periods. For more on this, see chapter 6.

3. This approach is a consequence of two complementary scholarly tendencies: First, following Neusner's work, which I present in this chapter, the Mishnah is generally considered as a product of the third century CE. Second, recent scholarship has marginalized the standing of the rabbis, and their literary product is therefore perceived largely as an expression of their own worldview rather than as a representation of wider Jewish circles (see S. Schwartz 2001). As I show, however, there is no need to return to traditional, naive perceptions of rabbinic authority and status to derive social and historical data from their literary activity.

4. See Krochmal 1961: 219; Hoffmann 1914: 15–28; Epstein 1957: 25–58.

5. For a survey of relevant research, see Ishay Rosen-Zvi (2012: 239–54). Rosen-Zvi claims that the description of the *sotah* ritual in the Mishnah, which appears to be a Temple practice, is actually an ideological construct of later tannaim.

6. See Lorberbaum 2015: 106–10; Berkowitz 2006. Cf. Urbach 1969: 47–57.

7. Notably, the use of an archaic style is a basic feature of Greek rhetoric within the Second Sophistic movement, concurrent with the activity of the tannaim.

8. See, for example, Neusner 1974–77: 21:315.

9. Neusner 1974–77. Following Mary Douglas's critique of his early work on purity (Neusner 1973b), which drew primarily from rabbinic ideological statements,

while ignoring the realm of law and practice, Neusner turned to a review of the rabbinic system of purity law, as an expression of their notions of purity.

10. Neusner 1981. Neusner ignores the linguistic and stylistic differences between different pericopes in the Mishnah (Cohen 1983: 52). Furthermore, as Hayim Lapin (1995: 24n66) notes, Neusner himself demonstrates that, at times, a literary unit (which he terms an "intermediate division") is interrupted due to the integration of another literary unit. This proves that the redactor of the Mishnah had additional sources at his disposal.

11. Cohen 1983: 48.

12. Neusner (2006) bases his claim on an example from the beginning of tractate Makshirin. In a discussion on this unit, I have demonstrated that while the Mishnah did, indeed, rephrase the position of the House of Hillel, one can reconstruct the early content of their tradition through a comparison of textual parallels. See Furstenberg 2016b: 305–11.

13. On the rabbis' methods of creative interpretation of earlier traditions, to produce new laws and address new cases, see Rosenthal 1994.

14. Epstein 1957: 61. The approaches of R. Akiva's disciples in transmitting the disputes between the Houses of Hillel and Shammai, following R. Akiva's amendments, are discussed therein (73–79).

15. For a sharp formulation of this critique, see S. Schwartz 2001: 8–9.

16. Hayes 2008: 291.

17. Friedman 1999; Hauptman 2005.

18. See, for example, Furstenberg 2012, 2018, 2021. Each of these articles reveals a different aspect of the changing study culture of the rabbis, which I have been able to discern through the literary gaps between the different layers of the Mishnah.

19. In spite of the tendency to tie together purity laws and the laws pertaining to the Temple, there is an important distinction between them. While the destruction of the Temple abruptly brought an end to the practical application of sacrificial law and led to the creation of a purely theoretical field of study, purity continued to be a practical issue throughout the tannaitic period. One must not, therefore, assume the antiquity of laws relating to purity law but rather be aware that the preservation of ancient legal traditions had a major role in the shaping of the current practice in tannaitic literature.

20. Shemesh 2009: 3–7. In his book, Shemesh demonstrates each of the models with specific rulings. I suggest here a multidimensional model, which enables us to distinguish, within a complete halakhic field, between those aspects that were held in dispute between the Pharisees and their opponents and those aspects of rabbinic law that are the product of later development.

21. Rabban Gamaliel, one of the Pharisees in the Sanhedrin, is mentioned in Acts 5:34 as a teacher of Torah who is respected by the entire people. Paul is one of his students (Acts 22:3). Shimon b. Gamaliel is mentioned in Josephus, Life, 38, 190.

Josephus famously mentions two Pharisees who flourished during Herod's rule, Pollio and Sameas (Josephus, Ant. 15:3; see also 14:172), whose names seem to allude to the rabbinic figures Shma'aya and Avtalyon or Shammai and Hillel.

22. See, for example, Matt. 23; Josephus, Ant. 13:298, 400–401; Josephus, Ant. 18:15, 17; Pesher Nahum 2:4–10.

23. See m. 'Erub. 6:2; t. Yoma 1:8; t. Sukkah 3:1, 16; t. Roš Haš.1:15; t. Ḥag. 3:35; m. Mak. 1:6; t. Sanh. 6:6; m. Menaḥ. 10:3; t. Menaḥ. 10:23; m. Parah 3:7; t. Parah 3:8; m. Yad. 4:6–8; t. Yad. 2:20.

24. See, for example, J. Baumgarten 1972b; Werman 2006.

25. Concerning the Pharisees see, for example, Smith 1956; Neusner 1973a. With regard to the rabbis, Catherine Hezser (1997) offers a noninstitutional image of rabbinic activity within small and relatively marginal study circles. On the other hand, see Haim Shapira (2007) for a balanced description of the institutional framework of the rabbis after the destruction of the Temple, with an understanding of the limitations of their authority.

26. According to Morton Smith (1956), Josephus sought to enhance the Pharisees' status due to the circumstances surrounding his writing of *Antiquities*. Smith's method was refuted by Daniel Schwartz (1983). Steve Mason (1991) also arrives at the conclusion that Josephus's testimony regarding the dominance of the Pharisees is reliable. Matthew's testimony on this issue (primarily in chap. 23) is also worthy of trust; see Mason (1990). For an opposing stance, see David Goodblatt (1989). For a description of the rabbis following the destruction of the Temple in sectarian terms, see Hayim Lapin (2012: 112).

27. Jaffee 2001: 84–99; Fraade 2011: 370–78.

28. See, for example, Shemesh 2009: 95–98.

29. Cohen 1984.

30. According to Cohen, the rabbis did not consider themselves Pharisees (since this is perceived as a negative term). Thus, he points out that Rabban Yohanan b. Zakkai, in m. Yad. 4:6, does not identify himself as a Pharisee and even appears to level an additional claim against them: "Have we nothing against the Pharisees excepting this?" This statement, however, should be understood within the framework of Rabban Yohanan b. Zakkai's study with students, as they address an early source that includes a dispute between the Pharisees and the Sadducees, in an attempt to justify the Pharisees' position. He is, therefore, not expressing any reservation toward them (although he may not be faithful to their original intention). See Furstenberg 2020a: 784n41.

31. As opposed to Cohen, in my article (Furstenberg 2018), I chart out a graded process of the acceptance of the rabbinic pluralistic ideoloy throughout the tannaitic period.

32. See, for example, Boyarin 2004: 44–67.

33. See Lapin 2006; Goodman 2007: 39–45.

34. This point is particularly emphasized by Sussman 1994: 187.

35. Cohen 2007: 139–40.

36. Cohen 2007 and Halbertal 2013 focus on the scholastic innovation of the rabbis. Without dismissing the validity of this general insight, it does not exhaust the forms of rabbinic study activity and the role of earlier traditions in shaping rabbinic law.

37. Sussman 1994: 196. See also Aharon Shemesh (2009: 129–35), who discusses the stringent tendency of priestly halakhah and its theological roots. Adiel Schremer (2000) explains this tendency against the background of the transition from an ancient oral tradition to the heightened concern for the interpretation of scripture.

38. See Knohl 1991. Compare, however, Fraade 2009b.

39. Neusner 1971: 1:305. See also Neusner 1973a: 83.

40. Harrington 1993: 26–43.

41. Harrington 1993: 248–60.

42. See, for example, m. Yad. 3:2, and R. Yose's reaction in t. T. Yom. 1:8–10.

43. For example, as opposed to Harrington's claim, there is no scriptural basis for the system of graded impurity established in the Mishnah (m. Teharot, chap. 2), a system that expands the spread of impurity far beyond its biblical roots and transforms impurity into an almost boundless threat.

44. Noam 2010. Beyond the centrality of purity for Jews of the Second Temple period (12), Vered Noam explained her choice of corpse impurity thus: "I believe that it is here, in particular, that we can isolate halakhic development and biblical exegesis, at least somewhat, from obvious external social and moral motivations, and approach the religious and ontological world of halakha in its pure form" (16). My research presents an opposing approach, which seeks to trace the variety of both internal and external influences that shaped the laws of purity as a mirror into a changing legal culture.

45. Noam 2010: 320. For a concise formulation of her position, see also Noam 2009.

46. Noam 2010: 325.

47. Noam 2010: 354.

48. Noam 2010: 250.

49. Aside from one source, whose original meaning is in doubt (t. Šabb. 1:18, p. 4; see Noam 2010: 78), the Houses and Hillel and Shammai address "tent impurity" only with respect to domestic space (m. 'Ed. 4:12; m. 'Ohal. 11:3–5) and do not extend it to any form of overhang.

50. Reich 2013: 206.

51. Regarding stone vessels, see Magen 1988. For a detailed description of the stamps on clay vessels that testify to their purity, see Yadin and Naveh 1989: 35; Sapir 1994.

52. Reich 2013: 231.

53. Adler 2014, 2017.

54. For an attempt to reconstruct the popular form of purity observance from the archaeological findings, see Miller 2010. A clear textual expression of the tension between the popular observance and the rabbis' approach to purity at a later period is found in y. Ber. 3:3 (6c), regarding the immersion of a seminal emitter. For more, see chapter 7.

55. Balberg 2014: 148–79. Previous studies have already pointed out the close affinity (as well as differences) between rabbinic ethical instructions, particularly those gathered in tractate Avot, and stoic ethical discourse. See, for example, Satlow 2003; Schofer 2005; Furstenberg 2020b. Mira Balberg's innovation is in the application of the ethical model to the refashioned legal space to realize these goals.

1. Biblical Foundations, New Conceptions

1. Purification before the Sabbath is mentioned in 2 Macc. 12:38. A Collection of Blessings from Qumran (4Q512) includes blessings for purification in preparation for Sabbaths and Holidays (J. Baumgarten 1992: 208).

2. Talmudic tradition attributed a decree regarding the impurity of glass vessels and the "Impurity of the Land of the Nations" to Yose b. Yo'ezer and Yose b. Yohanan (y. Šabb. 1:4 [3d]; b. Šabb. 14b). These decrees were understood to be targeted at imported vessels. On impure oil, see Josephus, Ant. 12: 119–120; m. 'Abod. Zar. 2:6; Goodman 1990.

3. The prevalent assumption in the Mishnah is that an impure person would make sure to distance himself from others and not contaminate his surroundings. See m. Tehar. 7:8. Menstruating women also took care not to impart their impurity to their surroundings, wiping away their spit so that it does not contaminate others (m. Tehar. 5:8; t. Tehar. 6:12).

4. This attitude is reflected, among other places, in T. Mos. 7:9–10: "They, with hands and mind, will touch impure things yet their mouths will speak enormous things, and they will even say: Do not touch me, lest you pollute me in the position I occupy." It is difficult, however, to ascertain which group the author is complaining of here.

5. See Ego 2014: 478–83, with respect to the fall of the angels in 1 En. 6–16.

6. As opposed to the plain meaning of the biblical texts (Lev. 5:2–3 and 15:31; Num. 19:20 and more), the rabbis explained that an impure person defiles the Tabernacle only when he enters it, not simply by not purifying himself. For a detailed discussion, see Noam 2008: 481–89.

7. David Wright (1987: 227–28 and 243–47) attributes this threat to the sanctuary to a fear of indirect contact. Jacob Milgrom (1991: 254–58, 310, 977), on the other hand, believes that the impurity contaminates the sanctuary from afar.

8. David Hoffmann (1953: 212–23) distinguishes between "the impurity of holy things," which is the result of sins such as the consumption of forbidden foods, and "the impurity of bodies." Tivka Frymer-Kensky (1983) distinguishes between healable impurities, and those that cannot be healed, and are therefore more threatening. Wright (1992) distinguishes between permitted and forbidden impurities.

9. Notably, while the Priestly Code subjects purity practices to the holiness of the sanctuary, the Holiness Code demands that the entire land of Israel be holy, lest it expel its inhabitants. In addition, Israel Knohl (1993: 173–74) argues that the Holiness Code expanded the obligation to keep one's body pure within the camp and, therefore, required the distancing of all impure people from the camp (Num. 5:1–4).

10. Alon 1977: 190–234.

11. Klawans 2000.

12. On the former, see m. Ber. 3:4–6; t. Ber. 2:12 (p. 8).

13. T. Demai 2:2. See chap. 6.

14. Alon 1977: 231.

15. Alon 1977: 223.

16. Compare the *Letter of Aristeas* 305, mentioned previously in this chapter, which addressed the issue of handwashing before religious rituals.

17. Josephus, Ant. 14:258; Runesson 2001.

18. Philo, *Laws* 1.262.

19. Sanders 1990: 262–63.

20. According to fragment 4Q266 from the Damascus Document, one who was captured by gentiles was considered impure and was barred from service at the Temple. Cf. *Avot de Rabbi Nathan* version A, chap. 8, p. 37 (Schechter ed.), which tells of a ḥasid and a wealthy woman who were taken captive and, upon their release, ritually immersed because they had eaten from the gentiles' food and therefore required purification. The strict practice of refraining from eating gentile foods is also specifically characteristic of Palestinian literature. Daniel did not partake of the king's bread (1:8), and Judith, too, did not eat of Holofernes's food (12:1–3) and took care to only eat pure bread (10:5). In the *Letter of Aristeas*, on the other hand, the translators are strict in their observance of dietary laws but at the same time partake of the king's foods. See on this Birenboim 2011: 21. See also Freidenreich 2011: 31–46.

21. For example, Eyal Regev (2000) includes the various purity phenomena under the category of "non-priestly purity." While Regev is careful to use only sources that are unequivocally attributable to the Second Temple period and also mentions the variety in the type of sources, which represent Pharisees, diaspora Jews, and "regular" Jews—to which he adds the archaeological findings of ritual baths and earthenware—he too, like Alon, suggests one overarching explanation. In his view, the observance of purity laws enabled each individual to personally internalize the consciousness of holiness, with the body serving as an alternative site of religious meaning.

22. Harrington 2019.

23. Harrington 2019: 169–220. Hannah Harrington's discussion includes rabbinic treatment of purity laws, which were presumably developed in response to the destruction of the Second Temple, even when they allude to Pharisaic observance (p. 171).

24. Josephus, A. Ap. 2.198 and 203.

25. Philo, *Laws* 3.63. The two laws are phrased similarly and forbid contact with any object until purification has taken place. Consequently, Philo requires ritual sprinkling following sexual relations. Scholars have offered various explanations for the addition of ritual sprinkling. Ed Sanders (1990: 264–70) sees it as a local Alexandrian practice. Joseph Baumgarten (1999: 85) links Philo's testimony with the practice hinted at in Qumran literature, of using the purifying water associated with the lustration water for purification of all impurities. Alternatively, it is possible that we are dealing with a simple mistake, resulting from the use of a common phrase (which usually appears in metaphorical contexts) in this paragraph.

26. 11 QT 49:16–17 and 50:13–14.

27. Milgrom 1992. For a detailed description of the purification process in Qumran, see the discussion below in chap. 5.

28. Tob 2:5, as well as v. 9, according to the long version of the book. See E. Eshel 1997: 9. According to Esther Eshel, ritual baths in proximity to cemeteries served for "first-day ablutions." Yonatan Adler (2009), on the other hand, believes that these ritual baths served those who came into contact with people who had contracted corpse impurity, and not those who had actually come into direct contact with a dead body.

29. Josephus, Ant. 18:36–38.

30. Ant. 3:261–62 (ed. Mason).

31. Josephus, J.W. 5:227.

32. This point was emphasized in Sanders's comprehensive critique of Alon and Jacob Neusner, who attribute a broadening of purity laws beyond the Temple boundaries to the Pharisees and Second Temple Jews in general. See Sanders 1990: 165. However, Sanders creates artificial distinctions between different sources of impurity. He claims that the impurity attached to crawling things in Leviticus 11 (as well as other dietary restrictions mentioned therein) was applied to all Israelites and not restricted to the priests (pp. 148, 199–205), while corpse impurity primarily preoccupied of those who came into contact with Temple worship; therefore, Sanders believed Jews were only troubled by the first type of impurity and made only limited efforts to protect themselves from the second (p. 188). This distinction, however, has no basis in contemporary sources.

33. Quoted in Josephus, Ant. 12:145–46 (ed. Marcus). For an interpretation and discussion, see Bickerman 2007: 357–75.

34. Bickerman 2007: 359.

35. The inscription, placed on a partition encompassing the Temple, is also mentioned by Josephus, J.W. 5:193–94; Ant. 15:417. According to Elias Bickerman (2007: 483–96), the worsening of the punishment for entering the Temple in the later version of the prohibition reflects the increased fear of defilement of the Temple in general. Daniel Schwartz (1990: 124–130) argues that the warning even possibly included proselytes.

36. See Orian 2016 for a comprehensive comparison of the mishnaic ten levels of holiness and Josephus's seven purities.

37. According to Albert Baumgarten (1994), due to the dispute regarding purity, the Essenes were distanced from the Temple courtyard but allowed on the Temple Mount like gentiles (Josephus, Ant. 18:19).

38. This similarity is noteworthy considering the extensive changes made to the Temple structure during Herod's time. The expansion of the Temple Mount presumably entailed the severer formulation of the prohibition. See Levine 1996: 14–15; Llewelyn and van Beek 2011: 15.

39. Josephus, A. Ap. 2:103–4 (ed. Mason).

40. Cf. Josephus, J.W. 5:193–94, 227.

41. Regarding the former, see Philo, *Laws* 1:261, 3:205; compare also to Josephus, J.W. 1:229.

42. 11QT 48:14–17; Yadin 1977: 1:215–18. For a more limiting definition of the phrase "Temple City," see Schiffman 1985 and compare CD 12:1–2. Cana Werman (2011) argues that the Qumranic sources diverted from the biblical scheme and delineated three arenas of purity—the Temple, Jerusalem, and the other cities of Israel—a model akin to that of the rabbis.

43. 11QT 45:8–10.

44. Sifre on Numbers, Naso 1 (ed. Kahana, 4). Compare Sifre Zuta on Numbers 5:1. For a discussion of these homilies, see Kahana 2011: 12–19.

45. T. Kelim (Baba Qamma) 1:12.

46. Noam 2010: 173; Orian 2016.

47. For supporting archaeological evidence, see Hartman et al. 2013. Hayim Lapin (2017) offers a model for the description of the economy of the city that was nourished by the Temple.

48. "And we are of the opinion that the sanctuary is the 'Tent of Meeting' and that Jerusalem is the 'camp' and that 'outside the camp' is outside Jerusalem, that is, the encampment of their settlements" (B 29–30; Qimron and Strugnell 1994: 49–51). David Henshke (1998) believes that according to sectarian law the slaughter of non-sacrificial animals was forbidden in a small area north of Jerusalem, where the ashes of the sacrifices (the *deshen*) were brought. According to Menachem Kister (1999b), we must assume that 4QMMT supports the stance of the Temple Scroll, which forbids slaughter for food purposes up to a distance of three days' travel from Jerusalem (see 11QT 52:13–15).

49. 11QT 47:7–16.

50. For all practical purposes, the rabbinic stance uprooted the prohibition in Leviticus 17 on slaughtering nonsacrificial meat. According to R. Ishmael in b. Ḥul. 16a (cf. Sifre on Deuteronomy 73), this prohibition existed only in the desert and was replaced in the Land of Israel with the permission to eat nonsacrificial meat (Deut. 12:21). Another explanation, attributed to R. Akiva, is that the passage in Leviticus 17 only forbids the slaughter of sacrificial animals outside of the Tabernacle. This appears to be reflected in the Sifra (e.g., Aharei Mot 6:1). This exegesis appears in the Samaritan translation of Leviticus 17:3 and in the Septuagint on the same verse, as well as in a version found in Qumran (Kister 1999b: 336). For a detailed discussion of the Karaite stance, against the background of Qumran and rabbinic Judaism, see Erder 2004: 249–67.

51. See t. Nid. 9:18; Maʻas. Š. 1:9. Compare Sifre on Deuteronomy 107. Yigael Yadin (1977: 1:247) learns from these sources that an earlier decree forbade the consumption of nonsacrificial meat but that it was rejected at some point. In my view it is questionable whether we may rely on the rabbinic narrative to reconstruct earlier historical stages. Nonetheless, it reflects the rabbinic attempt to explain how the prohibitive practice came into being.

52. Jub. 7:36; 32:14; 49:15–17. See Chanoch Albeck (2008: 14), who compares this stance to that of the Karaites but terms it "a strange theory by a sectarian author."

53. According to Shmuel Safrai (1965: 94–102), the law of the book of Jubilees reflects the practice before the Hasmonean period. In his opinion, the permission to consume sacrifices in all of Jerusalem is the result of the vast number of pilgrims who arrived in Jerusalem and the necessity of providing for their needs.

54. According to Hanan Birenboim (2009a: 9–12), the Temple Scroll, 4QMMT, and the "Animal Prophecy" share a vision in which the sphere of holiness will encompass the entire city, overtaking its residential areas.

55. Henshke 1998: 19.

56. The incongruity of the rabbinic stance with biblical categories was emphasized in Shemesh and Werman 2011: 122–24.

57. The stance of 4QMMT on this point is at variance with the opinion of the Temple Scroll (11QT 45:17–18), which forbids the zav from entering Jerusalem during his period of purification. For a discussion on the status of those undergoing purification in Qumran law, see chapter 5.

58. Reich 2013: 210. Notably, these findings are not exclusive to Jerusalem, as ritual baths were found in most of Judea, and they are dated up to the days of the Bar Kokhva revolt. See Adler 2014, figure 1; my discussions in chapter 6.

59. Compare m. Šeqal. 8:2. In a papyrus from Oxyrinchus a Pharisee priest claims: "I am pure, I immersed in the ritual bath of David, and I went down on one ladder and came up on another ladder." However, concerning the relevance of this description to Second Temple reality, compare Reich 1981 and Miller 2015: 104–52.

60. I should note that my description is fundamentally at odds with that suggested by Klawans (2000). In contrast to Klawans, I believe that the blurring of the distinction between the two categories was not unique to the Qumran sect and was basically shared by most groups. See further my discussion in the next chapter.

61. For a detailed analysis of the exegetical process, see Fishbane 1985: 114–23.

62. Klawans 1995: 291, 2000: 43–46.

63. Alon 1977: 146–89. According to Alon, "The Decree of Eighteen Matters" (y. Šabb. 1:5 [3c]), which was instituted on the eve of the Great Revolt and included a decree against gentile impurity, was intended to reinstitute an ancient halakhah that had lost its force with time.

64. T. Zabim 2:1; Sifra Zabim 11 (74c). For a detailed discussion of the nature of gentile impurity and its halakhic status in tannaitic literature, see Balberg 2014: 122–47.

65. Hayes 2002: 27–32.

66. See Olyan 2004: 11; Birenboim 2011: 15 (my translation).

67. See, for example, Jub. 11:16; 20:8, and see Hayes 2002: 53.

68. 2 Kgs. 18:4, in accordance with the commandment in Deut. 12:3.

69. Lev. 18:28; Ezek. 36:16–37.

70. Japhet 1997: 261–74.

71. Note that according to Alon, gentiles were considered to be defiled by idolatry impurity. Birnboim, on the other hand, believes that the notion of gentile impurity resulted directly from the social conditions of the Babylonian exile, and they were only secondarily associated with idolatry impurity. Considering that each of these impurities appears in different compositions, I believe that we should not derive these two impurities from one another. Both represent, independently, a new perception of the tangibility of impurity, characteristic of their time.

72. The defilement of the Temple at the command of the king is mentioned in 2 Maccabees 6:2, but the defiling factor itself is unclear. Was the defilement merely the result of the changing of the Temple name to "the Temple of Zeus of Olympia," or was it the result of what occurred in the Temple, which included acts of promiscuity and licentiousness and the sacrifice of forbidden things on the altar?

73. It should be noted that the testimonies regarding gentile impurity in Maccabees are less unequivocal. In 1 Maccabees 7:34–35, we hear that the priests and elders came to greet Nikanor, but he mocked them and defiled them. It is unclear how exactly the priests and elders were defiled, and whether Nikanor spat on them, as we find in the following case in the Tosefta: "It happened that Shimon son of Kimchit went out to speak to the king at eventide, and a line of spittle fell out of his [i.e., the king's] mouth and fell on his [i.e., Shimon son of Kimchit's] clothes, and his brother went in and served as High Priest in his place" (t. Yoma 3:20). It is similarly unclear how the soldiers in the citadel used to defile the surroundings of the Temple and greatly injured its purity (14:36). See Hayes 2002: 50–53.

2. Exclusive Paths to Purity from Qumran to Jesus

1. For a survey of sources concerning purity in Qumran, see Harrington 2004, 2006; Werrett 2007, 2013.

2. Klawans (2000: 90) even suggests that it was this revolution that led to the sect's isolation from their Jewish brethren, who were consequently deemed ritually impure.

3. I will not proffer a reconstruction of the historical development that led to the differences between the different groups of sources. On this, see Klawans 2000: 90–91; Regev 2003, 2007: 95–132. For criticism of these tendencies, see Holtz 2013.

4. Additional fragments dedicated to this issue are 4Q274, on the distancing of impure persons; 4Q276–77, on the preparation of waters of lustration; and 4Q514, on purification.

5. Some scholars have suggested that following its abandonment of the Temple in Jerusalem, the sect viewed itself as a Temple (1QS 9:5–6: "At that moment the men of the Community shall set apart a holy house for Aaron, in order to form a most holy community, and a house of the Community for Israel, those who walk in perfection") and, therefore, strictly observed purity in its boundaries. See Neusner 1973b: 50; Newton 1985: 42–43; García Martínez and Barrera 1995: 157. Hannah Harrington (2019: 207–13) emphasizes, "In accordance with the notion that the people of Israel can function as a sanctuary . . . the food of the community . . . was treated as if they were holy foods of the temple. However, it is quite clear that the level of purity for communal foods was lower than that required for sacrificial foods." See also Harrington 2004: 37–38.

6. Milgrom 1990: 93.

7. Noam 2009: 320–30.

8. For instance, the author of 4QMMT is also strict with regard to the impurity of animal hides (4QMMT 2:18–23; cf. 11QT 47:7–17), and he also believes that the purification process ends only after sunset (4QMMT 2:15–16 and 71–72).

9. As Menachem Kister (1999b: 340–42) notes, the explanation that appears here for the impurity of people with physical defects, which hinges on their mental disabilities, is at odds with the Community Rule, the Temple Scroll, and the War Scroll, which view the physical defects as offending the holiness of the angelic-like community.

10. According to the reading of Elisha Qimron and John Strugnell (1994: 148–50), 4QMMT is troubled by the grain sent by gentiles, which defiles the Temple (2:3–5). Furthermore, he seems to warn of the entry of children of mixed marriages to the Temple (2:48–49). The exact content of this prohibition, however, is unclear.

11. For a survey of this widespread notion, see Hayes 2002: 82–89. Compare *Aramaic Levi Document* 6:3–4 (Greenfield, Stone, and Eshel 2004: 74–75).

12. While the author of the Damascus Document only briefly discusses the status of Jerusalem, he shares the stringent approach of the Temple Scroll and forbids

sexual intercourse in the city (CD 12:1–2). In addition, with respect to bodily impurities the scroll also emphasizes that the process of purification concludes only with sunset on the eighth day (4Q266 6 ii). In addition, water of lustration is necessary for purification from other impurities (4Q272 1 ii 15). Cf. Himmelfarb 2001: 13–29.

13. A priest captured by gentiles is defiled (4Q266 5 ii 10). Additionally, gentile vessels are impure (4Q271 2 ll. 9–10).

14. For an analysis of the complex composition of this unit, see Kister 2018.

15. Following Klawans 2000: 52–56. Compare Regev 2003: 46–47.

16. According to Eyal Regev (2007: 95–132), this difference between the two compositions is key to reconstructing the history of the Qumran sect. The sectarians maintained ties with the Temple in Jerusalem so long as their claims related only to ritual impurity, and they even made attempts to convince the Temple leadership of their approach (as we learn from 4QMMT); once they identified moral turpitude in the people's behavior, however, they were forced to isolate themselves from them.

17. See also Pesher Habakkuk (1QpHab) 12:6–10.

18. See Sekki 1989: 73, 112–14. According to Arthur Sekki (in contrast to our analysis herein), there is a clear distinction between this holy spirit that resides in the people and the divine Holy Spirit. On the nature of this Holy Spirit, see Kister 2018.

19. Lev. 20:25, and compare 11:43. See Rabin 1958: 26.

20. This is also the impression we get from Psalms 51:13: "Take not Your holy spirit away from me."

21. See David Flusser (2007: 88–90), who compiles the relevant sources from rabbinic literature, Qumran, the New Testament, and the book of Enoch.

22. Mark 3:28–29. Cf. Matth 12:32; Luke 12:10.

23. See also Lev. 18:29–30, 20:3–5.

24. See Furstenberg 2016a on the transformation of the initiation process in Qumran into a purification rite.

25. Klawans 2000: 75.

26. On this, I follow Holtz 2013. Gudrun Holtz coins the apt term *constitutional impurity* in contrast to the biblical *sin impurity*, which is the result of sinful acts. As Holtz stresses, this conceptual change is tied to Qumran determinism.

27. Klawans (2000: 77) notes the affinity of the language of the Community Rule to that of Ezekiel 37:17: "Their ways were in My sight like the uncleanness of a menstruous woman." Only in the Community Rule, however, is the sin itself the source of impurity, not merely a simile for impurity, as it is in Ezekiel.

28. J. Baumgarten 1992: 209; Klawans 2000: 87.

29. Bracketed ellipses here and elsewhere appear in original edition.

30. Compare Birenboim 2003: 363 and Himmelfarb 2001: 36.

31. See 4Q277: "sin[ce h]e atones for the impu[re.] And a child should not sprinkle over the impure." The frequent usage of atonement language in this paragraph

testifies to the atoning essence of the water of lustration according to priestly law, as opposed to the Pharisee approach. See Werman 2011: 387.

32. Following the reconstruction in Qimron 2010–14: 2:30.

33. Klawans (2000: 82–85) understands this statement as implying that sin defiles. Compare Himmelfarb 2001: 33. I believe that it is possible that a change took place in the sectarian stance on this issue (see following note).

34. Furstenberg 2016a.

35. See, for example, the Testament of Dan 1:5–8: "And one of the spirits of Beliar was at work within me, saying, 'Take this sword, and with it kill Joseph; once he is dead, your father will love you.' This is the spirit of anger that persuaded me that, as a leopard sucks the blood of a kid, so I should suck the blood of Joseph."

36. See 4Q511 (Songs of the Sage[b]), fr. 48–51: "and through my mouth He startles [all the spirits] of the bastards to subjugate all the impure [spi]rits." See also 1QH 24:16, 26.

37. Jub. 12:20; on apotropaic prayers, see Flusser 1988; Eshel 2003.

38. Kister (1999a) believes that the prayer includes a request for divine moral support and protection from the "evil inclination" as well as rescue from physical suffering. To my understanding, the context here relates solely to the poet's sins, not to physical hardship.

39. As Flusser (1988: 215–16) demonstrates, there are significant parallels between this prayer and the Prayer of Levi in the *Aramaic Levi Document* (Greenfield, Stone, and Eshel 2004: 60–65), including the request for purification. Alongside this, however, one must note that the Psalms Scroll adds additional demonic forces, including the spirit of impurity, to the entity of Satan. Flusser (1988: 223) also notes that the request for purification is absent in rabbinic prayers.

40. Compare Ishay Rosen-Zvi (2011: 44–64), who speaks of the "reification of the Yetzer." See also Kister 2010.

41. Kister 1999a: 172; Furstenberg 2016a.

42. This notion is anchored already in the language of Jubilees 1:21: "Create a pure heart and a holy spirit for them. And do not let them be ensnared by their sin, henceforth and forever." Jubilees is based on Psalms 51:12—"Fashion a pure heart for me, O God; create in me a steadfast spirit"—but adds a reference to the holy spirit that has the power to purify man.

43. On the spirit that purifies carnal sin, see also Flusser 2007: 283–92 ("The 'Flesh-Spirit' Dualism in the Qumran Scrolls and the New Testament").

44. Josephus, Ant. 18:116–19; Matt. 14:1–12//Mark 6:14–29.

45. For a survey of possible understandings of John's baptizing activity, see Webb 1991: 183–205; Taylor 1997: 64–100.

46. Matt. 3:1–12; Mark 1:1–8; Luke 3:1–20. See also Acts 13:24, 19:4.

47. The references in Matthew and Luke to Isaiah 40:3 do not only allude to the act of going out to the desert—"A voice rings out . . . in the desert"—but also to the

future judgment: "Grass withers, flowers fade, when the breath of the Lord blows on them" (v. 7). Cf. Matt. 3:11–12; Luke 3:16–17.

48. Acts 11:18; compare Luke 24:47 and Acts 5:31.

49. Matt. 21:25–26; Luke 8:4–7. John garnered the authority to perform baptism as a result of his role as God's prophet. John's status as a priest might have contributed to his self-perception as worthy of providing expiation for the people, although he appears to have seen himself as a substitute for the Temple. See Webb 1991: 193, 203–5. Robert Webb further argues that the Jews who came to John were also critical of the Temple establishment.

50. Josephus, Ant. 18:116–17. This passage of Josephus is generally accepted as authentic. In contrast, Rivka Nir (2012), argues that it is an interpolation by a later Christian author.

51. John's baptism has been compared to the immersion for the sake of conversion to Judaism. As opposed to the regular, private immersion for purification purposes, the conversion immersion is overseen by a third party, who watches the conversion candidate (b. Yeb. 47b). But since there is no indication of immersion for conversion in Second Temple sources and it is first discussed by the rabbis of the early second century CE, it is doubtful whether it is relevant for the interpretation of John's actions. See Rowley 1940.

52. Flusser 1979: 84–89.

53. Klawans 2000: 142–43; Collins 2007: 138–40.

54. Some Christian sources portray baptism as an exorcism of the evil spirits who cleave to idolaters. See Kister 1999a: 176–77; Blidstein 2017. This conception had a major role in shaping the initiation procedure in the early church. See Furstenberg 2016a.

55. For instance, the words of the poet of the Psalms Scroll may be understood to refer to this sort of physical harm: "Let not Satan rule over me, nor an evil spirit; let neither pain nor evil purpose take possession of my bones" (11QPs^a 19 ll. 14–15).

56. See, for example, Dunn 2002; Fredriksen 1995.

57. See also Furstenberg 2008, 2020a.

58. Mark 1:40–45; Matt. 8:1–4; Luke 5:12–16.

59. Mark 5:25–34; Matt. 9:19–22; Luke 8:43–48.

60. Mark 5:35–43; Matt. 9:23–26; Luke 8:49–56.

61. Jesus's contact with the leper is in contrast to Luke 17:11–19, in which the lepers stand off and are careful not to defile others. Jesus's entering the house with a corpse is at the heart of Thomas Kazen's claim in the first half of his discussion on Jesus and purity. For a summary of his position, see Kazen 2010b: 197–98.

62. In Matthew 26:6, Jesus visits Simon the Leper, but it is unclear whether Simon was still suffering from leprosy at the time of this interaction. According to Papyrus Egerton 2 ("Unknown Gospel"), Jesus dines with lepers (see Kazen 2010b:

120). There are those who claimed that the very act of dining together with sinners is an expression of scorn toward purity law, but the sources themselves do not explicitly link the two. See Fredriksen 1995: 21–23.

63. On Jesus the purifier, see Chilton 2000: 83–102. According to Chilton, Jesus's basic commitment was to purity, and he was striving to replace the Pharisees as the arbiter of purity. Friedrich Avemarie (1997) adopts the approach that Jesus was careful to avoid impurity, but believed he had a "purifying power" that counteracted impurities. See Klutz 1999: 160–63. The central event in which Jesus's purifying activity is usually identified is his "purification" of the Temple by banishing the merchants and their customers and overturning the tables used by the money changers (Mark 11: 15–17; Matt. 21:12–17; Luke 19:45–48). Thus, for instance, Eyal Regev (2004: 397–402) believed that Jesus was troubled by the moral impurity caused by the merchants' corruption. This event, however, does not mention impurity, explicitly or implicitly, and one may suggest other explanations to Jesus's protest against the Temple. According to Hans Betz (1997), Jesus saw purity as an internal moral issue and, therefore, did not view the purity of the Temple as important.

64. In Mark, the spirits are regularly termed "impure spirits." In the other gospels, they appear under various names. Luke uses "impure spirits" in the following cases, sometimes in combination with "demons": 4:31–37, 8:26–39, and 9:37–43. Matthew consistently replaces "impure spirit" with other terms, with the exception of Jesus's instruction to his disciples and the logion on the impure spirit that returns to a man. See Wahlen 2004.

65. Later on, Jesus exorcises another impure spirit from the daughter of the Phoenician woman and then heals a deaf man, grants the power of speech to a former mute (Mark 7:24–37), and finally banishes a deaf-mute impure spirit (9:14–29).

66. Matthew 10:8 adds resurrection and the healing of lepers to the list of things the disciples are authorized to do. Alongside the healing and exorcism, Jesus also sends his disciples to "announce," but while this announcement in Mark centers on a call for repentance, according to Matthew and Luke, the disciples announce the coming of the Kingdom of God/Heaven (Matt. 10:7; Luke 9:2). Repentance and the coming of the kingdom are, of course, two sides of the same coin (Matt. 3:2).

67. Matt. 12:43–45; Luke 11:24–26 (quoted here according to Luke).

68. According to Harry Fledderman (2005: 496), this tradition, which attributed only relative power to Jesus, was considered an embarrassment among his disciples and, therefore, does not appear in Mark. Ulrich Luz (2001: 220–21) suggests that this saying originally expressed the general fear among exorcists that the evil spirits would return and harm their patients. Only in the context of the Q source, and later in the Gospels, did this saying come to express the specific challenges encountered by Jesus in his battle with the spirits.

69. Furstenberg 2008. See next chapter.

3. The Purity of the Pharisees

1. See Alon 1977: 219; Neusner 1960: 127; Sanders 1990: 197; Harrington 1995; Poirier 2003: 256.

2. The Pharisees make their first appearance during the reign of Jonathan the Hasmonean as one of the three philosophies (Josephus, Ant. 13:171–73).

3. For a survey of sources on the Pharisees, see Schürer 1973–87: 2:382–88; Mason 1991; Grabbe 1999; Saldarini 2001. Louis Finkelstein (1962: 101–44) suggests identifying the Pharisees with the urban plebian stratum, as opposed to the Sadducee aristocracy. For a survey of the possible organizational structures adopted by the Pharisees and their social profile, see Saldarini 2001: 280–89; Deines 2010.

4. Josephus, Ant. 13:398–411; J.W. 1:110–13; Matt 23: 1–15. Compare Pesher Nahum 2:8–10, which accuses that the "Seeker of Smooth Things" "with their fraudulent teaching and lying tongue and perfidious lip, misdirect many; kings, princes, priests and people together with the proselyte attached to them. Cities and clans will perish through their advice." See Berrin 2004: 91–99.

5. Rivkin 1969–70.

6. Büchler 1964: 1–5.

7. Alon 1977: 223.

8. Schürer 1973–87: 2:395–403. Anthony Saldarini (1992) describes the Pharisaic organizational scheme along the lines of voluntary groups familiar from the Greco-Roman world (for more see, chapter 6).

9. Deines 2010: 132.

10. Smith 1956. Compare Schwartz 1983; Mason 1991: 372–75.

11. See A. Baumgarten 1987.

12. Neusner 1973a: 66, 83.

13. A. Baumgarten 1997a: 91–100, 1998a.

14. Thomas Kazen (2010b: 87) aptly argues that the most unique characteristic of Pharisee purity was its consistency, the systematic implementation of purity laws. This is, indeed, a dominant component of Pharisee purity, but since the Pharisees' purity observance deviated from the foundation of biblical exegesis (as we will immediately demonstrate) and existed alongside competing approaches, this cannot be viewed as the single characteristic of Pharisee purity. As I noted in chapter 2, this tendency also characterizes Qumran purity laws.

15. Sanders 1990: 131–245. Roland Deines and Martin Hengel (1995) uncover Sanders's interest to bring Jesus back to the fold of the "Common Judaism" of the time, for if purity is not so important, one can also accept Jesus. On the other hand, James Dunn (2002: 454) believes that even small gestures among religious groups can lead to separationist tendencies, which he believes were at the heart of Pharisee purity observances.

16. Notably, even those who disagree with Neusner, based their claims primarily on biblical notions in order to describe the principles of Pharisee purity norms,

assuming that the Pharisaic way of life was, at its core, based on biblical interpretation. See, for example, Poirier 2003.

17. Noam 2008: 481–93. There is, therefore, a fundamental difference in this matter between Pharisaic and rabbinic law and the practice of Qumran sectarians, who were careful to anchor their halakhic rulings and practices on biblical exegesis.

18. See, for example, Hyam Maccoby (1999: 212–13), who believes that those who observed purity for the consumption of unconsecrated food believed themselves to be in God's presence due to the sanctity of the Land of Israel. John Poirier (1996) believed that the Pharisees observed purity in order to preserve the sanctity of the Torah they embodied.

19. See Bultmann 1963: 17–18, and in contrast Booth 1986: 74. For an analysis of the dialogue as a coherent unit, see Furstenberg 2008.

20. A partial parallel is found in Luke 11:37–39. This is a secondary version that combines the dispute over handwashing with the tradition regarding vessel purity that will be discussed further in this chapter. See Green 1997: 468; Nolland 1989–93: 664.

21. Commentators on Mark (see Collins 2007: 356) agree that the expression *katharizōn panta ta brōmata* is syntactically awkward. Possibly, according to some textual witnesses, this statement can be interpreted as referring to the digestive process (in neuter) that "purifies all foods." Compare the anecdote on Diogenes (Diogenes Laertius, 6:61). See Black 1954: 217; Guelich 1989: 378.

22. According to Barnabas Lindars (1988: 61), this is supposedly the most radical statement in all Jesus traditions. Daniel Boyarin (2012: 121), on the other hand, believes that this sentence is compatible with Jesus's original doctrine, assuming that "all the foods" include only the permitted foods consumed by contemporary Jews.

23. On the social profile of Matthew's community and their relationship with the Pharisees, see Sim 1998; Runesson 2008.

24. See Davies and Allison 1988–97: 516.

25. Ed Sanders (1985: 264) interprets the expression this way and, therefore, negates its authenticity. In his opinion, Jesus did not deviate from accepted halakhic norm. See also Räisänen 1982; Davies and Allison 1988–97: 528.

26. Lindars 1988: 66.

27. Booth 1986: 214; Davies and Allison 1988–97: 529.

28. Read this way, Jesus seems to express an approach similar to that of Philo. See Klawans 2000: 147–49.

29. Compare Booth 1986: 46.

30. Thus, Guelich 1989: 376. In Robert Guelich's opinion, Jesus had a tendency to shift from a narrow discussion to a wider issue, and he therefore responds to the question regarding handwashing by relating to the wider issue of purity in general.

31. Sanders 1985: 266.

32. This is emphasized by Kister 2001: 152 and Kazen 2010b: 86.

33. Notably, already the talmudic tradition attributes this law to a rabbinic ordinance, which it ascribes to the famous occasion of the edict on the eighteen matters. See y. Shab. 1:7 (3c); b. Shab. 13b.

34. Kazen (2013: 187–88) contests my interpretation and the relevance of the early rabbinic traditions for the interpretation of Jesus's statement. He claims that this tension is apparent only from a rabbinic point of view, and he therefore prefers interpreting Jesus's message in a prophetic manner rather than as a legal argument.

35. The notion that hands may be defiled and purified separately from the body possibly stems from purity practices familiar from the Ancient Near East, in which the term *hand purity* (*šuluḫḫu* in Akkadian) became a general name for purity rituals and even religious ritual in general. Beyond that, water that was defiled by hands was threatening to the extent that one should not even look at it. A striking expression for this is found in the ceremony for consecrating divine idols (*mīs pî*). When the idol was carried from the river in the direction of the temple, the priest would recite an incantation, which he attributed to the god Marduk. The incantation expresses the fear that despite the earlier purification in the river, the idol would be defiled by people with impure hands or by water that had come in contact with unwashed hands. For that purpose, the priest is required to prepare "hand water" with which to purify his hands (C. Walker 2001: 223–25). Here we discover the power of impure hands to defile others and particularly liquids. See also Laessøe 1955: 31. It is therefore possible that the origin of the "tradition of the elders" regarding handwashing is in Babylonian perceptions that made their way into Judean practice.

36. On person-to-vessel transfer, see the charts in Milgrom 1991: 953 and onward. According to scripture, various sources of impurity may defile people externally, but not through digestion. Jesus's statement is precise and contrasts things that come out of the body—zov and bleeding—with that which enters it (food).

37. Poirier (1996: 226) compares the Pharisaic concern with hand purity and modern table etiquette. Just as modern people fear disease will invade their bodies and, therefore, wash their hands and maintain the cleanness of their food, so too the Pharisees had such fears. This is a convincing portrayal of the Pharisees. Poirier, however, goes on to explain the particular care taken by the Pharisees to distance sources of impurity from their bodies as designed to create a holy body, from which one could produce prayer and religious learning. In my view, this addition is unnecessary and is foreign to the perception of purity presented by the Pharisees.

38. B. Šabb. 14b–15a.

39. The assumption that hand impurity was first instituted with respect to holy foodstuff led scholars to reconstruct extremely complex histories of this legal field or to artificially distinguish between different types of handwashing. See Büchler 1964: 94–98; Urbach 1984: 18–19; Maccoby 1999: 156 (following the Talmudic reconstruction, Maccoby rejects the New Testament testimony regarding the handwashing polemic); Milikowsky 2000: 152.

40. M. Hag. 2:5–7 is an early unit (see chap. 4), which assumes that unconsecrated food must be consumed in purity and with pure hands. The talmudic discussion, on the other hand, rejects the necessity of handwashing before eating unconsecrated food. The Palestinian Talmud suggests that handwashing for unconsecrated food is only a preventive measure to ensure this practice is maintained also with respect to terumah (p. Hag. 2:5, 78b). The Babylonian Talmud (b. Hag. 18b) takes this even further, claiming that with regard to unconsecrated food, handwashing is not intended for purity purposes but as a ritual before eating bread. A straightforward reading of the Mishnah, however, implies that also ordinary food must be eaten in a state of purity. While the hand imparts only light impurity, through the mediation of the liquids found at every meal, it threatens unconsecrated food as well (see m. Par. 8:7; m. Tehar. 2:1).

41. Sanders (1990: 229) believes that handwashing was practiced specifically on Sabbaths and holy days, due to their sanctity. However, while we know of purification practices in preparation for the Sabbath, there is no evidence that handwashing was reserved for this day. I have demonstrated elsewhere that the Hebrew terms denoting handwashing are borrowed from Greek. Additionally, the House of Shammai's opinion regarding the order of actions consistently correlates to that familiar from Greco-Roman literature regarding dining customs. The House of Hillel systematically deviated from the familiar order, delaying the handwashing until after the drinking of the wine, moving it up immediately after the meal and distancing the sullied napkin from the table. All of this, apparently, in order to ascertain that the meal would be consumed in purity. See Furstenberg 2016b: 96–107.

42. On the sectarian context of Jesus's woe sayings, see Furstenberg 2020a.

43. Compare Robinson, Hoffmann, and Kloppenborg 2000: 268–72. Harry Fledderman (2005: 536) also adopts this reconstruction, although the editor generally tends to regard Luke's language as more conservative.

44. This distinction could make sense only if we disconnect the last phrase ("all is pure for you") from its immediate context and read it as a general statement. Cf. Titus 1:15: "To the pure, all things are pure."

45. The difference between the versions in Matthew and Luke, respectively instructing purification and almsgiving, has been explained by some commentators as the result of two variants of the original Aramaic: *zky* versus *dky*. See Kloppenborg 1987: 58. But the fact that the language deployed by each matches their ideology mitigates against this strictly linguistic explanation. See Garland 1979: 144–45.

46. See, for example, Davies and Allison 1988–97: 3:296–99.

47. This approach has been put forth by Neusner 1975–76: 486–95, esp. 488, but he has misinterpreted the rabbinic texts. Compare Maccoby 1982.

48. According to Menachem Kister (2001: 148–50), Jesus evoked the legal issue to excite his listeners, but he used it merely as a rhetorical point of departure before shifting his focus to the moral plane.

49. M. Tehar. 8:7. As commentators have noted, Simeon brother of Azariah presents the ancient law in a different formulation, but agrees with R. Eliezer about its substance. According to both, the exterior of vessels contaminated by liquids can only render other liquids impure.

50. The following source exemplifies the concern: "[If] a dish full of pure liquid with an impure exterior is resting on a board on which a loaf of the priestly tithe has been placed, and the liquid overflowed onto the dish's exterior, it [=the liquid] is rendered impure by the dish's exterior. If it fell on the board and rendered it impure, the board in turn renders the loaf impure" (Sifre Zuta on Numbers 19:11).

51. See m. Kelim 25:7–8.

52. T. Kelim (Bava Batra), 3:7.

53. The Pesher on the Psalms refers to the Pharisees thus: "Its [interpretation] concerns the Man of Lies who misdirected many with deceptive words, for they have chosen worthless things and did not lis[ten] to the Interpreter of Knowledge" (4Q171 [4QpPs^a] 1–10 i 27). On the Pharisees as "Seekers of Smooth Things" in Qumran literature, see VanderKam 2003.

54. For an analysis of the entire unit in this Mishnah, see Furstenberg 2020a.

55. 4 QMMT B 56–58. On the degree of similarity between the cases discussed in the rabbinic and sectarian texts, see Elman 1996.

56. The last of the anti-Pharisaic charges recorded in the Mishnah also concerns the improper inclusion of the "pure" and "impure" in the same place, although not in the strict sense of ritual impurity. In m. Yad. 4:8, a Galilean sectarian complains that the Pharisees write the name of Moses alongside the name of the gentile ruler in their contracts. Arguably, the name of the non-Jewish ruler soils the good name of Moses.

57. Daniel Schwartz has suggested interpreting this dispute in terms of the general distinction between nominalism and realism. He argues that, from a natural perspective, a liquid is a single entity, a concept that makes discriminating between "parts" of a liquid a legal abstraction. See D. Schwartz 1992. For a thorough criticism of this approach, see Rubenstein 1999. In this case, it is hardly convincing that the Pharisaic view is less natural and intuitive, since the direction of the stream moves away from the liquids at the top toward the impure substance. The issue at stake is rather the degree of separation, as 4QMMT makes explicit. See Furstenberg 2015.

58. For a source-critical analysis of these units, which represent an early redaction of laws concerning food purity, see Furstenberg 2012.

59. See, for example, "When do fish become susceptible to uncleanness?" (m. ʿUq. 3:8); "When do honeycombs become susceptible to uncleanness on account of their being regarded as liquids?" (3:10–11); "At what stage do olives become susceptible to uncleanness?" (m. Tehar. 9:1); "If a man desires to put grapes [into the wine-press] from the baskets or from what was spread out on the ground, The House of Shammai ruled: he must put them in with clean hands, for if he puts them in with unclean hands he renders them unclean. The House of Hillel ruled: he may put

them in with unclean hands, and yet he may set aside his terumah in a condition of cleanness" (m. Tehar. 10:4). For more on this topic, see below, chapter 5, pp. ???. The dispute between the two Houses concerning rendering fruits susceptible to impurity by means of liquids appears at the beginning of Mishnah Makhshirin.

60. See, for instance, m. Kel. 3:6 ("The plug of a jar is not regarded as connected") and 5:5, regarding the various parts of a jar.

61. See Sussman 1994; Shemesh 2009.

62. This policy may by implied from m. Ḥag. 3:6–8 (see chap. 6 of this volume). For an overview of lenient approaches among the Pharisees toward the sacred, see Knohl 1991; Regev 2006.

63. This dispute appears in m. Par. 2:7, t. Par. 3:7–8, and 4QMMT B 13–15. For an alternative explanation of the dispute, see Birenboim 2009b.

64. As Mira Balberg (2014: 48–73) demonstrates, this notion was developed extensively in later rabbinic works. See also Regev 2000.

4. Outsider Impurity and the Forms of Judean Sectarianism

1. Am ha-aretz is frequently conceived as the backbone of Jewish society during the Second Temple period. See Schürer 1973–87: 2:395–99. This position was promoted by Morton Smith (1956: 73, 1959: 356). Following Smith, Ed Sanders coined the term "Common Judaism" for describing this form of nondenominational Judaism (Sanders 1994: 45–314), which he also associated with am ha-aretz. This group has also a central historiographical role in the description of Jewish society outside the rabbinic circle post-70 CE. For a portrayal of those Jews who renounced the rabbis' authority, see Goodman 1983: 102–4. Sacha Stern (1994: 114–19) identifies am ha-aretz with the common people.

2. Unlike the accepted historiographical use of the term *am ha-aretz*, I suggest (Furstenberg 2013a: 290) that this designation was an internal rabbinic term that had meaning only within rabbinic halakhic discourse. That said, this does not undermine its value for studying the Judean society of the Second Temple period. We should not view the laws regarding am ha-aretz as a direct portrayal of the social state of affairs but rather as an organizing and distinguishing category that was applied by the Pharisees, and later the rabbis, in order to operate safely in the social arena. One can therefore assume that structural changes occurring in the social sphere would be reflected in a reorganization of the halakhic realm, as we see in chap. 6.

3. The features of the later laws of am ha-aretz, as they were shaped by the Galilean rabbis of the second century, are discussed in chapter 6. As we will see, this innovation required a reformulation of some of the earlier rabbinic traditions.

4. See b. Pesaḥ. 49a–b. On the redaction and intention of the discussion there, in light of the elitist notions of the Torah scholars of Babylonia during the late Talmudic period, see Rubenstein 2003: 123–42.

5. This work was later translated into Hebrew. The references here are to the Hebrew edition. See Büchler 1964: 1–5.

6. For a critique of Büchler's approach, see Alon 1977: 214–15, followed by Oppenheimer 1977: 6–7.

7. Oppenheimer 1977: 10–18.

8. Some scholars view the term *am ha-aretz* as denoting peasants (as in the case of "pagans"). See Zeitlin 1932–33; Finkelstein 1962: 761; Miller 2006: 327–38. Rabbinic sources, however, do not locate the am ha-aretz in a nonurban context, and there is therefore no real grounds for this interpretation.

9. Salomon Zeitlin 1932–33 deduces from the fact that ammei ha-aretz were accused only of lack of observance of tithe laws that this group was careful to observe the Sabbath, holidays, and additional laws.

10. See also m. Hag. 2:7; m. 'Ed. 1:14; t. 'Ohal. 5:11–12. From the Tosefta, we learn that R. Joshua discussed this topic with one of the students of the House of Shammai.

11. The fact that the contrast between Pharisees and ammei ha-aretz did not, at its outset, relate to the realm of tithing is implied in m. Dem. 6:6: "The House of Shammai say: One may sell his olives only to an associate. But the House of Hillel say: One may sell them also to anyone who is known to give tithes." Anyone known to give tithes is distinguished from the *associate*, who was known to observe laws of purity. The Gospels testify that Pharisees differed from others in matters of tithing. See Matt 23:23/Luke 11:42; Luke 18:9–14.

12. For a survey of the textual indications of this new characterization of the am ha-aretz, see Furstenberg 2013a: 311–18.

13. For the development of this term in biblical literature see Gunneweg 1983.

14. See Schürer 1973–87: 2:398n59.

15. The following Tosefta would seem to contradict this claim: "There is a story that some Boethusians once hid the willows under some great stones on the Sabbath eve; but when this had become known to the ammei ha-aretz they came and dragged them out from under the stones on the Sabbath, for the Boethusians do not acknowledge that the beating of the willow suspends the Sabbath" (t. Sukkah 3:1). Here, however, am ha-aretz is opposed to the sectarian Boethusians. This is not a neutral term for the entire nation but rather reflects a sectarian confrontation. This is a particularly likely explanation if we identify the "Boethusians" with the Essenes (see Sussman 1994: 195).

16. See, for example, the Peshitta translation of Ezra 10:11, which parallels the Hebrew and Aramaic verbs of separation. In tannaitic language the verb *b.d.l.* is used very seldom to denote distancing and is rather used in the meaning of distinction (as it is used in the Bible); *p.r.š.*, on the other hand, does not appear in the Hebrew Bible with the meaning of separation and distancing at all, and this is a renewed meaning in rabbinic language.

17. Olyan 2004.

18. It is reasonable to see the terminology of Ezra as the source for the name of the Pharisees (Cohon 1960). At the same time, it appears that there were different explanations for this name already during the Second Temple period (A. Baumgarten 1983).

19. As is apparent in the opening of the Damascus Document, the sectarian authors presented themselves as the first returners from exile to the Land of Israel. They identified, to an unprecedented degree, with the returned exiles but completely ignored the historical occurrences in the Persian period, thus becoming, in their own eyes, the first returned exiles from the Babylonian diaspora.

20. The terms in use in sectarian literature are similar to those Ezra applies. The use of the verb *b.d.l.* to designate the sectarian separation from "the sons of the pit" or the men of injustice appears in the following places: CD 6:14–15, 7:3–4; 1QS 5:1, 5:10, 8: 11–13. The prohibition of intermingling, which appears in this form and meaning only in Ezra 9 and Daniel 2, is devoted in the Community Rule to rules of distancing from nonsectarians: "And he shall not fraternize with him with regard to his goods or his advice" (1QS 7:24).

21. This term appears in 4QMMT, according to the text suggested by the editors: "[And you know that] we have separated ourselves from the multitude of the peop[le . . .] [and] from mingling in these affairs, and from associating wi[th them] in these things" (3, 7–8; Qimron and Strugnell 1994: 53). For an explanation of the unique use of the root *p.r.š* here, see Qimron and Strugnell 1994: 111; Schwartz 1996: 67–80. For an alternative filling in of the sentences, according to which the author is referring to the people of Israel who had separated themselves from the nations, see Bar-Asher Siegal 2011.

22. See Shemesh 1997.

23. Compare to Josephus's assessment of the Sadducees, who "have a rather harsh disposition even towards one another: encounters with their peers are as uncouth as those with outsiders" (J.W. 2:166).

24. This paragraph has stood at the center of the ongoing scholarly debate concerning gentile impurity during the Second Temple period. According to Alon 1977, it proves that gentile impurity was a widespread notion. On the other hand, Jonathan Klawans (1995: 299–300, 2000: 79–82) suggests that contact with gentiles was considered defiling only by the Essenes themselves, in accordance with their unique notion of impurity. Christine Hayes (2002: 63–67) also assumed that this was a sectarian stringency, based on the fear of the ritual impurity carried by gentiles, but I see no good reason to accept this narrow interpretation. Josephus is comparing the sectarian practice to familiar practice, and the affinity to Acts 10 seems to confirm it.

25. Most exegetes assume that there is no difference between the two terms. However, *koinon* may be interpreted, in the current context, as something that has been defiled (see also Romans 14:14). It appears that these cases reflect an extension of the lexicon regarding impurity, and they contain a distinction that does not appear

in the Hebrew Bible, between that which is impure from its very nature and that which has been defiled by something else.

26. Compare Acts 15:7–12; Gal 2:11–18.

27. Dibelius 1956: 109–22; Conzelmann 1987: 80–81; Pervo 2009: 266–69; Peterson 2009: 330–31. Richard Pervo and David Peterson assume that the original meaning of the vision was intended to completely abolish the laws of kashruth and that Luke, the author of Acts who placed the vision here, wished to add to this meaning the social meaning as well. They believe that the mixing of kashruth laws and the social issues of contact with gentiles represent Luke's Christianity and does not have a Jewish source. Dibelius, as I understand him, suggests a more moderate approach, according to which the vision was only intended to permit foods of gentiles, as Peter himself responded to his opponents at the beginning of chapter 11.

28. Klawans (1995: 300–302) (and following him Hayes 2002: 49–50) attempts to dismiss the significance of this source as a testimony for the observance of gentile impurity during the Second Temple period. He notes that Peter was content with stating that associating with gentiles is only forbidden according to Jewish practice but does not defile, but he ignores the link between the beginning of Peter's speech and its end, where Peter rejects the definition of gentiles as impure. While this text does not state that all forms of contact with a gentile defile (similarly to contact with an impure animal), those manifestations of association with gentiles that were forbidden were explained as deriving from the immanent impurity of the gentile.

29. For a survey of positions regarding gentile hosting, see Tomson 1990: 230–36; Wahlen 2005: 506–8.

30. On the relationship between 4QS and the later Community Rule (although it is paleographically earlier), see Metso 1997; Hempel 2006.

31. CD 15:6–15 provides a different process of oath-taking and entering the covenant. On the difference between the Damascus Document and the Community Rule regarding the commitments undertaken in order to join the sect, see Furstenberg 2016a.

32. At this point, the text adds that the obligation is to adhere to the interpretation of the Law of Moses specifically "in accordance with the council of the men of the Yaḥad" (4QS^d 7). The parallel text in 1QS 5:9–10 suggests a more developed sectarian framework, which includes the sons of Zadok.

33. The syntax of this phrase links it quite poorly to its surroundings. It may plausibly be considered a later addition, intended to emphasize the impurity of the men of injustice. Thus, although the scribe of 1QS begins a new paragraph at this point (5:13) and seems to begin a new subject ("He shall not enter the water to touch the purity of the men of holiness"), it is clear from the earlier 4QS version that this detached phrase complements the original list of strictures. See Licht 1965 (128–29).

34. Scholars have suggested different reconstructions of the process through which the sons of Zadok gained control over the Qumran community. See Vermes 1996; A. Baumgarten 1997b. Cana Werman (2000), on the other hand, dismisses the

standing of "the sons of Zadok" among the Qumran sect. The Qumran author might be applying the term from Ezekiel *sons of Zadok* symbolically, as seems to be the case in CD 3:19–4:4.

35. The addition "unless at its price" is revealing, as it limits the prohibition to gifts, as the only type of giving that might lead to social bonding. A similar move can be found in tannaitic literature as well. In t. 'Abod. Zar. 3:14 (according to the genizah version), we find the following: "And you may sell to them, but not give them presents. In what case does this apply? In a case of a gentile that he is not acquainted with, or that was passing from place to place, but if he was his neighbor or his friend he is allowed to receive a present, since it is like a sale."

36. Klawans 2000: 79–91. Hanan Birenboim (2003) suggests a more careful wording of the relationship between both elements. In his opinion, impurity is not the direct result of sin but, rather, is a ritual expression of the physical lowness of man, which is also the source of sin.

37. Shemesh (1997: 232) explains: "upon closer investigation we find a profound difference between the rulings of the *Rule of the Community* and the mishnah just cited. For rabbinic halakhah would undoubtedly permit an *am ha-aretz* to eat with *ḥaverim*, provided he was willing to undergo a ritual cleansing of his body and of his clothing. Not so for the sect." In his estimation, am ha-aretz is impure only because he is not meticulous in preserving his own purity, while those who are not members of the sectarian community are intrinsically impure.

38. Jacob Nahum Epstein (1957: 50–51) provides evidence for the relative antiquity of these *mishnayot*. First, in m. Hag. 3:7, Yose b. Yoezer and Yohanan b. Gudgeda are mentioned as maintaining sacrificial-level purity for all foods, while the Tosefta, refers to later rabbis, Rabban Gamaliel and Onkelos. To this we can add the use of the term *Pharisees*, which appears only in early rabbinic traditions (as opposed to the term *ḥaber*, associate). On the antiquity of additional parts of this section of Tractate Hagigah, see chap. 6.

39. Compare e.g. m. Qidd. 4:5; t. B. Bat. 7:3 (p. 152).

40. Shemesh 1997: 232. The contrast between this rabbinic approach and the notion of spiritual purification according to the Qumran writings is highlighted by Joseph Baumgarten (1992: 209).

41. Seemingly, one may wonder about the order of actions in this mishnah. If a person already belongs to a particular group and is known to be a member of the group, why does the mishnah first state that he has immersed and only later than he is "held" for that level of purity. This would imply that a process of being held for a particular level of purity takes place only after the act of purification and is not a prerequisite for immersion (see Balberg 2014: 153n16). However, it is difficult to determine the order of actions from the mishnaic formulation. Additionally, it is possible that this mishnah relates specifically to the reality of Jerusalem. In this situation, even one who has not strictly observed a certain level of purity desires to be part of the fitting level of purity. For that purpose, immersion is not enough, but rather, one

must affiliate himself with that same group of pure people. In any event, purification is not a matter of private intent.

42. The accepted interpretation of the verb *huhzak* in the Tosefta and the Talmuds testifies to the transformation of purity observance into a private matter that only small numbers of people practiced. It, therefore, depends solely on a personal determination, not on group affiliation. This is characteristic to the end of the tannaitic period (see chap. 7).

43. Following Rava's words: "the law as to midras uncleanness is different, for it is feared that his wife, when in a menstruous condition, sat upon these clothes" (b. Ḥul. 35b).

44. In his article "The Levitical Uncleanness of the Gentiles" (Alon 1977: 146–89), Gedalyahu Alon claimed that tannaitic literature preserves a variety of stances regarding gentile impurity: some equate it with the impurity of the zav; some compare it to the impurity of swarming things; and still others compare it to corpse impurity. However, a close examination of these sources reveals that solid evidence exists only for the first of these categories.

45. Sifra, Zabim 1:1 (74d); t. Zabim 2:1.

46. See, for example, m. Neg. 3:1; m. Nid. 7:3; m. Zabim 2:1; m. Miqw. 8:4.

47. On urine, see m. Tehar. 4:4; m. Makš. 2:2. On spit, see m. Tehar. 5:8; m. Sheq. 8:1; t. Tehar. 4:5.

48. M. Tehar. 5:7 (the opinion of those commentators who believe the concern is a concern with gentile impurity appears to be correct). See also t. Tehar. 6:11 (p. 666).

49. Mira Balberg (2014: 139–47) suggests that by defining a gentile as one who has experienced zov, the rabbis sought to challenge his masculinity, and thus also his humanity, since genital emissions are considered a feminization of the masculine body. This suggestion is compelling, but I believe it is unnecessary. Of all the types of impurity that the rabbis could have chosen for defining the inherent impurity of the gentile, only zov, abnormal genital discharge, is a severe impurity that derives from one's body.

50. See m. Zabim, chapter 5; see also Sifra Zabim 4:14 (78b).

51. M. Hag. 3:2: "He that carries anything possessing midras uncleanness may carry [at the same time] terumah, but not hallowed things."

52. For example, Josephus, Ant. 13: 298.

53. According to Adi Ophir and Ishay Rosen Zvi (2018: 201), the rabbinic distinction between the degrees of gentile impurity and am ha-aretz impurity is another testimony to the consolidation of a binary dichotomy between Jews and gentiles among the rabbis. Arguably, however, it is already rooted in Pharisaic social policy.

54. The story of Rabban Gamaliel the Elder is adduced to support the lenient position of the rabbis. A man may marry off his mature daughter to an am ha-aretz, if he stipulates that she is not required to prepare pure foods for him. However, it should be noted that this early story does not explicitly mention am ha-aretz, and it

is hard to assume that Rabban Gamaliel would give his daughter to such a priest. A better supposition is that Rabban Gamaliel (like Yoḥanan b. Gudgudah in m. Ḥag 2:7) maintained a high level of purity—that is, purity for hallowed things—and the priest, who maintained purity only at the level of eating terumah, was considered relatively impure by comparison (see Lieberman 1955–88: 5:1310). This story cannot prove that as early as the Second Temple period a lenient approach toward marriage with 'ammei ha-'aretz was prevalent.

55. Following this unit on marriage with am ha-aretz, the Tosefta adds another dispute between R. Meir and the sages concerning the very definition of am ha-aretz: "Who is an am ha-aretz? Whoever does not eat his ordinary food in the state of purity, the words of R. Meir. The sages say: whoever does not tithe." Elsewhere I have argued that this is a later addition that was intended to redefine the status of am ha-aretz with respect to tithing, as a result of the decrease of purity observance toward the end of the tannaitic period. Hereafter, the neglect of purity matter was insufficient to consider one as an am ha-aretz. (See Furstenberg 2013a and chap. 7 in this volume.)

56. On this characteristic difference between the homogenizing tendencies of Qumran law and rabbinic law, which celebrates the creation of interim categories, see, for instance, Noam 2010: 109.

5. Inclusion and Marginalization

1. Cecilia Wassén (2016) has recently addressed the question of how members of the Qumran sect participated in the sect's meals in a state of impurity. While she attempts to distinguish between the different meals of the sect, I outline their coherent halakhic system of graded purity. See below n. 18 regarding some of the differences between our approaches.

2. J. Baumgarten 1980: 157–60; Schiffman 1994; Birenboim 2009b: 254–58; Himmelfarb 2010; Wassén 2016.

3. For a survey of relevant verses, see Birenboim 2006: 257–58; Himmelfarb 2010: 200–202.

4. Lev. 15:21. See also, for example, Lev. 11:24–25, 27, 31–32, 39–40; 14:46; 15:5–8, 10–11, 17–19, 21–23, 27; 17:15; 22:5; Num. 19:7–10, 22.

5. Lev. 15:13. See also Lev. 15:28 and 14:8–9 (leprosy).

6. Such a conclusion may be deduced from Numbers 19:19, concerning the purification from corpse impurity, which includes bathing in water on the seventh day but achieving purity only at nightfall.

7. Leviticus 22:6–7 rules that one who touched a swarming thing or an impure person may eat holy foodstuff only after bathing and waiting for sunset. The midrash (Sifra Emor 4:4) deduces from the language of this verse that the full process is required only of the priest, who eats holy foodstuff, while an Israelite may eat ordinary food immediately after bathing.

8. See m. Neg. 14:3; Sifra Zavim pereq 5:11, pereq 9:2: the zav and zava cease to defile unconsecrated foods and vessels after bathing. Interestingly, in both cases the Sifra distinguishes between the bathing required to stop contamination and the role of bathing for the sake of entering the Temple (see pereq 5:14 and pereq 9:4). In order to be eligible to bring the sacrifices, one must bathe on the previous day, but this is not necessarily identical to the bathing on the seventh day, which is intended to prevent further contamination.

9. The laws of immersion for a woman who has given birth are the subject of a dispute between the Houses of Hillel and Shammai. According to the House of Shammai, the woman does not immerse at the beginning of the pure days, but only at their end, whereas according to the House of Hillel, the woman must immerse in order to begin counting her pure days, and she therefore does not immerse at the end of the pure days (m. Nid 10:7). The comparison to tevul yom is thus valid according to the opinion of the House of Hillel.

10. M. Par. 3:7; t. Par. 3:8.

11. 4QMMT B 13–16.

12. Compare to Sifre Numbers 124: "What does the word 'pure' come to instruct us? [Pure] of any impurity. And who is this [person]? This is the *tevul yom*." See Kister 1999b: 330–35.

13. Pace Himmelfarb 2010. She rightly underlines the affinity of the scrolls to the language of scripture, but it is evident at this point that 4QMMT is opposing an alternative practice.

14. Hanan Birenboim (2009b) follows the first explanation. He assumes that all agreed that tevul yom was considered pure outside the sancta, and the dispute was whether the red heifer that was slaughtered outside the Temple was considered a sacrifice. Lawrence Schiffman (1994) follows the latter explanation.

15. Furthermore, the assumption that purification comes about only at the end of the day is so dominant that even when bringing a sacrifice on the eighth day, the purification takes place only in the evening (4QMMT B 71–72 [leprosy]; 4Q266 9 ii 1–4 [zava]). This position has no foundation in scripture and is the result of Qumranic homogenization of the purity system.

16. See the research by Milgrom 1990: 90–95, 1991: 968–76, 1995: 67–68; and especially 1992.

17. Milgrom 1992: 568–70.

18. Scholars have suggested other, and in my view less convincing, understandings of the eating restriction. Birenboim (2009b: 258–59) claims that immersion is intended for the consumption of pure, unconsecrated food, while complete purification was required for eating consecrated food. As we shall see, however, unconsecrated "purities" could be eaten only after the seventh day, and holy foodstuff awaited the termination of the eighth day. Thus, one could not eat any pure food before the end of the purification period. Wassén (2016: 115) argues, but in my

opinion doesn't sufficiently prove, that the first-day ablution allowed one to join regular communal meals, since only special meals on the Sabbath and holidays were eaten in purity.

19. Philo, *Laws* 3:63.

20. According to Birenboim, there is no real difference between the two systems. In his view, both groups solved the tension between the verses that present immersion as sufficient for purification and those that require sunset in the same manner, by distinguishing between holy and unconsecrated foods. However, since the Qumran sources do not relate to the final immersion, but to a different immersion, they evidently are not concerned with the role of the immersion on the last day but rather with the implications of immediately removing the source of impurity.

21. Although he would refrain from consuming foods that had come into direct contact with the source of impurity; see the section in this chapter on purification from corpse impurity.

22. The rabbis apply two terms to describe this stage: (1) *me'orav shemesh*, that is, one whose sun has set and, therefore, may eat terumah, and (2) *mechusar kippurim*, that is, one who has not yet brought a sacrifice and, therefore, cannot yet eat sacrificial foods.

23. M. Kelim. 1:5; m. Neg. 14:3; m. Parah 11:4.

24. This tripartite system is at the basis already of the positions of the Houses of Hillel and Shammai. This is also the difference between Yose b. Yoezer, who was considered the most pious in the priesthood, and Yohanan b. Gudgada, who ate all unconsecrated food in accordance with the purity required for hallowed things (m. Hag. 2:7).

25. Ostraca found in Masada included the following inscriptions, among others: "pure for the holiness," "fit for the purity of the holiness," "unfit for the purity of the holiness" (see image on front cover). According to Yigael Yadin and Joseph Naveh (1989: 35), these jugs contained wine and oil intended for Temple libations, implying that liquids for libations were stored outside Jerusalem. Itzhak Sapir (1994: 143) suggests that these jugs served a group of inhabitants who ate their unconsecrated foods as if they were sacrificial foods. Considering the fact that outside of rabbinic literature, there was only a binary distinction between what is merely "pure" to what is "pure for hallowed things," it is plausible that the marked jugs in Masada were intended for priests, who ate their terumah there.

26. Compare to Temple Scroll, 11Q49: 19–21: "And they shall be clean by the evening from the dead person, so that they can approach all their pure things," and 4QMMT B 71–72: "[when they have the uncleanness of leprosy] one should not allow them to eat any of the ho[l]y things until the sun sets on the eighth day."

27. As we mentioned, this immersion takes place at a different stage in each system. "First day ablution" in Qumran and the so-called last day ablution in Pharisaic law.

28. According to some sources, the immersion is intended to permit the consumption of tithes; see, for example, m. Kelim 1:5; m. Neg. 14:3. Other sources, on the other hand, include unconsecrated food (m. Parah 11:4).

29. According to Qumran law, the terumah must be consumed in Jerusalem (see Shemesh 2003). This is also alluded to in some rabbinic sources; see chapter 6.

30. Noam 2008.

31. Compare to Josephus, J.W. 2:128–33; 1QS 6:4–5.

32. For a discussion of this fragment, see Kazen 2010a. Thomas Kazen's conclusions partially corroborate what I suggest here. Additional research includes J. Baumgarten 1999: 99–109; Werrett 2007: 245–49.

33. See, for instance, m. Zabim 5:6–7.

34. Milgrom 1995: 66.

35. Compare the ruling of 4Q514, discussed previously, which prohibits one who has purified from his discharge to eat before bathing.

36. From the following fragment (4Q274 2 a), it appears that the bed and chair of one who has had a seminal emission also transmit impurity, as do those of the zav. The difference between the two is, therefore, only the duration of the discharge, and this distinction affects the ways in which the two are distanced. One who has had a seminal emission, unlike the zav, can easily remove the source of impurity and thus continue functioning. The zav, on the other hand, is secluded until the discharge has ceased, and only then may he begin his purification process.

37. On the length of the woman's period in antiquity, see Dean-Jones 1989.

38. Bóid 1989: 285–87.

39. Kazen 2010a: 71–72 also relies on Samaritan halakhah to explain the status of a menstruating woman in this passage. In his opinion, also Qumran law demanded a "first-day ablution" following the onset of menses, although this is nowhere mentioned explicitly. In my view, even without assuming such a practice, Qumran law exhibits significant structural resemblance to the Samaritan and Karaite legal systems.

40. Elijah Beshyzi, *Aderet Eliyahu*, On Purity and Impurity, chapter 10 (122a–c); Aaron ben Elijha of Nicomedia, *Gan Eden*, chapter 4 (111a–b).

41. Josephus, Ant. 3: 261.

42. T. Šabb. 1:14. See the full quotation at the head of the introduction to this volume.

43. Sifra Zabim 2:2 (75c) mentions a designated piece of wood used for the menstruants to lie on.

44. While some scholars have assumed that the menstruants were sent away to a different house, the sources make it clear that they remained at home. Scholars were misled by m. Nid. 7:3, which rules that "all bloodstains, wheresoever they are found, are clean, except those that are found indoors or round a chamber of the 'impure women.'" However, this is a misreading of the word *tema'ot*, which simply refers

to "impurities." The Mishnah is therefore alluding to a place for disposing various impure substances, such as the miscarriages of the Samaritan women mentioned later in this chapter (and in t. Nid. 6:15). On this matter, see Rashi, b. Nid. 56b, s.v. *bet ha-tema'ot*; Alon 1977: 227–28; Margulies 1938: 114; Dinary 1980: 309; Sanders 1990: 156; Fonrobert 2000: 222n11.

45. The Sifra (Nedava 12:8, 23b–c) distinguishes between "days of strictness" and "days of leniency" and so appears to contradict our claim. This question is raised by the Rabad, ad loc.: "Days of strictness—these are the days of seeing, and days of leniency are the seven days of cleanliness. And I do not know what leniency there is during the days of cleanliness over the days of seeing?" However, one should note that this midrash relates specifically to contact with the sancta. In the realm of the sancta an additional period of prohibition exists, where one is forbidden to come in contact with the Temple although they are already pure for the camp, and it is possible that this is what is termed "days of leniency."

46. Sifra Zabim 9:12 (79c). Compare b. Šabb. 64b.

47. Later medieval sources develop a similar distinction between the days of bleeding and the seven days following. Beginning in the Gaonic period, it was common practice to hold a ritual cleansing between a menstruant's days of bleeding and the seven days following (Emanuel 2007). This practice is echoed in one place in the Talmud itself, in the story of the pious man who died young (b. Šabb. 13a–b and in *Avot de-Rabbi Natan* version A, chap. 2, pp. 8–9). According to this story, even Elijah is aware that the period of menstruation is divided into two parts and that a menstruant defiles vessels only at the beginning of the period. Elijah objects to leniencies regarding intimacy between a husband and wife during the second half of the menstruation period but accepts this distinction with respect to the treatment of pure foods (regarding the areas of distancing, compare Margulies 1938: 79, 114–18). This approach is similar to that found in sectarian law, and it would appear that it eventually made its way into mainstream rabbinic practice in the post-Talmudic period. Notably, however, at this stage the menstruating woman was considered a zava and was impure for a week beyond the days of her period.

48. For a study of this unit, see Noam 2010: 74–137.

49. Yadin 1977: 1:252–53.

50. Noam 2010: 106–12.

51. Noam 2010: 323.

52. Qumran law in general, in stark contrast to rabbinic law, does not offer post-factum solutions for less than perfect practice. See Shemesh 2009: 69–70 and 171n. 44.

53. Sifra Shemini 7:6 (53b).

54. Vered Noam (2010: 84–90) suggests that according to the Temple Scroll the house materials contract corpse impurity, while according to rabbinic law the house is unsusceptible to impurity, and only vessels in it may contrast impurity. Clearly,

however, it is not the materials themselves, such as wood and dust, that are contaminated according to the Temple Scroll but only the liquids in them.

55. Hanan Eshel (2000) emends "and vessels of wood or stone" and adds that stone vessels, which do not receive impurity, are rendered fit to receive impurity through contact with oil. This emendation is unnecessary, however: it is not the stone itself that is contaminated but only the liquid it has swallowed.

56. From these sources it would seem that oil is an especially potent carrier of impurity, and thus we find also in Josephus's statement regarding the Essenes (J.W. 2:123): "They consider olive oil a stain and should anyone be accidentally smeared with it he scrubs his body, for they make it a point of honor to remain hard and dry." See J. Baumgarten 1972a. To my understanding, there is no essential difference between oil and other liquids as far as their status as carriers of impurity. In practice, however, only oil served for anointing a person's body and vessels. Other liquids were not deliberately placed throughout the house, and if they were spilled, they were immediately wiped away or evaporated.

57. On the possible evidence for the practice of "first-day ablution" with regard to corpse impurity from the miqva'ot adjacent to cemeteries, see E. Eshel 1997. Compare Adler 2009.

58. T. Tehar.8:12 distinguishes between an associate, who is trusted to have waited three days, and an am ha-aretz, who must wait in front of witnesses.

59. Joseph Baumgarten (1995: 98, 1999: 108) interpreted the word *seal* as relating to a seal of a container. However, this interpretation disregards the context of the fragment. Furthermore, in this case the meaning of the word can be safely determined through the close rabbinic parallel (which will be discussed further in this chapter) in Mishnah Teharot 10:5. With respect to the same situation of gathering and harvesting of grapes, the Mishnah distinguishes between a grape with a stalk sealing it and one without.

60. I discuss the gradual creation of the initiation process according to the model of purification from bodily purity in Furstenberg 2016a.

61. This translation follows the transcription of Qimron 2010–14: 3:57. Compare J. Baumgarten 1999: 131–32 for alternative renderings and translation.

62. A break appears here, signifying the end of a sentence.

63. It is unclear what *bacha'im* are (pears? See LXX 1 Chr. 14:14), and these words were erased from the scroll.

64. J. Baumgarten (1999) fills this in as "if they press [olives in the olive press]."

65. J. Baumgarten (1999) fills this in as "squeezed (in purity)," but this verb does not appear anywhere else in Qumran literature.

66. See 1QS 6:20 (the second-year candidate), 1QS 7:20 (one who has been distanced from the community during the second year of distancing). For more, see Avemarie 1997.

67. See J. Baumgarten 1995: 93 and 1999: 90–91.

68. The idea that the teachings of the House of Shammai are closely associated with Qumran law was developed in Noam 2006.

69. Various elements within the dramatic description in the Babylonian Talmud have been adapted from other contexts. Compare t. Shab. 1:16 and y. Shab. 1:4 (3c) concerning the heated debate over the eighteen decrees.

70. Columella, *On Agriculture*, 12.52.3, addresses the role of storehouses, since the entire crop cannot be pressed in one day. Cato, *On Farming*, 3, warns against leaving the crop in the storehouses for too long. Compare t. Hal. 2:5, where it appears that the softening in the vat is the stage that comes immediately following the harvest.

71. On this process, see Cato, *On Farming*, 67.

72. See t. Tehar. 1:2. Cato, and following him Columella, reject this opinion, which is attributed to most farmers (Cato, *On Farming*, 64; Columella, *On Agriculture*, 12.52.18–19). According to both writers, olives that wait in the storehouses produce less oil, and the oil they produce is of lesser quality.

73. According to our interpretation, the salted olives were not intended to be eaten, but were rather salted as preparation for the press. This mishnah should therefore not be compared to the dispute between the Houses of Hillel and Shammai regarding pickled olives, where the House of Hillel holds the more stringent opinion (m. 'Ed. 4:6). Jacob Nahum Epstein (1957: 103) believed that the mishnahs contradicted one another and therefore reconstructed divergent traditions on this matter.

74. Columella, *On Agriculture*, 12.52.10; see Cato, *On Farming*, 65.

75. For possible identifications of these two surfaces, see Frankel 1999: 188.

76. Compare with the parallel case in m. T. Yom 4:1.

77. In general, it appears that the distinction between the levels of purity is characterized by the fact that while lower levels of impurity require liquids to impart impurity, higher levels of impurity are transmitted directly. Thus, for instance, in m. Hag. 3:2: "a vessel unites all its contents [for defilement] in the case of hallowed things, but not in the case of terumah." While regular foods connect through liquids (for instance, in m. Tehar. 8:8), with regard to hallowed things impurity spreads in a vessel even without liquids. Similarly in the adjacent law: "dry foodstuff may be eaten with unwashed hands, with terumah, but not with hallowed things."

78. As we saw at the beginning of the chapter, the intermediate stage of one who "counts to purity" is comparable to the tevul yom in tannaitic literature. And indeed, the presence of a tevul yom in the olive press also occupies the tannaitic sources. Here, however, we do not find any restrictions, and the tevul yom is allowed to come in contact with liquids (t. Tehar. 1:3). This difference demonstrates the similarities and differences between the two legal systems. While a person in a period of purification is still considered impure according to Qumran law and is therefore distanced from the olive press and its liquids, the tevul yom is considered pure for

unconsecrated foods in tannaitic law and can, therefore, participate fully in all agricultural activities, even around liquids.

6. Changing Social Contexts

1. Geonic Responsa, *Sha'arei Teshuva*, responsum 175 (Luria ed. 18b). See Nemoy 1930: 336–37.
2. Reich 2013: 231–32, 257–59.
3. Magen 1988: 109.
4. Neusner 1973b: 118–19. See also Fonrobert 2000: 2.
5. M. Parah 7:6; t. Parah 5:6; y. Ber. 6:1 (10a, according to ms. Vat. Ebr 133): "Rabbi Hagai and Rabbi Jeremiah went to the place of lustration waters. Rabbi Hagai hurried and blessed over them. Rabbi Jeremiah said: You acted appropriately! For all *mitzvot* require a blessing." Compare b. Nid. 6b: "As Ulla stated, 'The Associates' in Galilee keep their things in Levitical cleanness." For a discussion of all the testimonies to the continuance of purity practices and the consumption of terumah in purity during the Amoraic period, see Sussman 1969: 310–13n16.
6. See Cohen 1999: 968.
7. Nielsen 1993 (esp. the summary on 109–20 and 144–45). The scope of findings led Bruce Nielsen to ponder the possibility that the level of purity observance even increased, in some aspects, during the third and fourth centuries.
8. See Adler 2014, 2017, 2021; Sherman et al. 2020.
9. Magness 2012: 88, following Goodman 1994. Martin Goodman (1994: 353) explains the silence of the sources on this matter based on the supposition that the rabbis ignored these groups; however, there is not enough positive evidence to substantiate such a hypothesis. See also Joshua Burns (2006), who uncovers references to sectarian groups in rabbinic discourse reflecting social differentiation.
10. Miller 2010, 2015: 210–48. On the role of household religion for the development of rabbinic Judaism, see Sivertsev 2005: 211–71.
11. See Kiperwasser 2012.
12. See Safrai 1983: 131. As a (single) testimony to the spread of purity observance following 70 CE, Safrai quotes R. Yose's words to the son of R. Haninah b. Antigonus, in b. Bek. 30b: "from the day that the Temple was destroyed, the priests guarded their dignity by not entrusting matters of Levitical cleanness to everybody." This statement, however, indicates the decline of the public observance of purity, which led the priests to refrain from entrusting purity matters to those suspected of being ammei ha-aretz. Compare t. Demai 2:21.
13. At this point the Mishnah introduces additional conditions in the name of R. Judah, but these are of a different nature and are meant to encourage general moral behavior. It is therefore reasonable to assume that these were added at a later stage.
14. We should note that we find only three commitments under the headline of "four matters." Rashi, b. Bek. 30b s.v. "divrei ḥaverut," suggested that the obligation to

tithe that is mentioned with regards to the definition of the *ne'eman* is necessary also to become an associate. See also Lieberman (1955–88: 1.210). Compare Avot de Rabbi Nathan A, 41, p. 132, which completes the list using two items from R. Judah's additions in the Mishnah (see previous note).

15. Regarding the conditions for becoming trustworthy in matters of tithing (*ne'eman*), the Mishnah and the Tosefta document the same dispute between R. Judah and R. Meir. According to R. Judah, the candidate must tithe what he eats, what he sells, and what he buys, whereas R. Meir adds that he must also avoid being a guest in an am ha-aretz's home. The law regarding one who is "trustworthy regarding tithes" is therefore a later product of the Galilean rabbis, R. Judah and R. Meir.

16. Lieberman 1955–88: 1:209, 216.

17. T. Demai 2:10–12.

18. Jacob Neusner (1960) describes a tripartite process: faithfulness, initiation, and novitiate. Sections 2 and 11 both reflect the initial stages of the process, in which one merits faithfulness and ascertains that his hands and food remain pure. Later on, one expands his realm of observance to everything within his house and his clothing (following section 12 in the Tosefta and the Mishnah). Compare Oppenheimer 1977: 129–39.

19. 1QS (Community Rule) 6:13–23, 4QS^b 8–13; 4Q265 4 ii; Josephus, J.W. 2:137–39. From among all these sources, the Community Rule presents the most complex process, which includes several rounds of lots and investigation of the candidate. Despite the complexity of this process, it contains only three stages of purity: outsider impurity, defilement of liquids only and complete purity (see previous chapter). On the initiation processes in Qumran literature, see Furstenberg 2016a.

20. See Büchler 1964: 121, based on the language of Haggai 2:12: "If a man is carrying sacrificial flesh in a fold (lit. 'wings') of his garment, and with that fold touches bread, stew, wine." The fold of one's garment was used, among other things, to carry money or food.

21. T. Ḥag. 1:2; t. Tehar. 3:10.

22. As mentioned, Lieberman and his followers adopted a harmonizing stance, which locates the difference between the list of commitments that appear in the Mishnah and the Tosefta at the two ends of the process. But this reconstruction raises significant difficulties. According to this approach, one accepts the commitments in the Tosefta while still outside the association, including the commitment to eat unconsecrated foods in purity. Following acceptance to the association, one increases the level of his purity observance, including accepting "purities" on oneself. But the candidate has already ostensibly been required to eat in purity before the beginning of the process! In order to resolve this difficulty, Lieberman is forced to distinguish between "eating in a state of purity" and accepting the stringencies of "purities," which literary means "pure foods."

23. See Lieberman 1952; Fraade 2009a.

24. 1QS (Community Rule) 6:15–16; Furstenberg 2016a.

25. 1QS (Community Rule) 5:10–17.

26. Scholars have debated whether to identify the associates as Pharisees, depending on the role of purity in Pharisaic identity. While according to Schürer, Vermes, and Millar (1973–87: 2:398), associates are synonymous with Pharisees, Elias Rivkin (1969–70) insists on distinguishing the two groups, and he disassociates the Pharisees from any concern with purity. Hanan Birenboim (2006: 29–59), on the other hand, believes that both groups were strict observers of purity but that they belonged to different periods. In his view, the sources regarding the Pharisees relate to the Temple period, whereas associates are mentioned only in later sources, when associations were formed to bolster the observance of purity. In my view, although some of the sources on associates indeed belong to a later stage of rabbinic law, some of them, such as those attributed to the Houses of Shammai and Hillel, evidently go back to an earlier period.

27. Compare Oppenheimer 1977: 118. According to Goodman 1987: 83, there was partial overlap between the associates and Pharisees, and he refers to the associations as the Pharisees' "power base."

28. For an analysis of this unit and its textual development, see Furstenberg 2016b: 313–21.

29. M. Tehar. 7:1/t. Tehar. 8:1: R. Shimon; m. Tehar. 7:2–4/t. Tehar. 8:4: R. Meir, R. Shimon; t. Tehar. 8:1; t. Tehar. 9:1: R. Judah, R. Yose, R. Shimon; m. Tehar. 8:2: R. Yose; t. Tehar. 8:12: R. Judah; t. Tehar. 9:11: R. Shimon b. Gamaliel. An earlier rabbi is mentioned only once in relation to am ha-aretz (R. Akiva in t. Tehar. 9:6); however, there the issue is not the social contact with am ha-aretz but rather the purity of fruit belonging to an am ha-aretz who has accepted on himself to become an associate.

30. Rather, as we have seen in the previous chapter, the earlier stratum of these chapters addresses the susceptibility of the grapes and olives to impurity and is concerned with hand impurity.

31. T. Tehar. 8:2.

32. T. Demai 2:17–18. Another group of instructions concerning social contact with am ha-aretz appears in tosefta Demai 3:5–9, where the associate is described as participating in a feast hosted by an am ha-aretz. However, this source is not of our concern here, since it relates to a different (and I believe later) definition of the am ha-aretz as one who is not careful to separate terumah and tithes (see Furstenberg 2013a: 311–18).

33. We should note that in the Tosefta, the process of acceptance to the association is undertaken in the presence of others. In the Mishnah, on the other hand, we find only the expression "accept upon himself," and it does not relate explicitly to a social framework, an "association," that adopts the candidate into its midst. From the Mishnah, we would not have concluded that the associate becomes a member of an organization.

34. For a survey and characterization of these voluntary associations, see Ascough 2002; Kloppenborg and Wilson 1996; Perry 2011. For a description of the early church as a form of voluntary association, see Harland 2003.

35. Indeed, Albert Baumgarten (1998b: 100–105) rejects any connection between the two phenomena and emphasizes the unique features of the Jewish sects as opposed to the associations characteristic of Greco-Roman urban culture. For a different view, see Gillihan 2007.

36. See Ascough, Harland, and Kloppenborg 2012.

37. This term is equivalent to names given to the associations: *koinon, hetairia, kollegion*. The leaders of the associations were called *archisynagogei* (heads of the synagogue; Ascough 2002: 14–15). See Weinfeld 1986: 77.

38. See t. Demai 3:1. According to b. Git. 62a, the associate (olive presser or baker) who specialized in this service is paid for his service. See also t. Kel. 2:4: "a spoon priests use for kneading"; t. Demai 3:17; y. Demai 3:1 (23b): "priests who knead in a state of purity."

39. This version appears in the main textual witnesses of the Mishnah, but other witnesses offer an opposing version, following b. Ḥag. 26a: "Tax collectors who entered a house: the house is defiled. If there was a gentile with them—they are trusted in saying: 'We did not enter' but they are not trusted in saying 'we entered but we did not touch.'" For a discussion of the complicated history of the version of this mishnah, see Furstenberg 2016b: 335n40.

40. T. Tehar. 8:5; b. Ḥag. 26a. From the Babylonian Talmud, it appears that Mishnah Hagigah also addresses a case in which a gentile supervises the tax collectors and is therefore trustworthy. Alternatively, following the Tosefta, one can claim that the tax collector is only trustworthy because he is the sole source of information regarding his entry into the house.

41. Mark 2:13; Matt 9:9; Luke 5:27. See Furstenberg 2022.

42. Matt 1:19, 5:8, 18:7, and 21:32. According to William Walker (1978), it was only in Luke that a more positive approach toward them was developed.

43. Lucian, "Pseudologista," 30–31; Lucian, "Menippus," 11. A similar linkage appears in Dio Chrysostom (Oration 14:14), who says that pimping and tax farming are not forbidden by law but those who engage in them are punished by becoming hated by the rest of humanity. For these sources, see Collins 2007: 193–94.

44. M. B. Qam. 10:1; Sifra Kedoshim 10:13 (91c); *baraita* in b. Sanh. 25b; t. B. Meṣ. 8:26.

45. T. Demai 3:4, 2:17. The contrast between an associate and a tax collector is parallel to the contrast that appears in Jesus's parable regarding the tax collector and the Pharisee (Luke 18:9–14).

46. The interpretation of the rare adjective *medam'ot/madmi'ot* has been disputed. While in general the verb *dm'* in rabbinic literature relates to cases of mixture of terumah and unconsecrated fruits, in this case it seems to denote vessels intended

for terumah. See Moreshet 1980: 134–35. Presumably, the phrase here is equivalent to "vessels of *dema'*," mentioned a number of times in the Copper Scroll from Qumran and has been interpreted as "vessels for offerings," following the biblical meaning of *dem'* in Exodus 22:28 as "first fruits" (Puech 2015: 31). Lefkovits 2000: 505–45 interprets this phrase in the Copper Scroll more generally as "dedicated objects." These vessels are thus intended for the storage of consecrated produce, and they are identifiable by shape or markings, which ensure appropriate treatment. It further appears that due to their designation for the preservation of terumah, they also served to store valuables, which were thus kept safe from thieves, who distanced themselves from consecrated things (and sometimes were mistakenly given to the priest), as well as for the preservation of holy books, which were kept in a vessel as holy as them. See the Copper Scroll 8:3 (Puech 2015: 68): "tithe-vessels and books, do not touch them." On the use of these vessels for the storage of pure foods and scrolls, see Magness 2004.

47. For a useful survey of the differences between Judea and the Galilee with regard to religious observance, see Goodman 1999. Compare Freyne 1988: 176–213. With regard to purity in particular, there is evidence for observance in the Galilee during the Temple period. Immersion pools and stone vessels were found in Jewish settlements in the area, most conspicuously in the site of Magdala, and Josephus mentions the refusal of Jews to live in Tiberias, which was built on gravesites (Ant. 18:37–38). It does, however, appear that many details of the Galilean purity practices were different than those of the Jerusalem Pharisees. See Kazen 2010b.

48. B. Hag. 25a.

49. Y. Hag. 3:4 (79c). According to one suggestion, the detailed instructions in Mishnah Teharot for maintaining the purity of oil and wine relate to an unusual case, where they were prepared at a different time than usual. A second suggestion, similarly difficult to uphold, is that we are speaking of terumah that was being prepared together with holy foodstuff and therefore all were trusted regarding its purity.

50. Compare the attitude of the Qumran sectarians toward outsiders: "No one should associate with him in his work or in his possessions in order not to encumber him with blameworthy iniquity; rather he should remain at a distance from him in every task, for it is written as follows: 'You shall remain at a distance from every lie'" (1QS [Community Rule] 5:14–15).

51. According to the accepted interpretation, am ha-aretz is only concerned not to defile hollowed things. However, as the structure of the literary unit implies, the issue of trustworthiness is not limited to the sacrifices but also to the sale of pure foods throughout Judea in general. Thus, for instance, the first ruling teaches that "in Judea they are trusted in regard to the purity of wine and oil throughout the year; and only at the season of the winepresses and olive vats in regard to terumah." Commentators assumed that the oil and wine mentioned here are pure in the degree of holy foodstuff. We must note, however, that an explicit contrast between hallowed things and terumah

appears only at the end of the unit, in the final sentence: "And in Jerusalem they are trusted in regard to hallowed things, and during a festival also in regard to terumah."

52. With respect to each sphere, the Mishnah adds a paragraph (omitted here) that relates to specific border cases. Compare t. Ḥag. 3:29–30, where a similar, but shorter, unit appears, which includes only the domains of trustworthiness without the added commentary on it.

53. According to the first comment inserted into the Mishnah, one may be trusted with respect to the purity of the terumah, if he says that it also includes a portion of consecrated produce. Notably, this solution is required to ensure the purity of the terumah; one should not, however, deduce from this ruling that in regular trade one is only trusted regarding hallowed things.

54. For a discussion on the effect of the Temple on the marketplaces of Jerusalem and Judea, see Levine 2002: 343; Goodman 1987: 51–75. Eyal Baruch (1998) and Hayim Lapin (2017) contain a summary of the archaeological findings. These studies, however, do not directly illuminate the mishnahs and their interpretation.

55. See t. Demai 1:2, and the explanation offered in y. Demai 1:1 (21d): "At first they would prepare their wine in purity for the sake of libations" (parallel sources: y. Pesaḥ. 3:1 [29d]; b. Pes. 42b).

56. The rabbinic term is "unconsecrated foods that were prepared *together with* holy foodstuff." The Talmuds identify this term with "unconsecrated foods prepared *on the purity level* of holy foodstuff." The Babylonian Talmud (b. Ḥag. 20a), therefore, finds a contradiction between m. Ḥag. 2:7, according to which foods being prepared with holy foodstuff are more susceptible to impurity than the terumah, and m. Tehar. 2:8: "unconsecrated foodstuffs that were prepared together with holy foods are still regarded as unconsecrated food (with respect to conveying contamination)" (compare also y. Nid. 1:1 [48d]). These however are two different phenomena. On the one hand, there were those few individuals, such as Yohanan b. Gudgeda, who treated all their foods as if they were sacrifices. On the other hand, everyone was required to maintain the purity of the foods they brought to Jerusalem, to be able to consume them together with sacrifices.

57. As we saw in chapter 1, the rabbis prohibited the consumption of unconsecrated meat in Jerusalem rather than sacrificial meat. Notably, t. Nid. 9:18 includes in this sanction foods that were prepared together with this meat: "At first they would say that unconsecrated meat (in Jerusalem) is pure. Then they decreed that it defied the hands. Then again they decreed that it would defile through touch, and then they decreed that this meat is like an animal carcass, and it defiles through carrying. Finally they said that the whole vat that was prepared in order to be consumed together with unconsecrated meat is impure with respect to holy foodstuff as well as impure for terumah." This final decree seeks to limit the production of wine intended exclusively for unconsecrated usage. Thus, all foods in Jerusalem would potentially have been consumed as part of a sacrificial meal.

58. Gedalyahu Alon (1977: 89–102) reconstructs the events that ultimately led to the cessation of the bringing of terumot and tithes to Jerusalem during the time of John Hyrcanus II. In his view, toward the end of the Hasmonean period many were reluctant to hand over the priestly gifts to the Jerusalem aristocracy. Alternatively, and more plausibly, one could suggest that the different sources testify to diverse halakhic practices.

59. Josephus, Ant. 4:68–70. See Sanders 1990: 89–294, 1994: 155. In 4Q251 f. 9 ll. 1–3 commentating on Exodus 22:28 ("You shall not put off the skimming of the first yield of your vats"), we read: "[Let no man consume grain and wi]ne and oil until [the priest has waved] their choice part, *the firstfruits*. And let no man put off (the skimming of) the flow, for [wine] is the choice part of the flow [and] grain is the best part [...]." See Shemesh 2003: 157.

60. 4Q270 3 ii; See Shemesh 2003: 163–64. The alternative custom of a regular separation of dough for the priest (outside of Jerusalem) is documented on an ostracon from Masada: "Yehosef the baker \ to Yehudah son of Haggai \ One *Hallah* every week." See Stiebel 2011.

61. It is generally assumed that the specific impurity that was waived during the festivals was that of am ha-aretz. The Palestinian Talmud formulates this idea in the famous sayings that during the festival "Jerusalem makes all the people of Israel into *ḥaverim*, i.e. associates." See y. Ḥag. 3:6 (79d); b. Ḥag. 26a. Compare Levine 2002: 350. However, we should note that the fear of am ha-aretz's impurity is not made explicit in the tannaitic sources regarding the festivals. Furthermore, the Palestinian Talmud raises the possiblity that among those entering the Temple an impure person has indirectly defiled the court, or that impure liquids might have made their way there (y. Hag. 3:8 [p. 79d]).

62. Compare t. Hag. 3:34 (p. 393): "Tax collectors who invaded a house and wrote on it 'all that is in the house is pure,' are trusted with respect to *hattat* purity and are not trusted with respect to terumah purity, and in Jerusalem they are trusted with respect to purity of all vessels made for holy foodstuff." This however reflects the general tendency of the Tosefta to frame all these laws within the contrast between terumah and holy foodstuff.

7. The End of Purity

1. Büchler 1964: 101–12, as well as 52–59, 86–91.
2. T. Tehar. 3:9. Compare t. Ḥag. 1:2.
3. Thus, for instance, the demand to burn "purities" that have been defiled is relevant only in the case of terumah, which is strictly prohibited for consumption if defiled. See, for example, m. Tehar. 5:3–4 or b. B. Meṣ. 59b (the famous case of the "oven of Akkanai"). Thus, also, sources that prohibit eating impure "purities" implicitly refer to terumah. For example: "The son of an am ha-aretz who visited his

mother's father, his father does not have to worry that he was given 'purities' to eat. If it is known that he feeds him 'purities,' it is prohibited and his clothes impart midras impurity" (t. Demai 2:15). The rabbis fear that the grandson will eat impure terumah at his grandfather the priest's home (see b. Yeb. 114a).

4. Maimonides, *Mishneh Torah, Hilchot Tume'at Okhalim* (Laws of Food Impurity) 16:8.

5. M. Yebam. 1:4; m. 'Ed. 4:8; t. Yebam. 1:11.

6. The following teaching proves that the rabbis are referring to unconsecrated foods when discussing "purities" defiled by the menstruant: "R. Shimon says: 'And after that she shall be clean' (Lev. 15:28): After her action she shall be clean—once she immersed in water she is pure to deal with 'purities,' but the rabbis said she should not do so (until the evening), in order not to encounter a doubtful situation" (Sifra Zavim 9:2). In principle, a woman can deal with "purities" after she has immersed, but because of a fear that her counting might be retroactively canceled if she sees blood on the final day of the count, she is required to wait until evening. Only with regard to unconsecrated foods may one come into contact with "purities" after immersion before sundown, while terumah can be consumed only in the evening. Evidently then, the "purities" discussed in this source must be unconsecrated foods.

7. T. Demai 3:1.

8. T. Ter. 1:1.

9. See Büchler 1964: 107n12.

10. See b. Git. 62a; chap. 6 in this volume.

11. *Pesiqta de-Rav Kahana*, Ha-Hodesh, 3.

12. B. B. Meṣ. 78a.

13. Genesis Rabbah 48:14.

14. This difference between the two sources is congruent with the testimony of *The Differences between the People of the East and the Sons of Eretz Yisrael* of the Geonic period, which lists the differences between the customs in Palestine and in Babylonia: "People of the East—a menstruant undertakes all the needs of the house, with three exceptions: the pouring of wine, the making of the bed and washing [her husband's] hands and feet. And the people of the Land of Israel—she does not touch a moist object, or the vessels of the house, and only out of necessity was she permitted to nurse her son" (Margulies 1938: 79).

15. T. Sukkah 2:3; t. 'Edu. 2:2.

16. In spite of the fact that R. Zadok, too, was meticulous regarding eating in purity (m. Sukkah 2:5).

17. Ostensibly, we are speaking of Rabban Gamaliel of Yavneh. He is mentioned alongside Onkelos the proselyte also in t. Miqw. 6:3, and there, too, Onkelos is described as more stringent than Rabban Gamaliel. In t. 'Abod. Zar. 3:10, on the other hand, we are told that Rabban Gamaliel the Elder agreed with his son-in-law, Shimon b. Netanel the priest, that his daughter would not prepare "purities" in his house (for

fear that he would contaminate them, see the last section of chap. 4 in this volume). Since his son-in-law was a priest, one must assume that he ate his terumah in purity and derive that Rabban Gamaliel himself was more stringent and maintained a higher level of purity. One might, however, suggest that Rabban Gamaliel the Elder maintained a lower level of purity, that of unconsecrated foods, whereas his son-in-law was an am ha-aretz, who did not observe even this level.

18. Büchler 1964: 87. Gedalyahu Alon (1977: 159) suggests that this example was provided by later generations, when this practice became rare even among the rabbis. This supposition is, in fact, supported by textual criticism, as we see later in this chapter.

19. As Saul Lieberman (1955–88: 5:1309) notes, the Mishnah brings the examples of a priest and a Levite, while the Tosefta cites the practice of an Israelite and a proselyte, who testify that those of loftier pedigree were less stringent on matters of purity.

20. Compare the different traditions regarding Rabban Gamaliel's servant, who would inspect herself between each barrel for fear of contracting impurity. In Leviticus Rabbah 19:4, these barrels contained regular unconsecrated wine, whereas in y. Nid. 2:1 (49d) we hear that "she would handle wine for libations," and was therefore required to be particularly careful. In b. Nid. 6b, an additional story is brought regarding terumah loaves. Evidently, the different versions seek to adjust the tradition to the purity standards attributed to Rabban Gamaliel.

21. See *Tanna Debe Eliyyahu*, quoted in the next section.

22. Y. Shab. 1:3 (3b).

23. Yosef Tabory (1996: 199–250) further traces this trend in later sources.

24. Chapter (15) 16, (Braude and Kapstein 1981: 162–63, with modifications).

25. Neusner 1973a: 3:103; 1974–77: 19:103. See also Finkelstein 1962: 272–79.

26. Sifre on Numbers 116.

27. A similar picture arises also from a comparison to the parallel source in Sifre Zuta on Numbers 18:7. The Sifre Zuta does not specify who authored the midrash linking handwashing to the Temple washing of hands and feet. However, its attribution to R. Judah the Patriarch may have been concealed by the redactor of the Sifre Zuta due to personal enmity. See Lieberman 1968: 86–87.

28. Sifra Zavim 4:6 (71a).

29. Notably, these two conceptions of handwashing find expression also in a terminological difference. Mishnah Hallah 1:9; Mishnah Bikkurim 2:1 explicitly rule that one is obligated to wash one's hands only before consumption of terumah, contradicting the earlier Mishnah Hagigah 2:5, which mandates handwashing also for unconsecrated food (see the suggested solutions in y. Ḥag. 2:4 [78b] and b. Ḥag. 18b). Remarkably, the mishnahs in Hallah and Bikkurim employ the verb *r.h.z.* rather than the prevalent *n.t.l.* This verb surfaces only in the margins of tannaitic literature, and it resonates with the language of the biblical command that the priests wash their hands and feet before entering the Temple (Ex. 30:19).

30. See t. Yad. 1:4–5, 7, and 2:1.

31. As we saw in the previous chapter, one who knows how to observe the purity of his unconsecrated foods also knows how to preserve the purity of his terumah, and the associate therefore also provides the service of taking terumah in purity.

32. Y. Ḥag. 2:7 (78c). The main statement relevant to our issue is R. Yoḥanan's conclusion: "The laws of barriers, of indirect shifting, of the private domain, and of am ha-aretz do not apply with respect to ḥullin but only with respect to terumah" (compare t. Ḥag. 3:21).

33. See, among other places, m. Zabim 4:1; m. Tehar. 5:7–8.

34. Y. Ber. 3:4 (6c). See Margulies 1938: 108–9; for an analysis of the discussion in the Palestinian Talmud, see Kiperwasser 2012.

35. T. Shab. 1:13.

36. Y. Dem. 2:3 (23a).

37. See Secunda 2020: 104–33 on the separation from menstruants according to the Babylonian Talmud.

38. Margulies 1938: 79 (see discussion on pp. 114–18). Compare Avot de Rabbi Nathan, version A, 2, p. 9, in the story regarding the pietist who died at a young age.

39. The following ruling from the post-Talmudic Baraita de-Masekhet Niddah demonstrates nonrabbinic forms of separation from impurity: "Even if she sat on a stone, it is prohibited to touch it, since it absorbs and does not emit, but the beds and benches that she touched are not impure" (Tosefta Atikta, p. 13). This ruling is in direct contradiction to the classical rabbinic principles governing the spread of impurity (see also pp. 3, 16–18).

40. In this context the term *ma'asim* indicates court rulings. This corpus has come down to us through quotations in later rabbinic works as well as from the Cairo Geniza. For a general introduction on this legal genre and its place in Byzantine Palestine, see Newman 2012: 631–38.

41. Newman 2011: 212 (ruling 68). Hillel Newman discusses in detail the complex relationship between the different versions of this ruling.

42. Compare m. Tehar. 10:8, regarding the drying of the vessels of the wine- and oil presses to purify them.

43. Levine 1973: 110.

44. Newman 2011: 52–57, and see the additional bibliography there for further testimony to purity observance in Palestine during the Byzantine period.

45. See Fine 1997: 61–94.

BIBLIOGRAPHY

Adler, Yonatan. 2009. "Ritual Baths Adjacent to Tombs: An Analysis of the Archaeological Evidence in Light of the Halakhic Sources." *Journal for the Study of Judaism* 40:55–73.
———. 2014. "Tosefta Shabbat 1:14—'Come and See the Extent to which Purity Had Spread' An Archaeological Perspective on the Historical Background to a Late Tannaitic Passage." In *Talmuda de–Eretz Israel: Archaeology and the Rabbis in Late Antique Palestine*, edited by S. Fine and A. Koller, 63–82. Berlin: De Gruyter.
———. 2017. "The Decline of Jewish Ritual Purity Observance in Roman Palaestina: An Archeological Perspective on Chronology and Historical Context." In *Expressions of Cult in the Southern Levant in the Greco-Roman Period: Manifestations in Text and in Material Culture*, edited by O. Tal and Z. Weiss, 269–84. Turnhout, Belgium: Brepols.
———. 2021. "Ritual Purity in Daily Life after 70 CE: The Chalk Vessel Assemblage from Shuʿafat as a Test Case." *Journal for the Study of Judaism* 52:1–24.
Albeck, Chanoch. 2008. "The Book of Jubilees and the Halakhah." *Jewish Studies* 45:3–8. [Hebrew; original publication, 1930].
Alexander, Philip S. 1999. "The Demonology of the Dead Sea Scrolls." In *The Dead Sea Scrolls after Fifty Years: A Comprehensive Assessment*, 2 vols., edited by P. W. Flint and J. C. VanderKam, 331–53. Leiden, Netherlands: Brill.
Alon, Gedalyahu. 1977. *Jews, Judaism and the Classical World*. Jerusalem: Magnes Press.
Ascough, Richard S. 2002. "Greco Roman Philosophic, Religious and Voluntary Associations." In *Community Formation in the Early Church and the Church Today*, edited by R. N. Longenecker, 3–19. Peabody, MA: Hendrickson.

Ascough, Richard S., Philip A. Harland, and John Kloppenborg. 2012. *Associations in the Greco-Roman World: A Sourcebook*. Waco, TX: Baylor University Press.

Avemarie, Friedrich. 1997. "'Tohorat Ha–Rabbim' and 'Mashqeh Ha–Rabbim': Jacob Licht Reconsidered." In *Legal Texts and Legal Issues: Proceedings of the Second Meeting of the International Organization for Qumran Studies Cambridge 1995*, edited by M. Bernstein, F. García Martínez, and J. Kampen, 215–29. Leiden, Netherlands: Brill.

Balberg, Mira. 2014. *Purity, Body, and Self in Early Rabbinic Literature*. Berkeley: University of California Press.

Bar-Asher Siegal, Elitzur A. 2011. "Who Separated from Whom and Why? A Philological Study of 4QMMT." *Revue de Qumran* 25:229–56.

Baruch, Eyal. 1998. "The Economic Hinterland of Jerusalem in the Herodian Period." *Cathedra* 89:41–62. [Hebrew].

Baumgarten, Albert I. 1983. "The Name of the Pharisees." *Journal of Biblical Literature* 102:411–28.

———. 1987. "The Pharisaic Paradosis." *Harvard Theological Review* 80:63–77.

———. 1994. "Josephus on Essene Sacrifice." *Journal of Jewish Studies* 45:169–83.

———. 1997a. *The Flourishing of Jewish Sects in the Maccabean Era: An Interpretation*. Leiden, Netherlands: Brill.

———. 1997b. "The Zadokite Priests at Qumran: A Reconsideration." *Dead Sea Discoveries* 4:137–56.

———. 1998a. "Finding Oneself in a Sectarian Context: A Sectarian's Food and Its Implications." In *Self, Soul and Body in Religious Experience*, edited by A. I. Baumgarten, J. Assman, and G. G. Stroumsa, 125–47. Leiden, Netherlands: Brill.

———. 1998b. "Graeco-Roman Voluntary Associations and Ancient Jewish Sects." In *Jews in a Graeco Roman World*, edited by M. Goodman, 93–111. Oxford: Clarendon Press.

Baumgarten, Joseph M. 1972a. "The Essene Avoidance of Oil and the Laws of Purity." *Revue de Qumran* 8:87–96.

———. 1972b. "The Unwritten Law in the Pre–Rabbinic Period." *Journal for the Study of Judaism* 3:7–29.

———. 1980. "The Pharisaic Sadducean Controversies about Purity and the Qumran Texts." *Journal of Jewish Studies* 31:157–70.

———. 1992. "The Purification Rituals in *DJD* 7." In *The Dead Sea Scrolls: Forty Years of Research*, edited by D. Dimant and U. Rappaport, 199–209. Jerusalem: Hebrew University Magnes Press and Yad Izhak Ben-Zvi; Leiden, Netherlands: Brill.

———. 1995. "Liquids and Susceptibility to Defilement in 4Q Fragments." *Jewish Quarterly Review* 85:91–101.

———. 1999. *Halakhic Texts*, Qumran Cave 4:25, *Discoveries in the Judaean Desert* 35. Oxford: Clarendon Press.

Berkowitz, Beth. 2006. *Execution and Invention: Death Penalty Discourse in Early Rabbinic and Christian Cultures*. New York: Oxford University Press.
Berrin, Shani L. 2004. *The Pesher Nahum Scroll from Qumran: An Exegetical Study of 4Q169*. Leiden, Netherlands: Brill.
Betz, Hans D. 1997. "Jesus and the Purity of the Temple (Mark 11:15–18): A Comparative Religious Approach." *Journal of Biblical Literature* 116:455–72.
Bickerman, Elias J. 2007. *Studies in Jewish and Christian History*. Leiden, Netherlands: Brill.
Birenboim, Hanan. 2003. "For He Is Impure among All Those Who Transgress His Words: Sin and Ritual Defilement in the Qumran Scrolls." *Zion* 68:359–66.
———. 2006. "Observance of the Laws of Bodily Purity in Jewish Society in the Land of Israel during the Second Temple Period." PhD diss., Hebrew University of Jerusalem.
———. 2009a. "The Halakhic Status of Jerusalem according to 4QMMT, 1 Enoch, and Tannaitic Literature." *Meghillot* 7:3–17. [Hebrew].
———. 2009b. "Tevul Yom and the Red Heifer: Pharisaic and Sadducean Halakah." *Journal for the Study of Judaism* 16:254–73.
———. 2011. "Gentile Impurity in Ancient Judaism." *Cathedra* 139:7–30. [Hebrew].
Black, Matthew. 1954. *An Aramaic Approach to the Gospels and Acts*. Oxford: Clarendon Press.
Blidstein, Moshe. 2017. *Purity, Community, and Ritual in Early Christian Literature*. Oxford: Oxford University Press.
Bóid, Ian R. M. 1989. *Principles of Samaritan Halachah*. Leiden, Netherlands: Brill.
Booth, Roger P. 1986. *Jesus and the Laws of Purity*. Sheffield, UK: JSOT Press.
Boyarin, Daniel. 2004. *Border Lines: The Partition of Judaeo-Christianity*. Philadelphia: University of Pennsylvania Press.
———. 2012. *The Jewish Gospels: The Story of the Jewish Christ*. New York: New Press.
Braude, William G., and Israel J. Kapstein. 1981. *Tanna debe Eliyahu, The Lore of the School of Elijah*. Philadelphia: Jewish Publication Society.
Büchler, Adolf. 1964. *The Galilean Am Ha-Aretz*. Translated by Yisrael Eldad. Jerusalem: Mosad Harav Kook. [Hebrew].
Bultmann, Rudolf. 1963. *History of the Synoptic Tradition*. New York: Harper and Row.
Burns, Joshua E. 2006. "Essene Sectarianism and Social Differentiation in Judaea after 70 C.E." *Harvard Theological Review* 99:247–74.
Chilton, Bruce. 2000. *Rabbi Jesus: An Intimate Biography*. New York: Doubleday.
Cohen, Shaye J. D. 1983. "Jacob Neusner, Mishna, and Counter Rabbinics." *Conservative Judaism* 37:48–63.
———. 1984. "The Significance of Yavneh: Pharisees, Rabbis and the End of Jewish Sectarianism." *Hebrew Union College Annual* 55:27–53.

———. 1999. "The Rabbi in Second Century Jewish Society." In *The Cambridge History of Judaism*, vol. 3, edited by W. Horbury, 922–90. Cambridge: Cambridge University Press.

———. 2007. "The Judaean Legal Tradition and the Halakhah of the Mishnah." In *The Cambridge Companion to the Talmud and Rabbinic Literature*, edited by C. E. Fonrobert and M. S. Jaffee, 121–33. Cambridge: Cambridge University Press.

Cohon, Samuel S. 1960. "Pharisaism: A Definition." In *Joshua Bloch Memorial Volume, Studies in Booklore and History*, edited by A. Berger, 65–74. New York: New York Public Library.

Collins, Adele Y. 2007. *Mark: A Commentary*. Minneapolis: Fortress Press.

Conzelmann, Hans. 1987. *Acts of the Apostles*. Minneapolis: Fortress Press.

Davies, William D., and Dale C. Allison. 1988–97. *The Gospel According to Saint Matthew: The International Critical Commentary*. 3 vols. Edinburgh, UK: T&T Clark.

Dean-Jones, Lesley. 1989. "Menstrual Bleeding According to the Hippocratics and Aristotle." *Transactions of the American Philological Association* 119:177–91.

Deines, Roland. 2010. "The Social Profile of the Pharisees." In *The New Testament and Rabbinic Literature*, edited by R. Bieringer, 111–32. Leiden, Netherlands: Brill.

Deines, Roland, and Martin Hengel. 1995. "E. P. Sanders' 'Common Judaism,' Jesus, and the Pharisees: Review Article of 'Jewish Law from Jesus to the Mishnah' and 'Judaism; Practice and Belief.'" *Journal of Theological Studies* 46:1–70.

Dibelius, Martin. 1956. *Studies in the Acts of the Apostles*. London: SCM Press.

Dinary, Yedidya. 1980. "The Impurity Customs of the Menstruate Women: Sources and Development." *Tarbiz* 49:302–24. [Hebrew].

Dunn, James D. G. 2002. "Jesus and Purity: An Ongoing Debate." *New Testament Studies* 48:449–67.

Ego, Beate. 2014. "Purity Concepts in Jewish Traditions of the Hellenistic Period." In *Purity and the Forming of Religious Traditions in the Ancient Mediterranean World and Ancient Judaism*, edited by C. Frevel and C. Nihan, 477–92. Leiden, Netherlands: Brill.

Elman, Yaakov. 1996. "Some Remarks on 4QMMT and the Rabbinic Tradition: Or, When Is a Parallel Not a Parallel?" In *Reading 4QMMT: New Perspectives on Qumran Law and History*, edited by J. Kampen and M. Bernstein, 99–128. Atlanta, GA: Scholars Press.

Emanuel, Simcha. 2007. "The Seven Clean Days: A Chapter in the History of Halakhah." *Tarbiz* 76:233–54. [Hebrew].

Epstein, Jacob N. 1957. *Prolegomena ad Litteras Tanaiticas*. Jerusalem: Magnes Press and Dvir. [Hebrew].

Erder, Yoram. 2004. *The Karaite Mourners of Zion and the Qumran Scrolls: On the History of an Alternative to Rabbinic Judaism*. Tel Aviv: Ha-Kibbutz Ha-Me'uchad. [Hebrew].

Eshel, Esther. 1997. "4Q414 Fragment 2: Purification of a Corpse Contaminated Person." In *Legal Texts and Legal Issues: Proceedings of the Second Meeting of the International Organization for Qumran Studies, Cambridge 1995*, edited by M. Bernstein, F. García Martínez, and J. Kampen, 3–10. Leiden, Netherlands: Brill.

———. 2003. "Apotropaic Prayers in the Second Temple Period." In *Liturgical Perspectives: Prayer and Poetry in Light of the Dead Sea Scrolls*, edited by E. G. Chazon, 69–88. Leiden, Netherlands: Brill.

Eshel, Hanan. 2000. "CD 12:15–17 and the Stone Vessels found in Qumran." In *The Damascus Covenant: A Centennial of Discovery*, edited by J. M. Baumgarten, E. Chazon, and A. Pinnick, 45–52. Leiden, Netherlands: Brill.

Fine, Steven. 1997. *This Holy Place on the Sanctity of the Synagogue during the Greco Roman Period*. South Bend, IN: University of Notre Dame Press.

Finkelstein, Louis. 1962. *The Pharisees: The Sociological Background of Their Faith*. 3rd ed. Philadelphia: Jewish Publication Society.

Fishbane, Michael A. 1985. *Biblical Interpretation in Ancient Israel*. New York: Clarendon Press.

Fledderman, Harry T. 2005. *Q: A Reconstruction and Commentary*. Leuven, Belgium: Peeters.

Flusser, David. 1979. "The Baptism of John and the Qumran Sect." In *Jewish Sources in Early Christianity*, 81–112. Tel Aviv: Po'alim Library. [Hebrew].

———. 1988. "Qumran and Jewish Apotropaic Prayers." In *Judaism and the Origins of Christianity*, 214–25. Jerusalem: Magnes Press.

———. 2007. *Judaism of the Second Temple Period*. Vol. 1, *Qumran and Apocalypticism*. Grand Rapids, MI: Eerdmans; Jerusalem: Magnes Press.

Fonrobert, Charlotte E. 2000. *Menstrual Purity: Rabbinic and Christian Reconstruction of Biblical Gender*. Stanford: Stanford University Press.

Fraade, Steven D. 2009a. "Qumran Yaḥad and Rabbinic Ḥaburah: A Comparison Reconsidered." *Dead Sea Discoveries* 16:433–53.

———. 2009b. "The Temple as a Marker of Jewish Identity before and after 70 CE: The Role of the Holy Vessels in Rabbinic Memory and Imagination." In *Jewish Identities in Antiquity: Studies in Memory of Menahem Stern*, edited by L. I. Levine and D. R. Schwartz, 237–65. Tübingen, Germany: Mohr Siebeck.

———. 2011. *Legal Fictions: Studies of Law and Narrative in the Discursive Worlds of Ancient Jewish Sectarians and Sages*. Boston: Brill.

Frankel, Raphael. 1999. *Wine and Oil Production in Antiquity in Israel and Other Mediterranean Countries*. Sheffield, UK: Sheffield Academic Press.

Fredriksen, Paula. 1995. "Did Jesus Oppose the Purity Laws." *Bible Review* 11:20–25, 42–47.

Freidenreich, David. 2011. *Foreigners and Their Foods: Constructing Otherness in Jewish, Christian, and Islamic Law*. Berkeley: University of California Press.

Freyne, Sean. 1988. *Galilee, Jesus and the Gospels: Literary Approaches and Historical Investigations*. Dublin: Gil and Macmillan.

Friedman, Shamma. 1999. "The Primacy of Tosefta to Mishnah in Synoptic Parallels." In *Introducing Tosefta: Textual, Intertextual and Intratextual Studies*, edited by H. Fox and T. Meachem, 99–121. New York: KTAV Publishers.

Frymer-Kensky, Tikva. 1983. "Pollution, Purification and Purgation in Biblical Israel." In *The Word of the Lord Shall Go Forth: Essays in Honor of David Noel Freedman in Celebration of His Sixtieth Birthday*, edited by C. M. Meyers and M. O'Connor, 399–410. Winona Lake: Eisenbrauns.

Furstenberg, Yair. 2008. "Defilement Penetrating the Body: A New Understanding of Contamination in Mark 7.15." *New Testament Studies* 54:176–200.

———. 2012. "Early Redactions of Purities: Re-Examination of Mishnaic Source-Criticism." *Tarbiz* 80:507–37. [Hebrew].

———. 2013a. "Am Ha-Aretz in Tannaitic Literature and its Social Contexts." *Zion* 78:287–320. [Hebrew].

———. 2013b. "Hand Washing in Tannaitic Literature: From Purification to Sanctification." In *Minchat Yizchaq: Festschrift for Y. Sapir*, edited by I. Rozenson, 107–30. Elkana-Rehovot: Orot. [Hebrew].

———. 2015. "Controlling Impurity: The Natures of Impurity in Second Temple Debates." *Dine Israel* 30:163*–96*.

———. 2016a. "Initiation and the Ritual Purification from Sin: Between Qumran and the *Apostolic Tradition*." *Dead Sea Discoveries* 23:365–94.

———. 2016b. *Purity and Community: The Traditions of the Law from Second Temple to the Mishnah*. Jerusalem: Magnes Press.

———. 2018. "From Tradition to Controversy: The Changing Forms of Transmission in the Teachings of the Early Rabbis." *Tarbiz* 85:587–642. [Hebrew].

———. 2020a. "Jesus against the Laws of the Pharisees: The Legal Woe Sayings and Second Temple Inter-Sectarian Discourse." *Journal of Biblical Literature* 139:767–86.

———. 2020b. "Rabbinic Responses to Greco-Roman Ethics of Self–Formation in Tractate Avot." In *Self, Self-Fashioning and Individuality in Late Antiquity*, edited by M. Niehoff and J. Levinson, 125–48. Tübingen, Germany: Mohr Siebeck.

———. 2021. "From the Literature of Early Halakhah to Roman Law: The Development of Tractate *Bava Mesi'a*." In *The Disciples of Aaron: In Memory of Prof. Aaron Shemesh*, edited by D. Boyarin, V. Noam, I. Rosen-Zvi, *Te'uda*, 31:541–74. [Hebrew].

———. 2022. "Tax Collectors and Sinners as Addressees of Jesus's Activity." In *The Jesus Handbook*, edited by C. Jacobi and J. Schröter, 345–52. Grand Rapids, MI: Eerdmans.

García Martínez, Florentino, and Julio T. Barrera. 1995. *The People of the Dead Sea Scrolls: Their Writings, Beliefs and Practices*. Leiden, Netherlands: Brill.

Garland, David E. 1979. *The Intention of Matthew 23.* Leiden, Netherlands: Brill.
Gillihan, Yonder M. 2007. *Civic Ideology, Organization and Law in the Rule Scrolls: A Comparative Study of the Covenanters' Sect and Contemporary Voluntary Associations in Political Context.* Leiden, Netherlands: Brill.
Goodblatt, David. 1989. "The Place of the Pharisees in First Century Judaism: The State of the Debate." *Journal for the Study of Judaism* 20:12–30.
Goodman, Martin. 1983. *State and Society in Roman Galilee, A.D. 132–212.* Totowa, NJ: Rowman & Allanheld.
———. 1987. *The Ruling Class of Judaea.* Cambridge: Cambridge University Press.
———. 1990. "Kosher Olive Oil in Antiquity." In *A Tribute to Geza Vermes: Essays on Jewish and Christian Literature and History*, edited by P. R. Davies and R. T. White, 227–45. Sheffield, UK: JSOT Press.
———. 1994. "Sadducees and Essenes after 70 C.E." In *Crossing the Boundaries: Essays in Honour of M.D. Goulder*, edited by S. E. Porter, D. Orton and P. M. Joyce, 347–56. Leiden, Netherlands: Brill.
———. 1999. "Galilean Judaism and Judaean Judaism." In *Cambridge History of Judaism*, vol. 3, *The Early Roman Period*, edited by W. Hurbory, 596–617. Cambridge: Cambridge University Press.
———. 2007. "Josephus and Variety in First Century Judaism." In *Judaism in the Roman World: Collected Essays*, 33–46. Leiden, Netherlands: Brill.
Grabbe, Lester L. 1999. "Sadducees and Pharisees." In *Judaism in Late Antiquity*, vol. 3.1, edited by J. Neusner and A. J. Avery-Peck, 35–62. Leiden, Netherlands: Brill.
Green, Joel B. 1997. *The Gospel of Luke.* Grand Rapids, MI: Eerdmans.
Greenfield, Jonas C., Michael E. Stone, and Esther Eshel. 2004. *The Aramaic Levi Document: Edition, Translation, Commentary.* Leiden, Netherlands: Brill.
Guelich, Robert A. 1989. *Mark 1–8:26.* Dallas: Word Books.
Gunneweg, Antonius H. J. 1983. "'Am Haʿaretz': A Semantic Revolution." *Zeitschrift für die Alttestamentliche Wissenschaft* 95:437–40.
Halbertal, Moshe. 2013. "The History of Halakhah and the Emergence of Halakhah." *Diné Israel* 29:1–23. [Hebrew].
Harland, Philip A. 2003. *Associations, Synagogues, and Congregations: Claiming a Place in Ancient Mediterranean Society.* Minneapolis: Augsburg Fortress.
Harrington, Hannah K. 1993. *The Impurity Systems of Qumran and the Rabbis: Biblical Foundations.* Atlanta: Scholars Press.
———. 1995. "Did the Pharisees Eat Ordinary Food in a State of Purity?" *Journal for the Study of Judaism* 26:42–54.
———. 2004. *The Purity Texts.* London: T&T Clark.
———. 2006. "Purity and the Dead Sea Scrolls: Current Issues." *Currents in Biblical Research* 4:397–428.
———. 2019. *The Purity and Sanctuary of the Body in Second Temple Judaism.* Göttingen, Germany: Vandenhoeck & Ruprecht.

Hartman, Gideon, Guy Bar-Oz, Ram Bouchnick, and Ronny Reich. 2013. "The Pilgrimage Economy of Early Roman Jerusalem (1st century BCE–70 CE) Reconstructed from the $d^{15}N$ and $d^{13}C$ Values of Goat and Sheep Remains." *Journal of Archaeological Science* 40:4369–76.

Hauptman, Judith. 2005. *Rereading the Mishnah: A New Approach to Ancient Jewish Texts.* Tübingen, Germany: Mohr Siebeck.

Hayes, Christine E. 2002. *Gentile Impurities and Jewish Identities: Intermarriage and Conversion from the Bible to the Talmud.* New York: Oxford University Press.

———. 2008. "What Is (the) Mishna? Concluding Observations." *Association for Jewish Studies Review* 32:291–97.

Hempel, Charlotte. 2006. "The Literary Development of the S Tradition: A New Paradigm." *Revue de Qumran* 22:389–401.

Henshke, David. 1998. "The Sanctity of Jerusalem: The Sages and Sectarian Halakhah." *Tarbiz* 67:5–28. [Hebrew].

Hezser, Catherine. 1997. *The Social Structure of the Rabbinic Movement in Roman Palestine.* Tübingen, Germany: Mohr Siebeck.

Himmelfarb, Martha. 2001. "Impurity and Sin in 4QD, 1QS and 4Q512." *Dead Sea Discoveries* 8:9–37.

———. 2010. "The Polemic against the *Tevul Yom*: A Reexamination." In *New Perspectives on Old Texts,* edited by E. G. Chazon, B. Halpern-Amaru, and R. A. Clements, 199–214. Boston: Brill.

Hoffmann, David Z. 1914. *The First Mishnah and the Disputes of the Tannaim.* Translated from the German into Hebrew by S. Greenberg. Berlin: Gruenberg. [Hebrew].

———. 1953. *Das Buch Leviticus.* Translated by Tzvi Har-Sheffer and Aaron Lieberman. Jerusalem: Mosad Ha-Rav Kook. [Hebrew].

Holtz, Gudrun. 2013. "Purity Conceptions in the Dead Sea Scrolls: 'Ritual-Physical' and 'Moral' Purity in a Diachronic Perspective." In *Purity and the Forming of Religious Traditions in the Ancient Mediterranean World and Ancient Judaism,* edited by C. Frevel and C. Nihan, 519–36. Boston: Brill.

Horowitz, Chaim M. 1890. *Uralte Tosefta (Tosefta Atiqta): Fünfte Abtheilung.* Krakow: Josef Fischer Press. [Hebrew].

Jaffee, Martin S. 2001. *Torah in the Mouth: Writing and Oral Tradition in Palestinian Judaism 200 BCE–400 C.E.* New York: Oxford University Press.

Japhet, Sara. 1997. *The Ideology of the Book of Chronicles and Its Place in Biblical Thought.* Frankfurt am Main, Germany: Peter Lang.

Kahana, Menahem, I. 2011. *Sifre on Numbers: An Annotated Edition.* Jerusalem: Magnes Press.

Kazen. Thomas. 2010a. "4Q274 Fragment 1 Revisited—Or Who Touched Whom? Further Evidence for Ideas of Graded Impurity and Graded Purification." *Dead Sea Discoveries* 17:53–87.

———. 2010b. *Jesus and Purity Halakhah: Was Jesus Indifferent to Impurity?* Winona Lake, IN: Eisenbrauns.

———. 2013. *Scripture, Interpretation or Authority? Motifs and Arguments in Jesus' Halakhic Conflicts*. Tübingen, Germany: Mohr Siebeck.

Kiperwasser, Reuven. 2012. "The Immersion of *Baallei Qerain*." *Jewish Studies Quarterly* 19:311–38.

Kister, Menachem. 1999a. "Demons, Theology and Abraham's Covenant (CD 16:4–6 and Related Texts)." In *The Dead Sea Scrolls at Fifty: Proceeding of the 1997 SBL Qumran Section Meetings*, edited by R. A. Kugler and E. M. Schuller, 167–84. Atlanta: Scholars Press.

———. 1999b. "Studies in *4QMiqsat Ma'ase Ha-Torah* and Related Texts: Law, Theology, Language and Calendar." *Tarbiz* 68:317–71. [Hebrew].

———. 2001. "Law, Morality and Rhetoric in Some Sayings of Jesus." In *Studies in Ancient Midrash*, edited by J. Kugel, 145–54. Cambridge, MA: Harvard University Center for Jewish Studies.

———. 2010. "Body and Purification from Evil: Prayer Formulas and Concepts in Second Temple Literature and Their Relationship to Later Rabbinic Literature." *Megillot* 8–9:243–84. [Hebrew].

———. 2018. "Textual Growth, Midrash, and Anthropology in CD A 4:12–5:19: Some Aspects of Ruaḥ (ha-) Qodesh and the Self at Qumran and Ancient Christianity." *Revue de Qumran* 30:265–92.

Klawans, Jonathan. 1995. "Notions of Gentile Impurity in Ancient Judaism." *Association for Jewish Studies Review* 20:285–312.

———. 2000. *Impurity and Sin in Ancient Judaism*. New York: Oxford University Press.

Kloppenborg, John S. 1987. *The Formation of Q: Trajectories in Ancient Wisdom Collections*. Harrisburg, PA: Trinity Press.

Kloppenborg, John S., and Stephen G. Wilson. 1996. *Voluntary Associations in the Graeco-Roman World*. New York: Routledge.

Klutz, Todd. 1999. "The Grammar of Exorcism in the Ancient Mediterranean World." In *The Jewish Roots of Christological Monotheism*, edited by C. C. Newman, J. R. Davila, and G. S. Lewis, 156–65. Leiden, Netherlands: Brill.

Knohl, Israel. 1991. "Participation of the People in the Temple Worship: Second Temple Sectarian Conflict and the Biblical Tradition." *Tarbiz* 60:139–46. [Hebrew].

———. 1993. *The Sanctuary of Silence: A Study of the Priestly Strata in the Pentateuch*. Jerusalem: Magnes Press. [Hebrew].

Krochmal, Nachman. 1961. *Kitve Rabi Nahman Krokhmal*. Edited by S. Rawidowicz. London: Ararat. [Hebrew].

Laessøe, Jørgen. 1955. *Studies on the Assyrian Ritual and Series bît rimki*. Copenhagen: E. Munksgaard.

Lapin, Hayim. 1995. *Early Rabbinic Civil Law and the Social History of Roman Galilee: A Study of Mishna Tractate Baba Mesia.* Atlanta: Scholars Press.

———. 2006. "Origins and Development of the Rabbinic Movement in the Land of Israel." In *Cambridge History of Judaism. Vol. 4: The Late Roman-Rabbinic Period,* edited by Steven T. Katz, 206–29. Cambridge: Cambridge University Press.

———. 2012. *Rabbis as Romans: The Rabbinic Movement in Palestine 100–400 CE.* New York: Oxford University Press.

———. 2017. "Feeding the Jerusalem Temple: Cult, Hinterland and Economy in First Century Palestine." *Journal of Ancient Judaism* 8:410–53.

Lefkovits, Judah K. 2000. *The Copper Scroll 3Q15: A Reevaluation, a New Reading Translation and Commentary.* Boston: Brill.

Levine, Benjamin M. 1973. *Metivot: Talmud Qatan le-Seder Moed, Nashim, u-Naziqin.* Jerusalem: Mekor Publishing. [Hebrew].

Levine, Lee I. 1996. "The Second Temple of Jerusalem: Josephus' Descriptions and Other Sources." *Cathedra* 77:3–16. [Hebrew].

———. 2002. *Jerusalem: Portrait of the City in the Second Temple Period (538 BCE–70 CE).* Philadelphia: Jewish Publication Society.

Licht, Jacob. 1965. *The Rule Scroll: A Scroll from the Wilderness of Judaea: 1QS, 1QSa, 1QSb: Text, Introduction and Commentary.* Jerusalem: Bialik Institute. [Hebrew].

Lieberman, Saul. 1952. "The Discipline in the So-Called Dead Sea Manual of Discipline." *Journal of Biblical Literature* 71:199–206.

———. 1955–88. *Tosefta ki-feshuṭah: A Comprehensive Commentary on the Tosefta.* 10 vols. New York: Jewish Theological Seminary of America Press. [Hebrew].

———. 1968. *Sifre Zuta: Talmuda shel Qisrin.* New York: Jewish Theological Seminary. [Hebrew].

———. 1999. *Tosefet Rishonim.* 4 vols. New York: Jewish Theological Seminary of America Press. [Hebrew].

Lindars, Barnabas. 1988. "All Foods Clean: Thoughts on Jesus and the Law." In *Law and Religion: Essays on the Place of Law in Israel and Early Christianity,* edited by B. Lindars, 61–72. Cambridge: James Clarke.

Llewelyn, Stephen R., and Dionysia van Beek. 2011. "Reading the Temple Warning as a Greek Visitor." *Journal for the Study of Judaism* 42:1–22.

Lorberbaum, Yair. 2015. *In God's Image: Myth, Theology and Law in Classical Judaism.* New York: Cambridge University Press.

Luz, Ulrich. 2001. *Matthew 8–20.* Minneapolis: Fortress Press.

Maccoby, Hyam. 1982. "The Washing of Cups." *Journal for the Study of the New Testament* 14:3–15.

———. 1999. *Ritual and Morality.* Cambridge: Cambridge University Press.

Magen, Itzhak. 1988. *Stone Vessel Production in Jerusalem during the Second Temple Period.* Jerusalem: Society for the Protection of Nature. [Hebrew].

Magness, Jodi. 2004. "Why Scroll Jars?" In *Religion and Society in Roman Palestine: Old Questions, New Approaches*, edited by D. E. Edwards, 146–61. New York: Routledge.

———. 2012. "Sectarianism before and after 70 C.E." In *Was 70 CE a Watershed in Jewish History? On Jews and Judaism before and after the Destruction of the Second Temple*, edited by D. R. Schwartz and Z. Weiss, 69–89. Leiden, Netherlands: Brill.

Margulies, Mordechai. 1938. *The Differences between the People of the East and the Sons of Eretz Yisrael*. Jerusalem: Reuven Mass. [Hebrew].

Martin, Dale B. 1995. *The Corinthian Body*. New Haven, CT: Yale University Press.

Mason, Steve. 1990. "Pharisaic Dominance before 70 CE and the Gospels' Hypocrisy Charge (Matt. 23:2–3)." *Harvard Theological Review* 84:363–81.

———. 1991. *Flavius Josephus on the Pharisees: A Composition-Critical Study*. Leiden, Netherlands: Brill.

Metso, Sarianna. 1997. *The Textual Development of the Qumran Community Rule*. Leiden, Netherlands: Brill.

Milgrom, Jacob. 1990. "The Scriptural Foundations and Deviations in the Laws of Purity of the Temple Scroll." In *Archaeology and History in the Dead Sea Scrolls: The New York University Conference in Memory of Yigal Yadin*, edited by L. H. Schiffman, 83–99. Sheffield, UK: JSOT Press.

———. 1991. *Leviticus 1–16*. New York: Doubleday.

———. 1992. "First Day Ablutions." In *The Madrid Qumran Congress: Proceedings of the International Congress on the Dead Sea Scrolls, March 1991*, edited by J. T. Barerra and L. V. Montaner, 561–70. Leiden, Netherlands: Brill.

———. 1995. "4QTOHORA^a: An Unpublished Qumran Text on Purities." In *Time to Prepare the Way in the Wilderness: Papers on the Qumran Scrolls by Fellows of the Institute for Advanced Studies of the Hebrew University Jerusalem*, edited by D. Dimant and L. H. Schiffman, 59–68. Leiden, Netherlands: Brill.

Milikowsky, Chaim. 2000. "Reflections on Hand-Washing, Hand Purity and Holy Scripture in Rabbinic Literature." In *Purity and Holiness: The Heritage of Leviticus*, edited by M. J. H. M. Poorthuis and J. Schwartz, 149–62. Leiden, Netherlands: Brill.

Miller, Stuart S. 2006. *Sages and Commoners in Late Antique 'Erez Israel: A Philological Inquiry into Local Traditions in Talmud Yerushalmi*. Tübingen, Germany: Mohr Siebeck.

———. 2010. "Stepped Pools, Stone Vessels, and other Identity Markers of 'Complex Common Judaism.'" *Journal for the Study of Judaism* 41:214–43.

———. 2015. *At the Intersection of Texts and Material Finds: Stepped Pools, Stone Vessels and Ritual Purity among the Jews of Roman Galilee*. Göttingen, Germany: Vandenhoeck & Ruprecht.

Moreshet, Menahem. 1980. *Lexicon of Verbs Introduced in Tannaitic Language*. Ramat Gan: Bar-Ilan University Press. [Hebrew].

Nemoy, Leon. 1930. "Al-Qirqisānī's Account of the Jewish Sects and Christianity." *Hebrew Union College Annual* 7:317–97.
Neusner, Jacob. 1960. "The Fellowship in the Second Jewish Commonwealth." *Harvard Theological Review* 53:125–42.
———. 1971. *The Rabbinic Traditions about the Pharisees before 70*. 3 vols. Leiden, Netherlands: Brill.
———. 1973a. *From Politics to Piety: The Emergence of Pharisaic Judaism*. Englewood, NJ: Prentice Hall.
———. 1973b. *The Idea of Purity in Ancient Judaism*. Leiden, Netherlands: Brill.
———. 1974–77. *History of the Mishnaic Law of Purities*. 22 vols. Leiden, Netherlands: Brill.
———. 1975–76. "First Cleanse the Inside." *New Testament Studies* 22:486–95.
———. 1981. *Judaism: The Evidence of the Mishnah*. Chicago: University of Chicago Press.
———. 2006. "Why We Cannot Assume the Reliability of Attributions: The Case of the Houses in Mishna-Tosefta Makhshirin." In *The Mishnah in Contemporary Perspectives*, edited by A. J. Avery-Peck and J. Neusner, 190–212. Boston: Brill.
Newman, Hillel. 2011. *The Ma'asim of the People of the Land of Israel: Halakha and History in Byzantine Palestine*. Jerusalem: Yad Ben Zvi. [Hebrew].
———. 2012. "Early Halakhic Literature." In *Jews in Byzantium: Dialects of Minority and Majority Cultures*, edited by R. Bonfil, O. Irshai, G. Stroumsa, and R. Talgam, 629–41. Leiden, Netherlands: Brill.
Newton, Michael. 1985. *The Concept of Purity at Qumran and the Letters of Paul*. Cambridge: Cambridge University Press.
Nielsen, Bruce. 1993. "Earth, Seed and Food: The Social Setting of Levitical Purity Rules in the Judaisms of the First Four Centuries." PhD diss., Jewish Theological Seminary.
Nir, Rivka. 2012. "Josephus' Account of John the Baptist: A Christian Interpolation?" *Journal for the Study of the Historical Jesus* 10:32–62.
Nitzan, Bilhah. 1994. *Qumran Prayer and Religious Poetry*. Leiden, Netherlands: Brill.
Noam, Vered. 2006. "Traces of Sectarian Halakhah in the Rabbinic World." In *Rabbinic Perspectives: Rabbinic Literature and the Dead Sea Scrolls*, edited by S. D. Fraade, A. Shemesh, and R. A. Clements, 67–85. Leiden, Netherlands: Brill.
———. 2008. "The Dual Strategy of Rabbinic Purity Legislation." *Journal for the Study of Judaism* 39:471–512.
———. 2009. "Stringency in Qumran: A Reassessment." *Journal for the Study of Judaism* 40:342–55.
———. 2010. *From Qumran to the Rabbinic Revolution: Conceptions of Impurity*. Jerusalem: Yad Ben Zvi. [Hebrew].
Nolland, John. 1989–93. *Luke 9:21–18:34*. Dallas: Word Books.

Olyan, Saul M. 2004. "Purity Ideology in Ezra-Nehemiah as a Tool to Reconstitute the Community." *Journal for the Study of Judaism* 35:1–16.

Ophir, Adi, and Ishay Rosen Zvi. 2018. *Goy: Israel's Multiple Others and the Birth of the Gentile*. Oxford: Oxford University Press.

Oppenheimer, Aharon. 1977. *The Am Ha-Aretz: A Study in the Social History of the Jewish People in the Hellenistic-Roman Period*. Leiden, Netherlands: Brill.

Orian, Matan. 2016. "Josephus' Seven Purities and the Mishnah's Ten Holinesses." *Journal for the Study of Judaism* 47:183–211.

Perry, Jonathan S. 2011. "Societies: Collegia." In *The Oxford Handbook of Social Relations in the Roman World*, edited by M. Peachin, 499–515. New York: Oxford University Press.

Pervo, Richard I. 2009. *Acts: A Commentary*. Minneapolis: Fortress Press.

Peterson, David G. 2009. *The Acts of the Apostles*. Grand Rapids, MI: Eerdmans.

Poirier, John C. 1996. "Why Did the Pharisees Wash Their Hands?" *Journal of Jewish Studies* 47:217–33.

———. 2003. "Purity beyond the Temple in the Second Temple Era." *Journal of Biblical Literature* 122:247–65.

Puech, Émile. 2015. *The Copper Scroll Revisited*. Boston: Brill.

Qimron, Elisha. 2010–14. *The Dead Sea Scroll: The Hebrew Writings*. 3 vols. Jerusalem: Yad Ben Zvi.

Qimron, Elisha, and John Strugnell. 1994. *Miqsat Ma'ase ha-Torah*, DJD 10. Oxford: Clarendon Press.

Rabin, Chaim. 1958. *The Zadokite Documents*. Oxford: Clarendon Press.

Räisänen, Heikki. 1982. "Jesus and the Food Laws: Reflections on Mark 7:15." *Journal for the Study of the New Testament* 16:79–100.

Regev, Eyal. 2000. "Pure Individualism: The Idea of Non-Priestly Purity in Ancient Judaism." *Journal for the Study of Judaism* 31:176–202.

———. 2003. "Abominated Temple and Holy Community: The Formation of the Notions of Purity and Impurity in Qumran." *Dead Sea Discoveries* 10:243–78.

———. 2004. "Moral Impurity and the Temple in Early Christianity in Light of Ancient Greek Practice and Qumranic Ideology." *Harvard Theological Review* 97:383–411.

———. 2006. "Reconstructing Qumranic and Rabbinic Worldviews: Dynamic Holiness vs. Static Holiness." In *Rabbinic Perspectives: Rabbinic Literature and the Dead Sea Scrolls*, edited by S. Fraade, A. Shemesh, and R. Clements, 87–112. Leiden, Netherlands: Brill.

———. 2007. *Sectarianism in Qumran: A Cross Cultural Perspective*. Berlin: De Gruyter.

Reich, Ronny. 1981. "Mishnah Sheqalim 8:2 and the Archaeological Findings." In *Jerusalem in the Second Temple Period: Abraham Schalit Memorial Volume*, edited by U. Rappaport and M. Stern, 225–56. Jerusalem: Yad Ben Zvi. [Hebrew].

———. 2013. *Miqwa'ot (Jewish Ritual Baths) in the Second Temple, Mishnaic and Talmudic Periods*. Jerusalem: Yad Ben Zvi. [Hebrew].

Rivkin, Elias. 1969–70. "Defining the Pharisees: The Tannaitic Sources." *Hebrew Union College Annual* 40–41:205–49.

Robinson, James M., Paul Hoffmann, and John S. Kloppenborg. 2000. *The Critical Edition of Q*. Minneapolis: Peeters.Rosenthal, Eliezer S. 1994. "Tradition and Innovation in the Halakha of the Sages." *Tarbiz* 63:321–74. [Hebrew].

Rosen-Zvi, Ishay. 2011. *Demonic Desires: Yetzer Hara and the Problem of Evil in Late Antiquity*. Philadelphia: University of Pennsylvania Press.

———. 2012. *The Mishnaic Sotah Ritual: Temple, Gender and Midrash*. Boston: Brill.

Rowley, H. H. 1940. "Jewish Proselyte Baptism and the Baptism of John." *Hebrew Union College Annual* 15:313–34.

Rubenstein, Jeffrey L. 1999. "Nominalism and Realism in Qumranic and Rabbinic Law: A Reassessment." *Dead Sea Discoveries* 6:157–83.

———. 2003. *The Culture of the Babylonian Talmud*. Baltimore: Johns Hopkins University Press.

Runesson, Anders. 2001. "Water and Worship: Ostia and the Ritual Bath in the Diaspora Synagogue." In *The Synagogue of Ancient Ostia and the Jews of Rome*, edited by D. Mitternacht, O. Brandt, and B. Olsson, 15–29. Stockholm: Paul Äströms.

———. 2008. "Rethinking Early Jewish-Christian Relations: Matthean Community History as Pharisaic Intragroup Conflict." *Journal of Biblical Literature* 127:95–132.

Safrai, Shmuel. 1965. *Pilgrimage at the Time of the Second Temple*. Tel Aviv: Am Ha-Sefer. [Hebrew].

———. 1983. *In the Last Days of the Second Temple and in the Times of the Mishnah: Chapters in Social and Cultural History*. Jerusalem: Magnes Press. [Hebrew].

Saldarini, Anthony J. 1992. "Pharisees." In *The Anchor Bible Dictionary*, vol. 5, edited by D. N. Freedman, 289–304. New York: Doubleday.

———. 2001. *Pharisees, Scribes and Sadducees in Palestinian Society: A Sociological Approach*. Grand Rapids, MI: Eerdmans.

Sanders, Ed P. 1985. *Jesus and Judaism*. Philadelphia: SCM Press.

———. 1990. *Jewish Law from Jesus to the Mishnah: Five Studies*. Philadelphia: SCM Press.

———. 1994. *Judaism: Practice and Belief 63 BCE–66 CE*. Philadelphia: SCM Press.

Sapir, Itzhak. 1994. "Masada: On the Purity of Sacred Things. The Sectarian Religious Association of the Masada Warriors." *Judea and Samaria Studies* 3:137–46. [Hebrew].

Satlow, Michael L. 2003. "'And on the Earth You Shall Sleep': 'Talmud Torah' and Rabbinic Asceticism." *Journal of Religion* 83:204–25.

Schiffman, Lawrence H. 1985. "Exclusion from the Sanctuary and the City of the Sanctuary in the Temple Scroll." *Hebrew Union College Annual* 9:301–20.

———. 1994. "Pharisaic and Sadducean Halakha in Light of the Dead Sea Scrolls: The Case of *Tevul Yom*." *Dead Sea Discoveries* 1:285–89.
Schofer, Jonathan W. 2005. *The Making of a Sage: A Study in Rabbinic Ethics*. Madison: University of Wisconsin Press.
Schremer, Adiel. 2000. "They Did Not Read in the Sealed Book: Qumran Halachic Revolution and the Emergence of Torah Study in Second Temple Judaism." In *Historical Perspectives: From the Hasmoneans to Bar Kokhba in Light of the Dead Sea Scroll*, edited by D. Goodblatt and A. Pinnick, 105–26. Leiden, Netherlands: Brill.
Schürer, Emil. 1973–87. *The History of the Jewish People in the Time of Jesus Christ (175 BCE–135 AD)*. A new English version, revised and edited by G. Vermes and F. Millar. 4 vols. Edinburgh, UK: T&T Clark.
Schwartz, Daniel R. 1983. "Josephus and Nicolaus on the Pharisees." *Journal for the Study of Judaism* 14:157–71.
———. 1990. *Agrippa I: The Last King of Judaea*. Tübingen, Germany: Mohr Siebeck.
———. 1992. "Law and Truth: On Qumran-Sadducean and Rabbinic Views of Law." In *The Dead Sea Scrolls: Forty Years of Research*, edited by D. Dimant and U. Rappaport, 229–40. Leiden, Netherlands: Brill.
———. 1996. "MMT, Josephus and the Pharisees." In *Reading 4QMMT: New Perspectives on Qumran Law and History*, edited by J. Kampen and M. J. Bernstein, 67–80. Atlanta: Scholars Press.
Schwartz, Seth. 2001. *Imperialism and Jewish Society: 200 BCE to 640 CE*. Princeton, NJ: Princeton University Press.
Secunda, Shai. 2020. *The Talmud's Red Fence: Menstrual Impurity and Difference in Babylonian Judaism and Its Sasanian Context*. Oxford: Oxford University Press.
Sekki, Arthur E. 1989. *The Meaning of Ruach at Qumran*. Atlanta: Scholars Press.
Shapira, Haim. 2007. "The Court in Yavne: Status, Authority and Functions." In *Studies in Hebrew Law and Halakhah: Judge and Procedure*, edited by Yaacov Habba and Amichai Radzyner, 304–35. Ramat Gan: Bar-Ilan University Press. [Hebrew].
Shemesh, Aharon. 1997. "The Origins of the Laws of Separatism: Qumran Literature and Rabbinic Halakha." *Revue de Qumran* 18:223–41.
———. 2003. "The Laws of First Fruits in the Dead Sea Scrolls." *Megillot* 1:147–64. [Hebrew].
———. 2009. *Halakhah in the Making: The Development of Jewish Law from Qumran to the Rabbis*. Berkeley: University of California Press.
Shemesh, Aharon, and Cana Werman. 2011. *Revealing the Hidden: Exegesis and Halakha in the Qumran Scrolls*. Jerusalem: Bialik Institute. [Hebrew].
Sherman, Maya, Zeev Weiss, Tami Zilberman, and Gal Yasur. 2020. "Chalkstone Vessels from Sepphoris: Galilean Production in Roman Times." *Bulletin of the American Schools of Oriental Research* 383:79–95.

Sim, David C. 1998. *The Gospel of John and Christian Judaism: The History and Social Setting of the Matthean Community*. Edinburgh, UK: T. & T. Clark.

Sivertsev, Alexei. 2005. *Households, Sects, and the Origins of Rabbinic Judaism*. Boston: Brill.

Smith, Morton. 1956. "Palestinian Judaism in the First Century." In *Israel: Its Role in Civilization*, edited by M. Davis, 67–81. New York: Israel Institute of the Jewish Theological Seminary.

———. 1959. "The Dead Sea Sect in Relation to Ancient Judaism." *New Testament Studies* 7:347–60.

Stern, Sacha. 1994. *Jewish Identity in Early Rabbinic Writings*. Leiden, Netherlands: Brill.

Stiebel, Guy D. 2011. "Meager Bread and Scant Water: Food for Thought at Masada." In *Halakhah in Light of Epigraph*, edited by A. I. Baumgarten, 282–303. Göttingen, Germany: Vandenhoeck & Ruprecht.

Sussman, Ya'akov. 1969. "Babylonian Sugyot for Orders Zera'im and Teharot." PhD diss., Hebrew University of Jerusalem.

———. 1994. "The History of Halakha and the Dead Sea Scrolls." In *Miqsat Ma'ase ha-Torah, Discoveries of the Judaean Desert 10*, edited by Elisha Qimron and John Strugnell, 179–200. Oxford: Clarendon Press.

Tabory, Yosef. 1996. *The Passover Ritual throughout the Generations*. Tel Aviv: Hakibbutz Hameuchad. [Hebrew].

Taylor, Joan E. 1997. *The Immerser: John the Baptist within Second Temple Judaism*. Grand Rapids, MI: Eerdmans.

Tomson, Peter J. 1990. *Paul and the Jewish Law: Halakha in the Letters of the Apostle to the Gentiles*. Assen, Netherlands: Van Gorcum; Minneapolis: Fortress Press.

Urbach, Ephraim E. 1969. "The Sanhedrin of 23 and Capital Punishment." *Proceedings of the World Congress of Jewish Studies* 2.2:37–48. [Hebrew].

———. 1984. *The Halakhah: Roots and Development*. Giva'atayim: Yad LaTalmud. [Hebrew].

VanderKam, James C. 2003. "Those Who Look for Smooth Things, Pharisees, and Oral Torah." In *Emanuel: Studies in Hebrew Bible, Septuagint, and Dead Sea Scrolls in Honor of Emanuel Tov*, edited by E. Ban David and S. Paul, 465–77. Leiden, Netherlands: Brill.

Vermes, Geza. 1996. "The Leadership of the Qumran Community: Sons of Zadok—Priests—Congregation." In *Geschichte—Tradition—Reflexion; Festschrift für Martin Hengel zum 70. Geburtstag*, edited by P. Schäfer, 375–84. Tübingen, Germany: Mohr Siebeck.

Wahlen, Clinton. 2004. *Jesus and the Impurity of Spirits in the Synoptic Gospels*. Tübingen, Germany: Mohr Siebeck.

———. 2005. "Peter's Vision and Confliction Definitions of Purity." *New Testament Studies* 51:505–18.

Walker, Christopher B. F. 2001. *The Induction of the Cult Image in Ancient Mesopotamia: The Mesopotamian Mīs Pî Ritual.* Helsinki: Neo-Assyrian Text Corpus Project.

Walker, William O. 1978. "Jesus and the Tax Collectors." *Journal of Biblical Literature* 97:221–38.

Wassén, Cecilia. 2016. "The (Im)purity Levels of Communal Meals within the Qumran Movement." *Journal of Ancient Judaism* 7:102–22.

Webb, Robert L. 1991. *John the Baptizer and Prophet: A Socio-Historical Study.* Sheffield, UK: JSOT Press.

Weinfeld, Moshe. 1986. *The Organizational Pattern and the Penal Code of the Qumran Sect: A Comparison with Guilds and Religious Associations of the Hellenistic-Roman Period.* Fribourg, Switzerland: Editions universitaires.

Werman, Cana. 2000. "The Sons of Zadok." In *The Dead Sea Scrolls: Fifty Years after Their Discovery*, edited by L. H. Schiffman, E. Tov, and J. C. VanderKam, 623–30. Jerusalem: Israel Exploration Society.

———. 2006. "Oral Torah vs. Written Torah(s): Competing Claims to Authority." In *Rabbinic Perspectives: Rabbinic Literature and the Dead Sea Scrolls*, edited by S. D. Fraade, A. Shemesh, and R. A. Clements, 67–85. Leiden, Netherlands: Brill.

———. 2011. "The Price of Mediation: The Role of Priest in the Priestly Halakhah." In *The Dead Sea Scrolls and Contemporary Culture*, edited by A. Roitman, L. H. Schiffman, and S. Tzoreff, 377–409. Leiden, Netherlands: Brill.

Werrett, Ian C. 2007. *Ritual Purity and the Dead Sea Scrolls.* Boston: Brill.

———. 2013. "The Evolution of Purity in Qumran." In *Purity and the Forming of Religious Traditions in the Ancient Mediterranean World and Ancient Judaism*, edited by C. Frevel and C. Nihan, 493–518. Boston: Brill.

Wright, David P. 1987. *The Disposal of Impurity.* Atlanta: Scholars Press.

———. 1992. "Unclean and Clean (OT)." In *The Anchor Bible Dictionary*, vol. 6, edited by D. N. Freedman, 729–41. New York: Doubleday.

Yadin, Yigael. 1977. *Temple Scroll: With Introduction and Commentary.* 3 vols. Jerusalem: Israel Exploration Society. [Hebrew].

Yadin, Yigael, and Joseph Naveh. 1989. *Masada I: The Yigael Yadin Excavations 1963–1965 Final Reports.* Jerusalem: Israel Exploration Society.

Zeitlin, Salomon. 1932–33. "The Am Haarez." *Jewish Quarterly Review* 23:45–46.

SUBJECT INDEX

abnormal genital discharges (including *zav* and *zava*), 1, 19, 21, 28, 56, 58, 74, 87, 103–104, 111–112, 114, 116–117, 120–126, 129, 132, 138, 176, 179
Adler, Yonatan, 144
Akiva, 4, 124, 151, 159, 165
Alon, Gedalyahu, 21–24, 37, 64, 67, 140
am ha-aretz, 36, 64–65, 84–110, 146–164, 166; level of impurity, 104–105, 179–180; marriage with, 88–89, 106–109, 153; meaning of term, 87–89; social separation, 102–108, 151–155; trustworthiness, 155–160
Antiochus the Third, 27–28, 31–32
archeological evidence for purity observance, 2, 13–14, 24, 27, 34, 117, 145–147, 165, 184
associates, association (*haverim, havura*), 23, 64–65, 87, 101–108, 126, 146–155, 157, 168, 186
atonement, 35, 39, 46, 48–49, 54–55, 98

Balberg, Mira, 11, 15
Bar Kokhba Revolt, xii, 4, 14, 86, 144, 183–185
Baumgarten, Albert, 66
Baumgarten, Joseph, 132
Belial, Mastema, Satan, 20, 44, 47, 50–52, 55
Birenboim, Hanan, 38
Blasphemy, 45–46

bodily vs. sin impurity, vii, 21–22, 35–39, 41, 47, 53–55, 72, 90, 96
Büchler, Adolf, 64, 85–86, 106

child training, 149, 166–167
clay vessels, 104, 126–129, 177, 181
corpse impurity, 25–31, 56, 74, 124–130, 134, 153, 177
critical analysis of rabbinic sources: additions to texts, 167–171; revision of sources, 145–146, 156, 169, 171–173; duplications, 177–178; reinterpretation, 100–101, 179; dating traditions, xii, 3–7, 106–107, 148, 154, 162

degrees of impurity, 73, 77, 99, 112–118, 139
Deines, Roland, 65
demons, impure/evil spirits, 50–52, 55–59, 68, 74, 94, 120
dietary laws (*kashruth*), 71–72, 76, 90–92, 162

early Halakhah: affinity between Qumran and the House of Shammai, 133–134; scholarly models, 7, 9–10; shared cross-sectarian traditions, 84, 98–99, 101–102, 104, 110, 111–112, 117, 139–140
eating ordinary foods in the state of purity, 23, 24, 63, 67, 99–100, 116–118, 167–169, 173–174

SUBJECT INDEX

economic considerations of purity policy, 30, 32, 160–163
eschatology, ix, 20–21, 41, 47, 50, 52–58
Essenes, ix, 74, 89–90, 92, 98, 102–103, 105
Ezra and Nehemiah, 36–39, 43, 88–89, 102, 106, 109–110

Flusser, David, 54

Galilee, 1, 14, 85–86, 153–154, 159, 163–164, 185, 187
genealogical impurity (holy seed), 37, 43
gentile impurity, viii, 19, 24, 28–30, 36–40, 43, 49, 55, 66, 89–97, 104–105, 109–110, 179

hand-washing, 12, 14, 23, 56, 69–75, 110, 137–140, 174–178; biblical foundation, 174–176
Harrington, Hannah, 11–12, 24–25
Harvest, 130–135
Hasmoneans, vii, 39, 63–68, 86, 102
Hayes, Christine, 37
Henshke, David, 33
holy foods, 99, 116–118, 160–161, 171–173
holy spirit, 20, 43–47, 52–55, 57, 98
Houses of Hillel and Shammai, 1, 4, 6, 10, 73, 75, 80–81, 85–87, 106, 119, 123, 130, 132–140, 147–150, 169, 172–173

idol Impurity, 36, 38–39, 68
illness, 19, 50, 56–58, 68
initiation procedure: in Qumran, 49, 51, 85, 131–132, 150; in Rabbinic Havura, 63, 85, 147–150
intention, 99–100, 133–135, 168, 185
Intermarriage, 36–37, 43, 89–90, 93, 107–110

Jerusalem: bringing priestly gifts to, 161–162; degree of trustworthiness in, 158–163; in Qumran literature, 30–31, 33, 42; permitted meat in, 28, 31–33; purity of, 27, 30–34, 38, 42, 114, 158, 168
Jesus, and the Law, 56–57, 69–79; as healer, exorcist and purifier, 56–59
John the Baptist, ix, 53–55, 57
Judea, 14, 144, 156–164, 185

Karaite law, 122
Klawans, Jonathan, 22, 37, 41

leprosy, 19, 21, 26, 28, 30, 33, 56–57, 72, 74, 114, 119, 123–124, 177
Lieberman, Saul, 147–148
liquid impurity, in Qumran law, 124–132, 139; in Rabbinic law, 67, 78, 106–107, 137–140, 146–149, 178, 181

Magen, Itzhak, 143
Magness, Jodi, 145
menstrual impurity (*niddah*), 119–124, 144, 167, 169, 179–181
midras impurity, 101–105, 171–173
Milgrom, Jacob, 42, 114, 120
Miller, Stuart, 145
Mishnah: as a historical source, 3; contradictions in, 153, 156–160; credibility of traditions, 5; description, xi–xii; source-criticism, 5, 7, 68; style, 4

Neusner, Jacob, on the Mishnah, 4–5, 10; on the Pharisees: 65–67, 83, 175
Newman, Hillel, 181
Noam, Vered, 11–13, 42, 118, 126

Oil: carrier of impurity, 125, 128; gentile, 19; production, 131–132, 135–137, 152, 157–162
Olyan, Saul, 38

Paul of Tarsus, 29
Peter the Apostle, 53, 70, 90–92
Pharisees: attacked by other groups, viii, x, 58, 68–82, 113, 123; eating in the state of purity, 63–68; ideology, vii, 20, 63, 83, 102, 110; lenient policy, 10, 66, 79, 82–83, 110, 129, 168; meaning of name, 64, 88; relation to "associates", 150–151; relation to the rabbis, xi, 7–8; social status and organization, x, 8, 63–66, 105; sources of information, x, 6–9
prayer, 48, 50, 51
Priestly Code, ix, 26, 33, 74, 82–83
priestly gifts (Heave offering, *terumah*, first fruits), 73, 75, 81, 86, 99–104, 112, 116–118, 138–140, 143–144, 153–154, 157–162, 166–169, 175–176

SUBJECT INDEX

priests, 8, 10, 23, 37, 42, 44, 63, 66–67, 78–80, 82, 86, 95, 103, 117, 144, 159, 166–168, 172, 174–177, 182
punishments, lost privilege for purification, 49, 96; exile, 21, 36, 39; cutting off (*karet*), 46–47
purification: after sexual intercourse, 19, 23, 25, 30, 34, 115, 145, 180; gradual, 112–124, 127, 130–132; after coming in contact with corpse, 25–26, 34, 42, 49, 114, 124–130; before Shabbat, 19; in preparation for prayer, 19, 23–24; first day immersion/ ablution, 25, 30, 114–116, 124–125, 127–129, 131; of food utensils, 64, 75–79, 125–129

Qumran: election, 47–50; exegetical approach, 12, 42, 49, 112, 126–129; separatism, vii, 43–44, 88–89, 92–97, 150; stringency, 42–43

Rabban Gamaliel (the Elder/of Yavnah), level of purity, 7, 106, 135, 170–175
Red heifer, 25, 82, 113, 125, 129, 144, 177
Reich, Ronny, 143
Repentance, 35, 53–55, 57–58
Ritual Baths (*miqva'ot*), 14, 34, 143–145, 177
Rivkin, Elias, 64
Rule of the community, textual history, 92–97

Sacrificial meat, 28, 31–34, 99–100, 112, 117, 161, 168, 172
Sadducees, ix, 8–9, 79–80, 84, 113
Samaritan law, 121
Sanders, Ed, P., 24, 67
Schürer, Emil, 65
Sectarianism, 8, 15, 84–110
separation: biblical command, 36, 82, 88; of foods and vessels, 79–82; of menstruants, 19, 26, 28, 44, 119–124, 143, 169, 180; second Temple tradition, 108–110, 154
Shemesh, Aharon, 7, 89, 92
Shimon b. Eleazar, 1, 2, 10, 14, 123, 180
Smith, Morton, 65
stone vessels, 14, 143–144
susceptibility to impurity, 80–81, 133–138, 158, 170
synagogue, 24, 57, 154, 181–182

tax collectors, 155–160, 185–186
Temple (in Jerusalem): alternatives to, 25; considered to be defiled, ix, 21–22, 35, 42, 44–45; distancing impure persons from, viii, 27–31; impact of its destruction on purity practices, 14, 143–145, 172, 183; in the Mishnah, 3; pilgrimage to, 19, 29, 82, 117, 161–162; warning inscription, 28
tevul yom, 81, 112–118, 140
Tiberias, impurity of, 26
Tosefta (in relation to the Mishnah), xii, 5, 6, 23, 78–79, 86, 100, 106–107, 114, 147–158, 153, 168–180
tradition of the elders, x, 8, 64–74, 102, 105

Usha, 4

Vermes, Geza, 65
voluntary associations (Greco-Roman), 151, 154–155, 163

Wine, production, 133–135, 137–139, 152, 157–162; impurity, 81, 125, 128

Yadin, Yigael, 126
Yavneh, 4, 8, 81, 172

Zav, zava and *Zov. See* Abnormal genital discharges

SOURCE INDEX

HEBREW BIBLE
Genesis
23:7   87
Exodus
19:6   66
Leviticus
4:27   87
5:2–3   21, 74
7:19   74
10:10   80
11:32–38   27
11:35   126
11:38   130
12:1–5 113, 117
12:7   49
13:45–46   21
14:31   49
14:8   33, 114
15–19   21
15:13   112
15:15   49
15:21   112
15:30   49
16   21
17:3–4 31
18:2–28 36
18:24   21, 35, 44
18:28   21
19:31   21, 36, 46

20:20   87
20:25   45
20:3   21, 35, 36, 44
21:7, 13–14 37
22:2   22
Numbers
5:1–4   21, 30
15:30–31   45–46
19   21
19:15   126
35:34   21, 35
Deuteronomy
7:3   36
12   33
2 Kings
15:5   87
18:4   38
23:8   38
Jeremiah
1:18   87
2:7–23 21
33:8   47
Ezekiel
20:3–44 21
22:1–6 35, 44
22:15   21
31:16–37   21, 47
36:17   35
36:25   53

255

Psalms
  51   48
Ezra
  6:21   37, 88
  9:1   88
  9:2   42
  9:11–12   36, 37
Nehemiah
  10:29–31   88, 93
  10:38   162
  12:44   162
  13:5   162
  13:7–9   37
  13:29–30   37
2 Chronicles
  29: 5, 15–16, 18   38
  34:3–8   39

SECOND TEMPLE LITERATURE
1 Maccabees
  1:54   39
  4:43–46   39
  13:47–48   39
2 Maccabees
  1:18   39
  2:16–18   39
  10:3–7   39
Book of Jubilees
  7:36   33
  10:1, 9   50
  22:16–20   50, 90, 92–95,
               108
  23:14   33
  49:15–17   33
Judith
  11:13   162
  12:6–10   24
Letter of Aristeas
  106   34
  305–306   23
Philo, Special Laws
  1:152   162
  3:63   23, 25, 115
Tobit
  1:6   162
  2:5   26

QUMRAN LITERATURE
Damascus Document
  4:13   44
  4:17   44
  4:20–5:14   44
  6:14–7:4   43–44
  7:3–4   45
  12:15–17   128
  16:4–5   51
1QH (Hodayot)
  11:21–24   52
  19:10–11   47
  19:13–15   52
1QM (War Scroll)
  14:8–11   5
1QpHab (Pesher Habakuk)
  8:11–13   35
  12:7–10   35
11QPsa
  19:14–15   50
1QS (Community Rule)
  2:25–3:7   49
  3:3–9   98, 101–102
  4:10   47
  4:20–22   52, 55
  5:13   49
  5:7–20   95–97
  11:7–15   48
4QMMT
  B 13–16   113
  B 22–23   31
  B 29–31   30, 31
  B 49–58   43
  B 52–54   168
  B 56–58   80
  B 58–59   31
  B 59–61   33
  B 67–68   33
4QS^d
  i 5–10   93–97, 108
4Q274 (Tohorot)
  1   119–124
  3   130–131, 139
11QT (Temple Scroll)
  45–51   42
  45:7–10   30, 114

47:7–16	32	8:49–56	56
48:14–17	30, 123	11:24–26	58
49:5–21	124–130	11:38–41	56, 75–82
49:16–17	25, 114	Acts	
49:20–21	114	10	91–92
50:13–14	25	11:15–18	53

Additional Qumran Texts

4Q284a	131–132, 137, 139	21:26–30	29
4Q414	49		

FLAVIUS JOSEPHUS

Against Apion

4Q510	51	2:103–4	29
4Q511	50	2:198, 203	25
4Q512	48		

Judean Antiquities

4Q514	114	3:261–262	26, 29
4Q560	51	12:145–146	28
8Q5	51	18:36–38	26
11Q11	51	18:116–119	53

Judean War

NEW TESTAMENT

Matthew		2:150	89
3:1–12	53	3:261	123
8:1–4	56	5:227	26
9:19–22	56		
9:23–26	56	RABBINIC LITERATURE	
12:43–45	58	**Mishnah**	
14:1–12	53	Bava Qamma	
15:11	71	7:7	32
15:1–20	69–75	Berakhot	
23:25–28	56, 75–82	1:1	113
Mark		8:2–4	75
1:1–8	53, 57	Demai	
1:21–28	57	2:2–3	104, 106–109, 146–150
1:40–44	56, 57		
2:1–12	57	Eduyot	
3:28–29	46	5:6	176
5:25–34	56	Hagigah	
5:35–43	56	2:6	99–102, 110
6:7–13	58	2:6–8	171–172
6:14–29	53	2:7	102–105, 110, 179
7:1–23	56, 69–75	3:1–3	178
7:3–4	64	3:4–6	157–163
7:15	71	Kelim	
7:19	72	1:5	116
Luke		1:8	28
3:1–20	29	5:10	82
5:12–16	56	19:2–3	82
8:43–48	56	25:6	78

Makhshirin			3:1	168
5:9	80		3:4	154, 157
Negaʿim			Eduyot	
14:3	116		2:2	170
Niddah			Hagigah	
1:1–2	167		1:2	149, 166
Ohalot			3:1–2	100
18:1	134		3:3	171–173
Parah			3:21	179
3:7	113		Kelim	
5:5	177		1:1:12	31
7:6	144		3:3:7	78
11:4	116		Negaʿim	
Sheqalim			6:2	32
7:2	32		Niddah	
7:4	32		9:18	32
8:1	34		Parah	
Teharot			3:8	113
1:14	73		5:6	144
2:2	73		Shabbat	
2:8	161		1:14	1, 123
7:3–5	151–152		1:15	87
7:6	155–157		Sukkah	
8:1	152		2:3	170
8:4	152		Teharot	
8:7	78		1:5–6	161
9	135–137		3:10	149, 166
10:1–3	152, 159		8:5	155
10:4–5	137–139		Terumot	
Tevul Tom			1:1	168
1:1	81		Yadayim	
Yadayim			1:7	177–178
1:2	177		Zavim	
4:6–8	79–80		2:1	104
Zavim			**Sifra**	
3:2	154		Zavim	
5:10	124		1:1	104
5:12	73, 138		4:6	176
Tosefta			9:12	124
Avoda Zara			**Sifre on Numbers**	
3:8–10	106–109		1 (Naso)	30
Demai			116 (Korah)	175–176
2:2	146		**Palestinian Talmud**	
2:10–12	147–149		Berakhot	
2:17	157		3:4	180

6:1	144
Demai	
2:3	180
Hagigah	
2:7	179
Shabbat	
1:3	173
1:7	134

Babylonian Talmud
Shabbat
   17a   133
Bava Mesia
   78a   169
Yevamot
   15b   171

Additional Rabbinic Sources
Genesis Rabbah
   48:14   169
Pesiqta de-Rav Kahanah
   Ha-Hodesh 3   169
Tanna debe Eliyahu
   16 (15)   174

YAIR FURSTENBERG is Associate Professor of Talmud at Hebrew University, where he serves as chair of the department. Among his publications are *Jewish Martyrdom in Antiquity: From the Books of Maccabees to the Babylonian Talmud* and the edited volume *Jewish and Christian Communal Identities in the Roman World*.

For Indiana University Press

Brian Carroll, Rights Manager
Gary Dunham, Acquisitions Editor and Director
Anna Francis, Assistant Acquisitions Editor
Brenna Hosman, Production Coordinator
Katie Huggins, Production Manager
David Miller, Lead Project Manager/Editor
Dan Pyle, Online Publishing Manager
Nancy Smith, Artist and Book Designer
Stephen Williams, Marketing and Publicity Manager